SKIP ALL THAT
Memoirs

Robert Robinson was born in Liverpool in 1927 and was brought up in the London suburbs. As a journalist he has written columns for the *Sunday Times*, *The Observer* and the *Sunday Telegraph*, but he is best known for his long-running broadcasts on the radio and television. He is married with three children and lives in Chelsea.

Robert
ROBINSON

SKIP ALL THAT

MEMOIRS

ARROW

This edition published by Arrow Books Limited 1997

1 3 5 7 9 10 8 6 4 2

First published in the United Kingdom by Century
Random House UK Ltd,
20 Vauxhall Bridge Road, London SW1V 2SA

Arrow Books Ltd
Random House UK Ltd,
20 Vauxhall Bridge Road, London SW1V 2SA

Random House Australia (Pty) Limited
16 Alfred Street, Milsons Point, Sydney,
New South Wales 2061, Australia

Random House New Zealand Limited
18 Poland Road, Glenfield,
Auckland 10, New Zealand

Random House South Africa (Pty) Limited
Endulini, 5a Jubilee Road
Parktown 2193, South Africa

A CIP record for this book is available from the British Library

Papers used by Random House UK Limited are natural,
recyclable products made from wood grown in sustainable forests.
The manufacturing processes conform to the environmental
regulations of the country of origin.

ISBN 0 09 917772 2

Typeset by Palimpsest Book Production Limited,
Polmont, Stirlingshire
Printed and bound in the UK by
Cox & Wyman Ltd, Reading, Berks.

'My Mother and Father were honest
   though poor –'
'Skip all that!' cried the Bellman in haste.

The Hunting of the Snark

I think the Bellman put paid to the Baker's story at this point because he thought he was going to hear more than he wanted to: he may have felt the Baker's opening gambit to be a preliminary to many a shy boast. So 'Skip all that' is a wise injunction, though if it is too studiously observed no book of memoirs would ever get written.

CONTENTS

HEARING THE LAST OF CAPTAIN FERGUSON

PHYLLIS THE MAID from Firlecroft said, 'I thought we'd heard the last of Captain Ferguson,' and Mrs Morse said, 'Yes. I shouldn't think it would rain, should you?' They were hanging out the sheets.

They had a side door in the avenue which ran between our two houses. This garden door had a gap underneath it, and once when Bob Russell and I were crouching down and shouting cheeky things through the gap, Phyllis sloshed a bucket of water over us.

The houses in the Lane were called: Lyndhurst, Holmedene, Ty Nant, Winton, Golf View, Vriog, Cartref, The Crossing, Bourne, Kismet, Westoe, Kylemore, Woodlands, Trefusis, Caseta, Eynsford, Shields House, Raydene, Belle Vue, Killarney Villa, Granville, The Elms, Dacre Villa, Gainsborough, Zenda, Colon Villa, Lynton, Firlecroft, Beverley, Dawlish, Roseland, Rathlea, Verona, Sutherland, Wynberg, Candytuft, The Haven, Toupet, Woodstock, Barley Cottage, Redcroft, Somerton, Sheafton, Windermere, Martinsholz, Carisbrooke, Orillia, Temple Newsam, and Ivy House.

I found the names in a red book in the loft when we moved into Beverley. It had been left there by Mr Dorking the previous tenant, along with a pair of big leather gauntlets and an old-fashioned lamp for the front of a motorbike, which my father told me was years out of date. The name of each householder appeared in brackets after the name of each house. When I opened the book in the light of the little window in the gable that was covered in cobwebs, I saw Mr Dorking's name was in the list as Mr Dawkins. But I went on thinking of him as Mr Dorking.

There was the brook on the other side of the Lane opposite our house, and beyond it there were fields. These fields had been pasture, part of the farm on which the Lane and the avenues had been built in 1909, and then they'd been turned into a golf course that rolled down to the brook as part of the amenity of a suburb

1

further to the east. A few years before we arrived at Beverley the tees and the greens had fallen into disuse and the golf course was fields again, tussocky where the bunkers had been, though there was still the house called Golf View. I thought of the Lane as the edge of the world, with the brook between it and the fields as between us and a wilderness. Since the brook was Beverley Brook and our house was called Beverley I felt proprietorial. Once on a day of heavy rain the brook overflowed and the Lane became a river. Everyone stood on their doorsteps, watching the water. A man came swimming up what was ordinarily the road. It was Captain Ferguson, though I only recognised him at a second glance, since he was wearing a bathing-cap.

The house he lived in was further up the Lane and on the other side from us, on the bank of the brook. It had a plaque on it saying Barley Cottage 1820 and it was a relic of the farm. The farm had been called Blagdons and a man called William Palmer, citizen of Wandsworth, bought it in 1907, then sold off the land. He knew the London and Southampton Railway was inventing suburbs by planting railway stations in the empty fields and leaving the business of sticking names on them to the builders who put up the houses. Palmer who never farmed the land took his profits and went to live in New Zealand. But I didn't feel the Lane was new, I felt it was very old. I felt the fields were still there underneath the houses and one day I would learn how to roll the brick back and uncover the landscape as it was before anyone had ever seen it.

There were respectable men who didn't have jobs in those days, for this was the Thirties. They knocked on our doors, lugging big suitcases made of something that looked like leather but was stiffer and wasn't quite the right colour. The cases were filled with pen-knives and combs and little hand mirrors. When the ladies who lived in the houses opened the doors they stared into the suitcases and bought a nailfile for threepence. I know my mother did this, and only took the item she bought because she thought the man on the doorstep wanted the coppers she gave him to be part of a transaction. One day I was climbing trees with Frank and Wilf Smith on a little bit of ground across the Lane by the brook: it was left-over land that would be built on when someone got round to doing it, but meanwhile it was covered with brambles and small black gnarled trees. An old chap with a moustache and a hooked nose came across the Lane, carrying one of those suitcases, and sat down under the tree we were swinging on. Could the tree have been a hornbeam? The old gentleman with the suitcase looked like the embossed figure on the front of the *The Magic Walking Stick* that my father had just bought me. He was lame, and as he sat at the bole of the tree he told Wilf and Frank and me how he'd been wounded in the Great War, and was lucky to be alive. Well, he added, when I say lucky. He'd been a proper salesman before 1914, a commercial traveller for a firm that made fire-extinguishers, but his job had been given to someone else when he got back – 'this chap hadn't been dodging the column, it wasn't that, but he'd been an officer and I was in the ranks, and I think that made the difference.' I was sitting cross-legged with my arms round my knees and said to him, 'And now you're only a pedlar.' The old man started to cry.

I was glad it wasn't Captain Ferguson who'd taken the old chap's job; he couldn't have taken it, because he didn't have a job himself. There were no outward signs that this mattered to him and after I'd met the old man selling from door to door I supposed it not mattering was something to do with Captain Ferguson being an officer. Now and again he did go after a job. He went to see about one at the Metal Box Company, then a small new concern housed in what looked like a garage with brick battlements a mile or so away near Shannon Corner. He banged his umbrella on the floor of the empty outer office and cried, 'Is there nobody here to attend to me?' He told my father this, stopping by the front gate as my father was pushing the mower. I heard them through the open window of my bedroom. It was a summer night in 1934, about eight o'clock. My father said, 'Hard lines'.

'I've done a great deal of cycling,' Captain Ferguson said, warning me not to stand on the pedals. Someone told me he had called out the guard in India in the Great War because he mistook the Colonel's dog for a dacoit. It hadn't occurred to me that India was in the Great War. Captain Ferguson often wore breeches and long boots like Cecil B. de Mille, and when he saw someone walking towards him down the Lane at dusk under the elm trees he would hold out his leg and make his little dog Patch jump over it, back and forth. It might be a stranger, who would ask him if he was on the right road for getting a bus to Malden, and Captain Ferguson would say 'No' very sharply, as though the error were an impertinence. In his re-directions Captain Ferguson would incorporate the fact that he had lived in the Lane for twenty years and that when he arrived in 1915 there had been cows at the end of his garden, implying that their absence now was an instance of declining standards. He would tell, or more properly instruct, the stranger that prior to his service in India he had logged the number of Gothas flying over the Lane on their way to drop bombs on Croydon Aerodrome. He would sternly explain that it was not possible to do this effectively unless you lay at full length on the bedroom floor using binoculars. He brought home to the stranger the dedication involved in carrying out this manoeuvre by strenuously miming it. When he called the aeroplanes Gothas he sounded as if he had inside information about their design.

Boys jumping over the brook from the fields to get back to the Lane knew there was a risk in dodging through Captain Ferguson's garden since he believed they were after his raspberries. He caught Bob Russell once and clasping him by the shoulder marched him down the Lane to confront his parents. Other boys said they'd seen Bob being led along and that he'd smiled at them in a silly way as though he was trying to fool them into thinking Captain Ferguson was some kindly old relative.

Bob lived four doors along from us with his mum and dad and his older sister Margaret, and his grandad. Bob's grandfather was famous for having once met Dickens. The great writer had called at the cobbler's shop where Bob's grandad worked, to pick up a pair of shoes, and he invited the young fellow to go with him for a drink. Bob Russell's grandfather said he couldn't as he had his work to get on with, and Dickens congratulated him and said his mother had reason to be proud of him. I thought it was nice of Dickens to go round offering drinks to humble people in shops, but why had he asked Bob's grandfather to do something he gave him full marks for refusing? Perhaps it was a sort of test. Bob's grandad was over ninety but Bob's mother said the doctor said he had the heart and lungs of a boy of twelve. Two days later I began a diary in a small red notebook with the words 'Russell's grandfather died'. Nothing else ever matched the initial entry, so the rest of the pages stayed blank.

When we were about four or five I used to tell Bob that though the inside of our houses belonged to our parents, the roofs were ours. That's where we had another life, up on the ridge of the tiles in the morning, warming ourselves in the sun as we sat on our hunkers next to the little red hooked thing at the apex of the gable. I told him tales of what I'd seen and thought while strolling the tiles and Bob would join in as though he'd been there with me, but after a bit he found he didn't want to go on talking like this and would say, 'That's enough of that,' sounding just like his mother. When Captain Ferguson came by it was Bob who asked him for cigarette cards. Captain Ferguson smoked Kensitas which gave away flags of all nations printed on little silk rectangles, but since we were collecting Kings and Queens of England from Player's I expected Bob to swap them whenever he could but I never saw him doing this. I was a bit sorry Captain Ferguson bought Kensitas because for the price of twenty they gave you four more which they stuck on the side of the packet in a secondary compartment labelled 'Four For Your Friends'. I felt Captain Ferguson hadn't really noticed this because I thought getting four free cigarettes was something he wouldn't have had anything to do with.

Captain Ferguson had a sister, his only visible relative, who tootled up the Lane in a butter-coloured Hillman Minx. It was a drop-head coupé, the hood made out of some black material that looked as though it had been fried in batter. On each side of the hood there was a chromium-plated hinge shaped like the *forte* mark on a sheet of music, but I never saw Miss Ferguson getting to grips with them – the hood was never down even on the finest of days, and sometimes when she was unloading the car I'd breathe on the chromium and polish it with my sleeve as though I'd spotted a mark, just to draw her attention to the mechanism; but she never took the hint. Captain Ferguson didn't drive, but had once begun a course of lessons. These he quickly abandoned because he refused to turn right. He explained to my father that to turn right was to court certain death from oncoming traffic. My father forbore to query this, though afterwards commented that the bloody fool only had to wait for the road to be clear.

Miss Cicely Ferguson lived in Epsom and when she visited her brother to go to the theatre she might stay on at Barley Cottage for a night or two. Her hair was a strange phosphorescent shade of burnished stair-rods which she hid under a cowl as though ashamed of it. Sometimes you saw a hint of it alight round the edge, as though the cowl were on fire inside. If she didn't like it, why didn't she just dye it? 'She doesn't believe in touching it up,' my mother said, the phrase rebuking the flightiness of such a procedure.

Telephones weren't an ordinary part of life as it was then lived in the Lane, telephones were to be found in some houses, but they were icons, a ritual presence, used mostly at times of crisis. So when Captain Ferguson dropped in he would arrive unannounced and simply knock at the door. My father and he would sit opposite each other, either side of the fire, and Captain Ferguson would read items aloud from the *Daily Telegraph*. He had a way of plucking up his trousers at the knee very deliberately, one after the other, then holding the paper open at its full broadsheet width. I took both actions to be formal emblems of adulthood. He would stay just a little bit longer than it would take each of them to smoke a Kensitas and a Craven A (my father's chosen cigarette), while my mother did her knitting. My father weathered the visits with unbreachable politeness, but in a corner of my mind as I sat on the sofa reading an ancient *Greyfriars Holiday Annual* (another bequest from Mr Dorking who had left six or seven behind, dating from as early as 1919) I felt my father was on the alert, not quite at ease. As though Captain Ferguson's oddity, when he left, couldn't quite be wrapped up and thrown away in the phrase 'Bloody fool!', which my father often used.

Was my father odd too? He was an accountant with the United Africa Company in Kingsway. The UAC had amalgamated with the Niger Company and half the combined staff had lost their jobs. My father was one of the lucky ones, and had been moved to London – greatly to his satisfaction. He 'went to the office'. Some people, notably Mrs Wright (two houses along at Rathlea, and captain of the ladies' bowling team) or Mrs Russell further up at Verona, who was Bob's mother, used the phrase 'going to business', with an air of conveying that this was territory not open to enquiry. My father would walk down the Lane to the level-crossing and get the bus to Raynes Park station, then the train to Waterloo. What he did when he got to the office was a blank, he might have walked off the edge of the world each morning, returning at six with the *Evening Standard*. Once my mother, showing the sort of interest a politician takes in a stranger, said, 'You like figures, don't you?' and my father replied, 'No.'

He conducted himself in public in accordance with the conventions that went with being a householder in those latitudes, sometimes wearing a bowler, sometimes a trilby. Meeting neighbours in the street, he raised his hat to them whether they were male or female. At the weekends he wore plus-fours and gardened, taking me before lunch on Sunday to The Plough where he would have two halves of bitter and I would have a lemonade. We went on our bikes while my mother cooked the lamb (it was always lamb). My bike came from Gamages (all largeish shop-bought items came from Gamages, where members of the United Africa Company held credit cards. My mother was not a dressy woman, but grumbled at having to get her clothes from what seemed to be an indoor bazaar). But my father's bike was special: hand-made by a man in Kennington called Maurice Selbach. If Captain Ferguson had done a great deal of cycling, he offered no details of it, whereas my father described the heroic rides he had made as a young man, putting his bike and his haversack and his fishing-rods on the Liverpool tram to go to the terminus, then riding north through the Trough of Bowland, out of Lancashire into the Yorkshire Dales.

My father felt himself to be defined by his bike, it had played a great part in his life. To have a bike made specially for you might be considered an indulgence, but not when the bike had a moral significance to do with effort and the outdoors. It had given him freedom, and a licence to be solitary. He took his holidays alone, with his bike and his rods, in Yorkshire or Scotland; my mother and I went to the seaside. Occasionally he would make a stab at personalising the machine by calling it 'George' but the romantic style was foreign to him and this never sounded convincing; especially as there lingered about the usage a touch of the overweening, as though such fancies belonged a social notch or two beyond his reach, and he was aware of it.

At Christmas, he greeted people with the phrase 'The compliments of the season'. When responding to reports of mishap or inconvenience he would say 'Hard lines'. He sometimes used a style of his own when piqued: trying on a pair of trousers at Bentall's that were so long they cascaded over his shoes, his face was suddenly red with fury as he said to the assistant, 'Don't you see they make me look like a comedian?' The image he invoked was more or less to the point, but it was a curious way of putting it. I was hanging about waiting to get to the toy department and I felt I wouldn't have minded him saying things that were even odder. Then I could have boasted about him. Being a character is something people do to show they command their circumstances, but I suspected anything my father did that was out of the ordinary would be done by accident.

I sometimes wondered if other boys' fathers were odd or unaccountable at home in a way their behaviour in public wouldn't lead you to expect. John Bache's father often overstayed at the buffet at Waterloo, bringing home a bunch of flowers for his wife – 'a peace offering' as my mother described it – and would belch after finishing the evening meal, exclaiming 'Manners!' as though rebuking some third party. I was sprawled below eye-level on the carpet with his son, rigging up the wire we hooked round table and chair legs down which we were going to slide our Dinky Toy aeroplanes, and I suppose this little glimpse into the private life of Mr Bache came my way because he hadn't taken account of my presence. My father would never have been 'rude' in front of any friends of mine, and indeed in the presence of the family would go out into the hall to fart. My mother caught my eye once and said, 'He thinks no one can hear him.' Derek Paine's father would eat a whole fried egg in a single mouthful; I never saw him do this, but Derek assured us of it one morning while we were finishing breakfast and he was waiting for me to go out to play, making the point not boastfully but as though reserving a place for his father if the conversation became competitive.

But I couldn't imagine any other boy's father shouting as mine did. He shouted as one might fire a gun. At his own father, when a friend who was also an accountant and worked for VP ('Such lovely wine for five and nine') was to pay a visit, and my grandfather was refusing to cut his nails. But mostly he did it to my mother, always on the subject of her family, and it made her cry. She cried readily, and neither the shouting nor the crying seemed other than perfectly normal to me. At the same time, I couldn't imagine it featuring in the lives of anyone else. Mr Craigie was very strict, Mr Russell was under his wife's thumb, Mr Wright had a fat arse and a duck-footed walk and called his son 'dear', Vivian Tate's father gave him too much pocket-money, and David Parish's mother dressed him in pinafores. But I couldn't imagine any of them shouting. Equally, I couldn't imagine any of the mothers pulling faces or making jokes or using daft phrases as my mother did, though I noticed them trying to live up to her jokes which she didn't mind making in public. They'd try and join in, but only managed to sound like people stumbling about in a foreign language which they couldn't really speak. When my father was amused he laughed as furiously as he shouted, though not as loudly, the laugh distorting his face as though he were actually in pain. I saw no soft or tender passages between my parents, and when she was once in hospital I kissed her at my father's bidding as though I were doing it for both of us. I never doubted that marriage was like that, even in families where the father might not shout: that all the demonstrative, romantic stuff belonged to before you were married, and afterwards life at home for grown-ups was a procession of humdrum days.

He was a quiet, humorous, shy fellow, but he shouted. He detested my mother's family to such an extent I found it hard to understand how he had managed to court her. Her mother would say, 'Here's that little stiff fellow for you,' as my father promenaded outside the family house in Breeze Hill, Liverpool. Her family were always singing round the piano or doing imitations or dressing up in a foolish unorganised sort of way: my mother's eldest brother Bill borrowed a Gladstone bag from a pal, donned his father's top hat and knocked on the door of a neighbour saying gravely as the door opened, 'I have come to cut the children's hair.' My uncle Tom and my uncle Peter would sing 'The brothers Magee from old Tralee', and a friend from Makin Street would arrive to give his impression of a music-hall performer called Albert Whelan who, so my mother told me, made a feature of whistling while pulling on a pair of white gloves. Uncle Joe, her youngest brother, played the piano.

I cannot place my father in this room. He would have lingered outside waiting for my mother to appear, or one of her sisters – probably Rose, the youngest – to run out and tell him she'd got a headache or was washing her hair. Plucking up courage, he did call in the conventional way, but not before he wrote to my mother, 'Tell your Ma to make allowances for me as I am very shy (ahem!).' And once inside I imagine him screwed up like a violin string, waiting for my mother to turn her attention away from the laughter and the fooling and give that attention to him. Then what? A stroll in the darkness, along the pathways of Stanley Park, a *passeo* in which they would encounter other couples and be facetious in the style of the time. This I know for certain, since my mother kept a little scented box of my father's letters in a drawer of her dressing-table, and when I was marooned in their bedroom having measles I rifled the drawers and read them all, and read them again when it was chicken-pox, and again when it was mumps. The thread I see running through them is his desire to have her to himself: he wouldn't venture out into the aura of her enveloping family, he wanted to tuck her away in some corner with him where he couldn't be assailed. Perhaps because he'd been an only child.

In these letters he used French phrases. '*Comme d'habitude*', '*jusqu'à ce soir*', '*Toujours à toi*', 'Yours *à toujours*'. He liked to write '*Cherie*', sometimes '*Querida*'. He called her 'Dear', 'darling', 'dearest' – words I never heard fall from his lips in my childhood. '*Milles baisers*', he would scrawl, or 'I enclose 2 million and fourteen kisses, all of which I will count over in detail when I next see you. Always Yours, Ernest.' It must have been a very efficient post, for he wrote in the afternoon to make a date for the evening.

The word for the allowed-for degree of sexual rapprochement was 'spooning'. I think this meant kissing and embracing, probably of a fairly reserved order. 'I hope the weather will be fine so that we can sp—— (I mean, so that we can enjoy the fresh air – ahem!).' Fidelity was a constant topic, but having regard to the conventional limits set on physical contact, I think it just meant not paying attention to other chaps. 'Well, dearest, I hope you have been strictly true and have not been having anything to do with any fellows, or been out with the girls who have been after chaps. It's not a good way of putting it, but you know what I mean, *cherie*. If you do go out don't go larking with Molly.'

My grandmother's phrase 'That little stiff fellow' referred to his jerky way of walking, but it might have applied to his epistolary style as well. 'By the way, *ma cherie*, do you know if anyone sent me a Leap Year proposal? I received one and suspect one of your friends. I am not annoyed in any way, but would just like to find out for curiosity.' Rather stilted stuff. 'Don't be imagining that I am going with any other girl, and don't be worrying yourself with such thoughts if I should not see you until Monday. I know from my own experience how one is given to troubling over things of that sort. So take my advice, *cherie*, and don't do it. You'll have no reason to. Hurry up and get well and we'll have a good long spoon.' She had a cold and he expresses concern about it, but why would he suppose such sentiments 'sloppy'? 'I expect you will think the latter paragraph rather "sloppy", but, my love, it is sincerely meant. Cheer up, I think you will soon be all right and be ready to take up osculatory exercise (ahem!).' Perhaps he just wasn't much of a hand with the pen.

But then there's a letter that makes my theory that he wanted her all to himself sound a little elaborate. What happened prior to 16 May 1912, the date on the note? 'My God, I never remember feeling so upset as I have done this last day or two, and what makes it worse is the thought that I have broken your heart. I have no doubt that people will call me a scoundrel for leaving you as I have done . . . Believe me dear time after time when I have thought of you I have felt my eyes fill with tears . . . What makes it harder is that Ankers has not done as he said he intended to do; had he kept his promise to me and broken with Molly I would have felt a bit more comfort in having him with me, and it would have been a bit easier for you if you had Molly to go out with. As it is, he's putting Molly in a Fool's Paradise . . .'

What's all this? A couple of young men deciding to abjure womankind and one reneguing? On 13 June 1912 he writes, 'I remember telling you that I would make up a yarn to tell the boys, but afterwards I thought it best for your sake to tell them the truth . . . That I had parted with you, as I was only wasting your time, seeing that I did not intend to get married . . . If you think I was making a convenience of you during the winter . . . you must also think I am a very good actor to act with you the way I have done. I would not go to the trouble of playing the part of deceiver for so long with any girl on earth. . . .'

Sounds like funk to me. Yes, he married her in the end, but it might have been passive marrying, as people are said to be passive smokers; being in the vicinity of those who are continuously doing it, it could happen involuntarily. No question of pregnancy forcing the issue – that didn't happen till some years after the knot had been tied. 'Oh, mother,' my mother told me she said to my grandma, 'I think I've caught a cold.' 'You'll be dandling that cold on your knee in nine months' time,' my grandma replied. My father was a Protestant and came from Manchester and my mother's family were Liverpool Irish Catholics. My mother had no qualms about marrying him in an Anglican church. But long after they'd left Liverpool he was saying he'd disenfranchise that city because like Laputa the place came from an alien dimension and was only tethered to the world for malign purposes. After *they* left? I think I mean after he'd left. For my mother in a sense never did leave the place. She couldn't. She was helplessly addicted to her family and I think my father felt she'd never really married him. She accompanied him to London like a grown-up child on a visit to hostile territory. She couldn't wait for the holidays, to go 'home'. This must have been especially irritating if you'd married reluctantly, and your wife thought of marriage as an interruption. He never did get her to himself: even if he'd deserved to, it wouldn't have happened. I suppose this might make you shout. It's an explanation, there must be others. And explanations are less than anything they explain: there's lots of stuff they leave out, because if there were any loose ends it wouldn't be an explanation. Explanations don't explain things away.

My mother was one of eight – nine, when you count the brother who died in infancy. Her father was a drunk, or as they called it in those days, a dipsomaniac, and died when she was a girl; he'd come over from Ireland during the potato famine. 'If only he could have taken a glass of beer like other men,' she said, telling me how he'd go without drink for months then ask his wife for money: 'Lend us twopence, Lizzie.' The children dreaded this moment. He thought he saw flames burst out of the wallpaper and was taken from the house, raving, and put in a lunatic asylum. This dark figure was like a steel engraving in a poisonous Victorian primer, whereas my cantankerous grandad, my father's father Alfred, my real living grandad, took me out for walks and we'd count the little piles of dog muck along the way. I was three, and asked him about people dying – this was something I'd heard about. He laughed as though it was an old joke designed to alarm the gullible. He read Dickens and Smollett and I stood on the rungs at the back of his chair and wrinkled up his bald head between my fingers and said it looked like worms; 'The man's mad,' he said, going on reading. He was awkward by instinct, smoking Digger Mixture with greater relish because my mother disliked the smell. He insisted the ham he was eating must be salmon. He called jam 'preserves'. His family had been silk home-loom weavers and he said the bedroom he shared with his brothers in their house in Ashton-under-Lyne was big enough to house sixteen double beds put end to end. Once the brothers had heard a tapping on the window; it was only the branch of a tree but they thought it was a ghost and my grandad said, 'Speak again!' His grandfather John, born in the second half of the eighteenth century, would take off his wooden leg and stand it in the corner. 'Pass us that wooden leg, Talt,' he'd say from the chimney seat, 'and I'll gi' thee a penny.'

My grandmother Drusilla faded from view. I don't remember her death as an event. Before she married Alf she'd been a Sunday School teacher in the Unitarian church in Dob Lane, Failsworth, where her performances in annual plays drew the admiration of Ben Brierley, the Lancashire dialect poet. 'My dear Friend,' he wrote on 2 November 1884, after Drusilla had retired into domestic life, 'I personally much regret your absence from the School – especially in that department in which you have had no equal, I mean The Stage. Although I cannot hope now to see you taking the prominent position you have always taken in the past, with so much credit to yourself, I do hope to have the pleasure of seeing you again in some part worthy of your past performances.' Perhaps Brierley wrote the stuff. What sort of plays can they have been?

My mother's sisters turned up singly or in pairs from Liverpool. They handed out half-crowns and anecdotes in an openhanded frivolous way. But because there was no prior warning my father must have been knocked off balance. His initial alarm, arriving home from the office and finding outriders from the evil empire on the premises, was surely considerable, but he could stick it out for a couple of days knowing *they* knew that was his limit. Once, Rose stayed longer, and I see both her and my mother standing by a half-open door crying in unison as my father by the french windows shouted them out of the room, unwilling, unable to share the space.

But he always allowed space for Clarice. She and her mother lived in some style in Hampton Court, their flat richly bedight with antiques paid for by Clarice's boyfriend. Mother and daughter – aunt and cousin respectively of my mother – often called, and my father and Clarice would lend each other books: she spilt tea on his copy of Kipling's *Limits and Renewals* and had it re-bound in leather which must have cost more than he'd paid for the book in the first place. And they talked about motor cars, at least Clarice did, because she wanted to sell him the Lea-Francis her boyfriend had bought her. I was never particularly listening, passing through the room with a cup of tea or my homework in my hand, but fragments stuck. 'He says I have no conversation,' she more than once told my dad, speaking of the boyfriend. This figure was referred to as 'John', a ridiculous soubriquet since his real name was Slobodjik or Janovar or something like that which she avoided because I suspect she felt it made him sound like a waiter. He was a millionaire, and a pretty tidy one at that, but stratification, socially speaking, was more in evidence in those unreconstructed days, and certain sorts of foreigner, however rich, had mass but no weight. This would have been specially so if, like 'John', you'd made your way from somewhere like Transylvania where you'd learnt to suck blood, a knack you transferred to England, having turned yourself from a vampire bat into a property speculator.

From elliptical conversations engaged in by my aunts when they thought I wasn't listening (any subject with what might be described as an 'adult' bias was put into a code so primitive it had the effect of alerting me to topics of particular interest: certain words were pronounced in reverse after a style known in their childhood as 'Back Slang', and other words like 'divorce' or 'pregnant' were spelled aloud as though this rendered the message opaque) I gathered that Clarice had been engaged to a timber merchant in the Wirral (my aunts would normally have referred to the Wirral as 'across the water' since anywhere adjacent to, but separated from, Liverpool was considered to be wasteland not worth defining. But once it was incorporated into family history it was awarded honorary membership.)

It was while dining at the house of the timber man that 'John', up there on business to bespeak some panelling for a house he was building, met Clarice, and thereafter the timber merchant was heard of no more. Rose who went to the pictures a lot said 'John' looked like the man who played the deputy undertaker in films where Donald Meek was the head one. 'The same hollow cheeks, and a swarthy look,' Rose said. (Rose called it 'swahthy', and during rows with my mother about her family, nothing was more certain to fan the flames than my father insisting Rose needed elocution lessons: her eccentric pronunciation of 'Westminster' as 'Westminister' didn't seem to bother him, it was the smaller idiosyncrasies that infuriated him – he claimed she spoke of 'going to the pickchores', spoke of children as 'chuldren' and called chips 'cheps'.) But when I once heard her criticise Clarice's mother for encouraging the liaison, I was amazed that blame of any sort could attach to my great aunt Beatty.

The dramatis personae of Liverpool were engraved in stone and I was instructed in their immutable roles by my mother: of her two aunts, Beatty was the sacred one, whose wonderfulness was unquestioned, while Dolly was the profane, I think because of her addiction to fur coats (I never met Dolly, and there were conflicting accounts: aunts Rose and Lil said she was good company but aunt Marie and my mother thought Dolly's loud ways – she had warned my grandmother that only inferior people kept hens in the backyard – were at odds with a streak of parsimony, always illustrated by my mother pretending she was Dolly walking into her own sitting-room and throwing back the collar of a heavy fur coat, crying 'Who put that big fire on!')

Aunt Beatty's wonderfulness was never more in evidence than when she went to have her hair done. There she would give the benefit of what my mother called her 'lovely singing voice' to the ladies as they rolled her up in the tongs. Should there be any little display of modesty on my great aunt's part (so my mother explained) the hairdressing ladies would implore her to begin, and she would launch into 'Just a Song at Twilight' as they combed her out. I felt faintly embarrassed when aunt Beatty sang in our house while waiting for tea to be served, but as I swallowed my whack of the tinned salmon and the brown bread and butter I imagined she must have been a great draw at the salon she patronised, since all the other customers would be able to listen to her as well, and at no extra cost.

As a child I was much impressed with their flat in Hampton Court, which had an ornate Chinese cocktail cabinet in one of its many rooms, and a set of dining-room chairs that looked just like the ones I'd seen in the Charles Laughton film about Henry VIII. Clarice made presents to my mother of odd items of expensive clothing, such as hats or cardigans, and though the giving was entirely unaffected I thought my mother was too relaxed about being on the receiving end. And when Clarice would swing open the special cupboard fitted with orange-tinted mirrors where she kept what looked like hundreds of pairs of shoes, and my mother said to me, 'What about that, then!', instead of gasping with admiration I ground my milk-teeth and said like an envious ill-tempered old man, 'Mum, why don't *you* have as many pairs of shoes as Aunty Clarice?' They laughed, each in a somewhat different way.

Clarice was a stunningly good-looking woman in her thirties, about as unlike my homely fat aunts as Joan Fontaine, an actress people told her she resembled. Though she was my mother's cousin, and much younger, I called her aunt, though as the tips she gave me went from sixpences to half-crowns to cigarettes *and* half-crowns, plus an occasional off-colour joke, in the end I wasn't calling her anything (in one perspective, this process, a sort of graduation, covers aeons of time, but in fact was complete by the time I was sixteen). An example of the sort of joke she would tell me is as follows: a man who had had his member chopped off and an elephant's trunk sewn on in its place said, 'It's fine, except a bit embarrassing when buns are produced.' I judged this singularly unamusing story, at which I was obliged to laugh heartily to mask the blush it produced, to be from a cornucopia of similar duds from the comic foreigner she walked out with – my dad said the man had managed to buy a whacking great slice of Sussex from some old family because the present incumbent was gaga. When my mother spoke of 'John' I could tell two things: that the usage grated because she felt it was fraudulent, but that his financial status disqualified her from holding an opinion. I think she thought Clarice was in high society, though the boyfriend, being a peasant from the land of Vlad the Impaler, was finding it harder than he'd supposed to get into Boodles or some such. All this seeped into my ear sideways as I crouched over my logarithms. Clarice never sounded anything but bright, even when the burden of what she was saying was gloomy. I once heard her tell my father one of the bad dreams she was prone to – 'I was lying, dressed as a bride, in a coffin.' But she was smiling as she told him, just as she was when she told me the elephant's trunk joke. I wondered afterwards whether she had second sight.

*

Our house was on the corner of the Avenue and the Lane – the corner of the world. I stood under the apple tree and my dad opened his camera and pulled out the black concertina part. He put the palm of his hand round the little glass cube in which he saw the picture, and pulled the lever down slowly with his thumb. When my dad looked up at me after the click, I had no suspicion that we wouldn't all live for ever.

When I fell into the brook Bob Russell walked home behind me holding up my new overcoat from Gamages as it dripped with green slime: once, when I was three, I'd stepped out of our garden gate and he'd been pedalling by in his toy motor car – a blue one, made of wood – and I held one arm out and the other one up, like a policeman, and said Stop. He became my best friend.

Margaret from next door had red hair which she sometimes wore in a long plait. We played shops and gave tea-parties for her dolls in the garden, and she loved to brush my hair as though she were my mother. One Guy Fawkes night they all came into our garden – the two Margarets and Keith and Bob – and my dad was just putting a rocket into a milk bottle when Bob lit a sparkler and it slipped out of his hand into the big box my dad had put the fireworks in, and they all went off at once. Both the Margarets burst into tears, but I felt sorry for Bob as he held out the two jumping-jacks and the boy-scout rouser he'd brought with him. My dad said a bit sourly, 'If Bob Russell cut your head off, I think you'd forgive him.'

The Craigies were next door, then there was Keith's house, and next to that lived a young man called Bernard who was twenty and taught at the Sunday School. I was very little when I knocked on his door and didn't know why his mother laughed when I asked her if Bernard wanted to come out to play. Then came Bob's house, and next to him lived Mrs de Cruz. She had a handsome grown-up daughter who taught tap-dancing to little girls in the church-hall. When we bent down, peeping through the keyhole to see her in her tights, she suddenly opened the door. 'Cheek!' she magnificently cried, as we raced away.

These were quiet days in Malden and Coombe, moving very slowly. The sounds were soft: the squeak and chirrup of a hand-held garden spray, the patter of winter-wash on pear-trees; a lone car, drawing into the kerb across the gravel of a side-road; the shaking of milk-bottles in Natty James's cart as he pushed it to the side gate; the thump of a come-back ball, the creak of a swing in one of the long gardens, the muffled clank of a garden roller. I fainted from the sun one hot summer, but Dr Roberts was only a little way up the Lane. Bob Russell and I disappeared in our pedal-cars while search-parties were sent out far and wide – we came back from Cannon Hill covered in mud and singing and everyone laughed and marvelled at our daring – that's when Dr Roberts called us the two terrors of the known world. Nothing happened, everything was the same, you could hear the clock in the kitchen ticking but the hour hand never moved. My grandfather came to herd us back home in the evenings from over the fields and decoys jumped up from behind the grassy mounds to shout 'Grandad!' and then we all ducked down again, suffocating with laughter. Parachutes made out of handkerchiefs floated from bathroom windows and men painting the sills threw down tennis-balls they'd found in the gutters. There were birthday parties with green jellies and my name read out on Children's Hour, and my mother bustled out of the scullery on a summer's evening to join the boys in a game of cricket; she would insist on holding the bat in one hand, but I was proud of the scornful way she belted the ball over the fence for six and out.

This was the way it was before Captain Ferguson was hanged. When that happened, I think every mother and father kept the reports from their children as far as they could, but the censorship wasn't perfect. If you didn't overhear the grown-ups talking to each other in the street or over the fence or suddenly falling silent in kitchens and sitting-rooms, the Sunday papers were there, tucked by habit under cushions, and those who hadn't seen them knew friends who had. Just as when Billy Pratt offered to tell me how babies came and I thought I was terribly keen to garner the information, I found I didn't want to know. There was no chance of a reprieve since there was no element of extenuation in the event. The bed was soaked in blood, and Captain Ferguson's sister lay in it with her throat cut. It was his bed, and his knife, and after a strange preliminary deposition on his part that he had felt it his obligation to protect her from the depravity of other men, he appeared simply to cave in. On the morning of his execution Mrs Van Der Elst of the Society for the Abolition of Capital Punishment stood outside Wandsworth prison waiting for eight o'clock, accompanied by people who made a habit of turning up on these occasions to watch the minute hand flick past the hour. 'So she wasn't his sister after all,' I heard Mrs Smiles saying to Mrs Chamberlain, and Mrs Chamberlain catching sight of Ken and me looking up from the little red wheelbarrow we were filling with stones in their front-garden, said 'Off you go, boys.' But there'd been no deception. She'd been his sister as well.

After it happened I knew Captain Ferguson was timing me with a big watch in his hand as I ran down from Frank Allsop's house in Adela Avenue in the dark. Captain Ferguson was on the side of the witches, but he gave you a chance if you got back inside the time. But what was it? The witches sat against the wall in Douglas Avenue and I whistled as loud as I could when I ran past. He might have stood them down, but you couldn't be sure. Had you said the Lord's Prayer the magic number of times? Three times three times three. Would you get through the back gate before he stopped the watch? You never knew how much time he was allowing. I got ear-ache, bilious attacks, lay trembling in my bed in inexplicable panic. I developed a conviction that I had gone mad and people were in a conspiracy not to tell me, pretending I was sane when they knew I was not; and even if this could be denied, wasn't I mad in thinking it? My dad sat me on his knee and my mother took me into the big double bed between them and I fell asleep with my face on her arm. Captain Ferguson was going to come back and murder both of them, leaving me alone in the world until one day I would hear the door creak and he would appear in the empty passageway in the empty house, and draw his knife as he came towards me.

> When I was five the bad dreams came;
> Nothing after was quite the same.

Time after time the anxieties of childhood are floated away in dreams and fairy-stories, but then a day comes when the fantasies lose their power to discharge the real anxiety. My recurring nightmares showed how I'd failed in my attempt to incorporate what had happened as just an extra ingredient in a world that had stayed the same. Because it hadn't. Captain Ferguson changed it, not by altering the landscape but by destroying the certainties that had underpinned it. He had removed them for ever. Captain Ferguson had re-made the world by revealing that the only everlasting certainties were separation and death. Nothing was what it seemed. I would never hear the last of Captain Ferguson, I never could, for his was the world I was to live in for the rest of my days.

THE MONSTER

My father's roots were in an old-fashioned culture of self-improvement. He had served his time to the shipping and forwarding business at the firm of Paul and Preston in Liverpool, and pursuing his studies in his spare time had taught himself statistics and short-hand, French and Spanish: to 'better' oneself was something of a moral as well as a commercial imperative. His references are written out in longhand and in brown ink, plain straightforward statements with a measured tread that tell you not only about the man himself, but something about a society which knew when not be casual: 'TO WHOM IT MAY CONCERN: Mr Ernest Redfern Robinson has been associated with the American Express Company as bookkeeper for the past eight years. During that period he has fulfilled his duties with satisfaction to the Company and with credit to himself. We have the highest opinion of his integrity and honour and can confidently recommend him to any requiring his services. We may also be permitted to point out his value as an interpreter and/or translator of foreign languages which has been frequently of material assistance to us. He is leaving us entirely of his own accord to better his business career, and we wish him well in any new sphere to which he may be called.'

He had bettered himself. That meant he had improved his position but not changed his circumstances. There is greed and covetousness and envy and narcissism tucked away in the word 'ambitious', and my father had none of these characteristics. But ambitious also implies a willingness to exchange what is certain for what is not, and on this ground also my father could not qualify. First he asked me what I wanted to do and I answered promptly I should like to be a singer or a comedian. He thought I was joking, but when he realised I wasn't, the bitter way he clucked his tongue (a habit of his when truly disgusted) prompted me to add that I wouldn't mind being a journalist if I couldn't be either of the other two. He was instantly

19

seized by the huge odds against anyone thinking I was fit for such work. He said look, wouldn't it be a good plan to enter the executive branch of the Civil Service? I said that was for people who didn't go to the University. Or to be precise, Oxford.

Now he was really alarmed. Oxford wasn't anything he'd had to take account of – I think the closest he'd come to it was an account of the place by one Terence Greenidge, written in the Twenties, which he'd picked up from the book barrows of Faringdon Road where he often spent his lunch hour browsing. The book was called *Degenerate Oxford?* It was a spirited defence of homosexual style conventionally disguised as a tract against philistinism. My father didn't realise this, I'm pretty sure, but was taken by the descriptions of parties and drunkenness and the debts and the broken glass. It wasn't my morals he was worried about, although being as much in the habit of reading my correspondence as I was of reading his, he'd once or twice told me I was getting too fond of girls; it wasn't depravity that concerned him, it was expense. He had fantasies of me getting through my grant in a fortnight, joining the Bullingdon, hiring a manservant and hunting with the Quorn. I would then return to Malden and Coombe dressed in a velvet jacket and present him with the bills.

One evening I got back from school and he said Look, I've written it all down on this bit of paper. Just go up to your room and don't say anything until you've read it. I knew it must be serious because my 'room' was a chilly little place whose only function was to supply somewhere to go to sleep in. The main thing he now proposed was that I should try and get into the *Administrative* section of the Civil Service since this was for someone with a degree. And read for that degree at London University. I don't think he felt he had a chance of roping me in for this, because when I went downstairs he was already mending a puncture in his back wheel and scarcely looked up when I told him what I thought.

I said more or less this. That I had to go to the University, since it changed you – changed you like garlic and onion and alcohol changed you: a degree made you feel different: made people perceive you differently: changed your tribe. However, if you were to be entitled to the full woolly tie with the large knot as patented by the bunch of Audenesque missionaries at my school, the only degree that would work the magic was one from Oxford. This was a practical if somewhat romantic analysis of my feelings, but it wasn't at all the full strength.

The fuller version I didn't bother setting out, either for my father or anyone else, because it wasn't altogether amenable to description; you can't go round telling people you know a place you've never visited unless you wish to invite shuddering yawns and the presumption you've been reading *Sinister Street* or *Vile Bodies*. I don't mean I had any idea of the physical layout of Oxford, I wasn't certain about the Colleges and the University being the same thing, I didn't know about the river and which bit was the Isis and which bit the Cherwell, and when I sent in an application to read English I called it *Literae Humaniores* because it sounded about right. But Oxford was already in me because it was the original source of the high anxiety I had become hooked on. This addictive tension was generated by the swaggering but merciless gang who ran my peculiar school: to perform, to deliver, to astonish, was unflaggingly demanded, and they would search you for it, regardless of your wishes or capacity. We entered the place each morning and heard the sound of their whips whistling and cracking about our heads, unless it was a day when you encountered their even more fearsome approval, something they propped up against you like a stupendous menhir you had to keep upright. You were thrilled to the marrow by the way they treated you as an equal, and scared to death by the responsibility it enjoined. My school was like a continuous bout of scarlet fever, and it did for many. But like rats fed on warfarin there were those who developed an appetite for what might have poisoned them, felt pangs of deprivation if they didn't get it, and knew the anxiety they were famished without was available in its concentrated form at the original source, the place these men had started from. I was at Oxford before ever I got there. I brought it with me. I couldn't wait to stick my fingers into the sockets of the place and connect myself directly with the current.

All this was coming up like a boil towards the end of my life at this strange school. The place was constructed – you couldn't say 'built' because that suggests some identifiable personal endeavour – in 1935 and was indistinguishable from the factories which surrounded it. The authorities invited a man to run it who before he took the job was (according to witnesses) a mild creature who taught history at Whitgift. When he arrived in the barren wilderness between the Southern Railway and the Kingston By-pass he turned into a Monster. His face became red and fleshy, he wore a check overcoat that he must have dragged from the shoulders of a welshing bookie in lieu of winnings, and as he turned towards the parents of his boys he raised his lips from his teeth like Mr Hyde and told them they lived in a suburban slum.

This man called Garrett was able to send the blood out of his face at will, inducing a white-faced anger whenever tactics seemed to require it. The music master of Winchester, a man with a monumental stammer, came to lecture and the whole school laughed until it was hysterical, and small boys were sitting cross-legged in the pools of their helpless incontinence. Garrett beat them all, he beat every boy, he beat the whole school. When he came on to the dais at Assembly and sat in the seat of power while the hymns were being sung, his face, already a high tomato, suffused with extra blood as he laughed silently at the memory of some unutterable never-to-be-forgotten joke. He wrote to the parents of a boy who was later to become an enlightened prison-governor, ranting about their son's undescended testicles as though this were a personal affront. At all times he was rumoured to be on the point of marriage with a strange actress called Martita Hunt, but was in fact as queer as a coot (not that these two last conditions need have been mutually exclusive). Knowing him was like knowing an ogre who had the power to drag you up the essential beanstalk and show you the view. That he then insisted you distinguish the significant features of this panorama, that you tell him what you thought might usefully be rearranged, and that for the rest of your days you would question received opinion with the zeal of a knight pursuing the Grail, was the payment he exacted for the revelation he bestowed.

His thumbprint was everywhere. He tirelessly rallied boys, parents, governors with his radical assessment of the empowering nature of education, shamelessly importuning old Oxford chums to visit his bricky grove and fertilise it with their fame and aura: he must have had an unusually convincing style to persuade Eliot to present the prizes, but then he'd already talked Auden into writing the school song. This was of a banality that is only achieved by great contriving; I suspect Auden was not so much intent on dashing off a poem to order (something he was always surprisingly amenable to: he accepted five dollars from a woman who had recognised him in Schraft's in payment for an epithalamium for her daughter's wedding, scribbling the verses out on the pharmacist's pad as they both waited for their prescriptions to be filled) as making a pastiche of the genre –

> Man has mind but body also,
> So we learn to tackle low;
> Bowl the off-breaks, hit the sixes,
> Bend the diver's brilliant bow.

– and my suspicion is augmented by the fact that the only decent line in that verse was later recycled as part of a proper poem. As a boy of eleven the name Auden meant nothing to me and I rather wondered why we didn't have verses by a poet you'd heard of, like Wordsworth. But as I joined in, belting out his reach-me-down lyrics in the school hall, set to a rollicking tune by Thomas Wood, they did seem to have a clattering matter-of-factness that was curiously in tune with the raw concrete of the by-pass road and its shacky factories and bumbling traffic –

> Tractors grunt where oceans wandered
> Factories stand where green grass grew;
> Voices break and features alter,
> We shall soon be different too.

– 'Tractors grunt where oceans wandered' – how distinct the voice even when engaged in a technical exercise.

Cecil Day Lewis recited, Michael Redgrave sang, Harold Nicolson and the aged George Lansbury took us on romantic meanders through the political scene, Robert Graves judged the essay competition, David Cecil handed out the prizes, and Sybil Thorndike spoke of the therapeutic qualities of theatre. Theatre was a big thing at the school, and Garrett had initiated a tradition of an annual Shakespeare play, even contriving with his usual flair to have them reviewed in the *Evening Standard*, *The Times* and the *New Statesman*. How he smirked in telling the sixth-form that Mr Gielgud had asked Nevill Coghill rather tartly whether he had come up to London to see his Hamlet or the Raynes Park Macbeth. 'We must discount the obvious hyperbole,' Garrett added complacently. Then he forced tribute from the Ministry of Information in the shape of one of their much-admired ten-minute films which was devoted to our sixth-form discussion society, The Partisans. Coghill came from Oxford to judge the House Play competition and later, when he was my tutor, smilingly summed up Garrett as 'that old Monster'. But as monsters go, he was of the sacred order.

How did he manage it? 'You simply couldn't say no,' said Stephen

Spender, whose wife Natasha Litvin played the piano for us – the Bluthner that had belonged to Basil Wright and which Auden had left the cigarette burn on; Wright, producer of *Nightmail*, had given it to the school. 'Garrett was irresistible,' said Wright, 'Love at first sight.' But if all this had just been decor, a state grammar school with a stage army of nobs on call, it wouldn't have charged the particles, it couldn't have put the boys into a chronic state of over-excitement or stirred one parent to write and say he was suing the school for alienation of affection: he never saw his son, this father said, since from morning to night he was at the school, and when he wasn't there you couldn't get his attention for his mind and heart had been left behind, magnetised by something agitating that he couldn't let go of.

Garrett was delighted, for he saw the suburb as wasteland awaiting reclamation, and himself as just the man for the job. Of course, he would do it as an act of social piety, but his air was the air of a captain, if not an emperor, who would turn the entire district into a personal fiefdom: it would be a suburb, but a suburb of *his* school. Like many another unaligned radical of the day, his eye was fixed on the shining uplands of the romantic Left, where the new Jerusalem was to be superintended by an oligarchy of *bien pensant* clever dicks like himself. 'Whatever else you do in the holidays,' he told the school at the end of one term, 'make sure you get out of this suburban slum.'

Absurd, of course. The reality of life lived in middle- and lower-middle-class suburbs was casually disregarded by the *New Writing* crowd who invented a stereotype and reinforced it in poem after poem. Suburbia as miserabilium was central to the Macspaunday mob's boyish rebellion against mummy and daddy, and they made it their abiding metaphor. But metaphor based on a wishful fantasy is dreadfully attenuated, and when you read MacNeice's line about the Birmingham trams being like 'vast sarcophagi' you blush for its callowness, while the special fraudulence of *Keep the Aspidistra Flying* is always there to spoil the view when you feel like admiring Orwell's immaculate common sense.

The prejudices of the Faber & Faber tendency were not Garrett's natural inheritance, he had come by them second-hand being the son of a barber in Trowbridge. His scholarship from the local high-school to Exeter College, Oxford introduced him to an idiom which he found was much to his taste, and he brought it with him when he came to Raynes Park; Maurice Bowra was the style-guru of the homosexual gratin of that Oxford period, and whatever it was that Bowra imagined he was passing himself off as Garrett reproduced in an even fruitier version: to the besieging, booming voice was added an urgent scurrying walk in which the shoulders were held well back and the hasty duck-footed progress was of one anxious to catch someone with his trousers down. 'Walk the Garrett way,' John Grubb, junior English master had been heard to murmur, parodying the Mr Barratt shoe ads, '2, Mincing Lane.'

Garrett's air of being on the cultural barricades, about to take over the world, was preposterous. It arose from the prevailing intellectual climate in combination with his own bumptious and overbearing personality. But while in any wider application these impulses were merely foolish, they were nonetheless a true source of power and in my own view were what supercharged the school itself and made it singular. His crew was hand-picked. They were freebooting cosmopolitans who in their coloured hairy suits and bright woolly ties were as unsettling as a bunch of pirates sporting bandanas and flashing gold teeth. Three of them eventually held Chairs at universities, Claude Rogers and Rupert Shepard taught art, and Rex Warner was senior English master. Swank was built-in, elitism was pandemic, but the monstrous Garrett had a purpose: to confront the boys with a world beyond the by-pass road and provoke a questioning temperament. This last came direct from the University along with the Bowra imitations, but it was more than a style it was an instrument, something to go into the jungle with; using it, and provided good manners were observed (something of an obsession with Garrett) any boy's opinion was as good as the emperor's.

Except mine. Throughout the Garrett period I was in continuous trouble, condemned to spend my life in detention and beaten when I came out of it. Captain Ferguson was jumping out at me round corners, hiding my gasmask, stealing my gym-kit, losing books and transforming cheerful remarks into something called 'Insolence'. I couldn't get anything right because my spastic bids for survival never added up to a coherent strategy. My father was summoned and pooh-poohed Garrett's strictures – 'I suppose his behaviour might seem dreadful to a *schoolmaster*.' Garrett kept secret diaries in which he listed encounters with parents and long after both he and the school were at one with Nineveh and Tyre I saw what he'd written. 'Robinson. First-rate father.' Nice one, dad.

I was being bounced about on those energising quarks with

which the Monster bombarded his environment, and I suppose I was learning to stay in the saddle for longer periods at a time. I played rugger in a sly and nimble way, nimble, that is, at getting out of the way of hulking brutes who might otherwise have bumped into me. Rex Warner spotted this and made me full-back. 'You'll have to tackle them, then, won't you, or everyone will see,' said this mild-mannered man, coming as close to a triumphant jeer as he ever could. I was Caliban and Long John Silver in the school plays and it did nothing for my character. Riding backwards while sitting on the handlebars of my bike I collided with my best friend on the staff, Frank Coventry. 'We all know you're a clever little boy,' he said. 'Try and make it easier for us, please.'

Poetry – writing it or speaking it – won approval, for Garrett had compiled an anthology with Auden called *The Poet's Tongue*. It was in use throughout the school, and a more instantly enjoyable, entirely heterogeneous collection of poems I've yet to come across: making no distinction of light or serious, Auden and Garrett made a list of all the poems they liked and bunged them together alphabetically and anonymously (you had to look at the index to find out who'd written what). They did this, according to the introduction – a piece of prose which strikes the only ponderous note in the book – because they didn't want to over-awe the novice with 'the bias of great names'. Even when I was twelve or thirteen and couldn't imagine what poetry was for I thought if you were going to have the stuff at all this jumble of the narrative, the sonorous and the comic would do to be going on with until you could get your hands on a decent piece of prose, preferably the *Hotspur* – I suppose it was a compliment, coming from a schoolboy staring at a text book.

Garrett would have done the donkeywork, running down the copyrights and putting the book together, because Auden wouldn't have bothered (for circumstantial evidence in support of this claim, see Auden's apologetic thanks in the *incipit* to the *Oxford Book of Light Verse* which he supposedly edited: he says he owes so much to Mrs Dodds – wife of his friend Professor Dodds of Birmingham University – that it would be 'embarrassing' to go into details. It seems she'd assembled the greater part of the book while he was in Iceland with MacNeice.)

I think Garrett must have written the intro for there's a refined blokeyness about it that reminds you of a salesman pushing the goods by daring you to be left out of the swim – 'A great many people dislike the idea of poetry as they dislike overearnest people, because they imagine it is always worrying about the eternal verities. Those, in Mr Spender's words, who try to put poetry on a pedestal only succeed in putting it on the shelf. Poetry is no better and no worse than human nature; it is profound and shallow, sophisticated and naïve, etc., etc.' Of course, Auden used to do a natty line in schoolmasterly take-offs (*The Orators*) but only because he despised schoolroom propaganda; the brush-salesman patter would have been anathema to a poet who had written that poetry 'stubbornly insists on being read or ignored'.

And apart from the suspicion that it isn't good enough to be Auden, there's a tiny splinter of internal evidence that it was Garrett: the use of 'Mr' before Spender's name. A howling genteelism, he used it all the time in the school magazine to make it clear he was on calling terms with the celebs. (As a young man, my tutor Nevill Coghill had been Auden's tutor, and when Coghill retired some of us put together a Festschrift. At the dinner for Nevill in Exeter, Auden as a contributor was present. He was in his slippers, not the carpet-slippers but black velour with little rosettes to go with his dinner-jacket. I mentioned Garrett. He looked at me stonily. 'That schoolmaster', he said. And that's all he said.)

So with my bottom a *macedoine* of colourful bruises inflicted by the man that Garrett in his Talbot Baines Reed mode liked to call the 'Second Master' (there was a myth that Garrett couldn't beat because of some deficiency in the upper arm, but I think he liked watching) I entered for the Verse Speaking Competition at the suggestion of my friend Frank Coventry and won it with a recitation of 'Bat' by D.H. Lawrence. Coventry had steered me in the direction of this poem, perhaps because he thought a nice accessible descriptive piece, with plenty of attitude, would appeal to me. He coached me in speaking it aloud, although it made him smile to do it: he knew I was a show-off long before I knew it myself, but he himself had a special diffidence.

L.A.G. Strong (a governor of the school, co-opted by Garrett) was the judge and in his notes suggested I 'avoid the intrusive r in "a quick parabola under the arches"'. And I have, ever since, in all circumstances, obsessively; and even though the 'Second Master', a tall thin fellow called Gibb who was prone to wearing the top and bottom halves of separate suits, was the one who beat me, I have obeyed him – to the letter – in the single injunction he laid upon every boy. He taught geography but announced to all his classes, 'I care little how much any of you carry away from here in knowledge of prevailing winds or rain forests, but of one thing I am certain: no boy will ever leave this school without knowing how to spell "separate" and "Mediterranean".'

I took to wearing my pullovers back-to-front so that under them I could conceal one of those large-knotted ties, the badge of my betters. And I collided with Martita Hunt, twice. She was runner-up to Edith Evans when it came to playing eccentric grotesques, having a face like a North Country footballer and a voice like an aeolian harp in a stiff breeze. During the war she was a character-player in British films like *49th Parallel* where Eric Portman was the U-boat commander and she was the British grande dame who rounded on him with the words 'I must remember I am talking to one of the *herring folk*'. Later in *Great Expectations* she was Miss Havisham when Alec Guinness was Herbert Pocket (at Oxford during a talk at the OUDS Guinness told us how he had gone to Martita for lessons. She'd grabbed his upper lip and hooted 'Throw it away, darling, it's no use to you!')

Garrett was one of her walkers, and she would descend on the school to judge competitions or read poems. I'd had another go at the verse-speaking thing, and won again, this time with 'The Love Song of J. Alfred Prufrock'. Martita, who was judging, and had arrived with a middle-aged lady-in-waiting who smelt curiously of crème de menthe, graciously rose in front of the assembled school and said as a very special treat I should be allowed to choose a poem which she would recite. Baffled by so suddenly being thrust forward I heard myself asking her to give us the definitive reading of 'Prufrock'. I'd forgotten the line about 'a bald spot in the middle of my hair'. She shyed like a horse passing a lamp-post, and loosed off a batch of Shakespeare sonnets before you could say Ealing Studios.

And then one spring afternoon a group of the elect was invited to hear Miss Hunt give a reading of lyrics from the Silver Poets of the Seventeenth Century. Towards the end of the recital Garrett turned round and scanned the group sitting behind him. He was deciding which was the cleanest-looking boy, and picked on me. He whispered, 'Get the flowers that are in my study and present them to Miss Hunt when she finishes.' I withdrew with the solemn air of one whose purity fitted him to do the high priest's bidding. The school cat Stephen was sitting on the sofa ('The choice of name could only be put down to the early martyrdom expected by pessimists,' Garrett had noted) but Captain Ferguson was hiding in a cupboard and had put the 'fluence on the place. There were three lots of flowers and none of them looked like the sort of bouquet you gave an actress. I glanced wildly at the options: there was a bowl of bulbs, a vase of daffodils, and an elaborate arrangement of dried ferns. The bulbs were too dull, the daffs would drip – it must be the ferns. I grabbed them out of the Clarice Cliffe urn and got back as the applause was at its height, and as I crammed the ferns, crisp as a serving of Kelloggs, against the performer's enormous *balcon*, I knew Captain Ferguson had floored me again. Garrett gave her the bowl of bulbs afterwards but it was very nice of her to behave as though the ferns were a marvellously acceptable surprise, even as the crumbs were littering her chest.

The day came when Garrett left us. He was to be headmaster of Bristol Grammar School, and he had reason to hope this might be a staging post on his way to the headmastership of Harrow; two previous Harrow incumbents had come from Bristol. (His luck was out. When the Harrow job fell vacant on the death of R.W. Moore he sent in his application. But someone on the board of governors remembered what had been said all those years ago about Hensley Henson in the same circumstances: 'What Mr Garrett seems not to realise is that to be appointed headmaster of Harrow one must be either a scholar or a gentleman.') He wept, and shook hands with every boy as they filed past him. Some of the little boys wept too.

He was a great natural force, and would take his elemental powers with him. We lost them, but did they desert him too? Once he was away, did he have need of them, when the new circumstances may have made their exercise irrelevant? Power of this sort may depend on certain conditions for the magus to find it is available to him; at Whitgift, Garrett was an inoffensive nobody, quiet and biddable. At Raynes Park he was transformed, even as he had transformed.

The faintest of echoes rolled back from Bristol. Was there some hint of homosexual scandal at the school? Had a master been forced into withdrawing a too precise remark he had made about Garrett, substituting some such phrase as 'male orientated' for the word he'd actually used? My old friend and housemaster Peter Smith, himself a Bristolian, told me he'd been alarmed at Garrett's enormous intake of whisky, even to the extent of shushing him when they were at the bar of one of the Bristol hotels and Garrett, ogling the barman, cried out in his great trumpet-blast voice, 'Why did you never tell me this city had such gorgeous creatures in it?'

Dame Helen Gardner, who admired Garrett and served with him as a governor of the Shakespeare theatre in Stratford, told my wife, whose tutor she had been and whose friend she became, that the stroke Garrett suffered was at his mother's funeral. 'Mother always hoped I would marry Martita,' Garrett had said, 'but she had to make do with a boy.' The stroke crippled him and he couldn't continue. He resigned the headmastership and left the city, returning to what was undoubtedly his true heimat, close to what he always referred to as 'the beloved school'. He took a house in Wimbledon which he shared with a chaplain to the Archbishop of Canterbury.

Like a gyroscope set going at full speed the school took time to slow down and change its axis. The benign and clever Charles Wrinch was made Head. He came from Radley where he'd run the English department. What on earth was he doing, climbing aboard Garrett's garish whirligig, this civilised man whose great pleasure was the savouring of out-of-the-way texts? (Years later at my house Betjeman was quoting and couldn't place the source. 'Campbell,' said Wrinch, promptly but modestly). He stuck it for three years, then went back to teaching at Radley. His successor was Henry Porter, as nice and as good a man as anyone might hope to meet, as plain as the name he bore. Peter Smith said 'Henry specialises in unenthusiasm' and that made a change. The school's temperature came down, though as far as the Garrett virus went some of us were carriers, and perhaps would be, one way or another, for the rest of our lives. In a convalescent atmosphere it was easier to meet the conventional requirements, and since County Scholarships more or less came round with the rations in those days, I got mine, and Oxford was on. Frank Coventry now had his D.Phil and left to follow his vocation as a priest. William Walsh, later professor of Commonwealth Literature at Leeds, arrived to pass on the analytic style of his old tutor, Leavis, and I like to think he became a friend in the way Coventry had been: some boys are jaunty, but very hopeful of being looked after. Peter Smith put on the plays and when I went up to try for a place at Exeter, the Monster's old College, he wrote to Coghill telling him I'd be just the thing for undergraduate theatre. The kindness of these men was startling, in that it was resistant to the brash deficiencies of my temperament: it was unaffected and unfailing. For the moment, Captain Ferguson was on half-pay.

Reviewing the period, a social historian might suspect Garrett had been trying to set up a cod St Dominic's among the pickle factories, but it would be wide of the mark. It's true he liked to call the playing-field 'Big Side' and hand out grandiose titles like 'Prefect of Hall' and 'Prefect of Library', but all that was incidental, it was unassimilated left-over material, peripheral to the central endeavour: and the central endeavour was entirely idiosyncratic.

The truth is that Garrett was an oddity. He didn't know what he was doing, he was simply answering the call of his quirks and prejudices, which were often incoherent. He borrowed the school motto from Marx via Auden – 'To each his need, from each his power' – an irreproachably even-handed sentiment. But it went side by side with a wholly unreconstructed elitism. For example, you could find yourself either in Form Three or Form Three Special, and of course 'Special' meant 'clever'; the rich political incorrectness of the word, viewed from the perspective of a later day, is not without its charm. He boasted incessantly about the sorry commercial landscape of which the school was a part, and encouraged Frank Halliwell the senior chemistry master to design a cap-badge which would combine the major topographical eyesores of the location, viz. the by-pass road, the Southern Railway, and the concrete bridge which carried the one over the other. Halliwell turned out a metal chromium-plated job that was certainly a credit to scientific principles – the electric railway featured as a flash of lightning – and Garrett's only regret must have been that he hadn't managed to work in the fish-paste factory. This was snobbery of vintage quality, and seems to me to illustrate the cock-eyed merit of the man.

His school was unique, just as a picture is unique even when it is out of perspective, or a poem, even if it doesn't scan. Unique or just peculiar? Original or merely novel? A new star in the educational firmament or a comet burning out even as it is speeding nowhere? The place followed no tradition, nor did it initiate one: at that time, and in that place, it changed the world for me, but it's clear enough that it had no real location outside the imagination of the man whose monument it became. A pretty temporary monument, because it didn't long outlast him. Within fifty years it had gone from the face of the earth as though it had never been; what song the sirens sang is not beyond all conjecture, but Auden's curious ditty is forgotten and *The Poet's Tongue* lies buried in the rubble that packs the foundations of somewhere else entirely. I sometimes think I dreamt it.

GOOCH AND GEEK

Mr GEEK SAT at his usual table in the Bridge cafe in Great Mersey Street. He was a man whose teeth looked like a hand of cards fanned downwards. He lisped. Bridey the waitress came barging down the aisle bearing the plate of food and placed it in front of him. Geek stared at it, then picked up his knife. The cafe was full, for it was the dinner hour at the offices thereabout. Geek whispered a phrase to himself, and those near him on that occasion said that though he lisped they heard him clearly, perhaps because what he did next they had heard him threaten to do the day before. The words he uttered were 'Peas again!', and he rose to his feet and using the knife, catapulted the hard green little fellows all round the cafe, one by one.

Why had he done it? I asked the two other lads, the ones who were there when I arrived. They thought it was because Geek had got above himself: he was a senior manager and Jeff and Norman had to call him sir, but he gave himself airs that would have been appropriate only had he been the top man, a grey-haired well-bred figure who wore pince-nez and whose name was Gooch. It was odd there were two men called Geek and Gooch in the same office, but Gooch was of another dimension, and was never seen: I met him once, summoned to his office on my first day, where he lifted his mild severe gaze from a sheet of paper as I stood with my hands respectfully behind my back, and bade me mind my duties. So remote from the lino and cubicles of the rest of the office was his own hushed environment with its carpet and ticking clock that I felt he would pick up a quill pen when I had gone and continue painstakingly to inscribe on the paper in front of him the sort of curlicues that were seen on white five pound notes. He lowered his head and nodded slightly, and I left the room.

The war was on. Looking back I can see I was lucky to have been a boy in the war, for as a boy I'd had no experience of anything better, and the rationing and the blackout and the restrictions in general just seemed like ordinary life. Otherwise I'd have known what I was missing. The food was monotonous to someone like Geek who had been driven mad by endless peas, but in my own case never ever having been offered an omelette I was delighted to discover such things existed, when my mother was forced into making them after eggs turned into powder overnight. Like the mad theft of everyone's railings, which were discovered rusting in piles all over the country after the war, this 'dried-egg' replaced the natural product for no reason at all and at vast expense. It was either a scam by owners of factories which were good at turning things into powder, or one of a multitude of cock-ups at the Ministry of Bubble Blowing. The quiet inefficiency of a Civil Service run by rusticating academics anxious to 'do their bit' was masked or actually canonised by reference to the 'war effort'; a culture prolonged after the war when the only thing people couldn't do without was the habit of doing without.

In London, everyone was frightened of the flying-bombs. I was apprehensive when the siren went, my father always put a brave face on it as we dived under the dining-room table, but my mother was simply terrified. (She was a great trembler, but when we installed a Morrison shelter, a sort of metal cage that occupied our front room, you knew everyone in it was equally frightened, because the wire mesh shook noisily for a minute or two after each of us in turn climbed in. The trembling stopped after you got used to being inside the thing, and the certainty that you would be dead in short order was replaced by the knowledge that this had happened before and you were still alive.) But there was no reason my mother had to be terrorised like this night after night, since there was nothing to stop her taking off for Liverpool, where it had been all quiet for some time. I went with her largely because that was the way she wanted it; and for my own obscure reasons, I wanted it too. My father stayed on, living at his office where he was a member of the Fire-Service, and sleeping at night in a dormitory. I became an office boy.

This might seem strange. Why didn't my father fix me up at some school or other, and why didn't I kick up a row about it? Perhaps he thought we'd only be away a few weeks, and it wasn't worth it. But if we were going for that short a time, why bother wangling me a job at the Liverpool branch of the United Africa Company? We were staying with an aunt, and I suppose we made a contribution to the household expenses – was the office job to help out with this? I handed my wages to my mother – £2.10s – and she gave me back money for lunch and fares and six shillings as pocket-money, but I had a feeling this was a ritual rather than a necessity. Even in the panic of bundling us off, my mother sick with fear that we'd be killed before we reached Euston, it's odd my father's sense of priorities seems to have collapsed. Perhaps the bombs made it easy to forget about anything else. My own complaisance is very simply explained: I wasn't just running away from the bombs, I was running away from the School Certificate. The exam was prowling towards me out of the deep thickets of Captain Ferguson country and the necessity of doing spectacularly well haunted me day and night. Here was a magnificent, an unlooked-for reprieve.

Office life was remarkable for the total absence of expectation. The days arrived like patterns that had simply to be coloured in, one day's pattern being exactly the same as the next. I found it enormously refreshing. Dozing on the tram to the Pier Head, I knew no one had been baiting tiger-traps for me overnight, no chance of anyone else getting higher marks in the English essay, the competition had been suspended and there was no temptation (to which I had often succumbed) to stay at home feigning a bilious attack to avoid some exam or test in which I might not have come top by acclamation.

The mail would be waiting, wonderfully impersonal stuff full of ult and inst and even date and yours of, mail that would have nothing to do with me once I'd opened it and made my morning distribution to the men it was addressed to. These men seemed to take no more notice of it than I did, sticking it in in-trays as though that was all that had to happen, continuing to fill in ledgers with a smiling abstracted air, as though this too was simply a way of passing the time. How I relished it. Nothing to win, nothing to lose, and free to go out into this land of the harmless tramcar with no fear of being asked to explain myself.

Two walks fell delightfully to my lot, and I followed them daily, hardly believing you could be paid for dawdling along like a milk-maid in a fairy-tale. One would take me down Great Mersey Street to the Phoenix Mill, a name so much enhancing the mythical impression I was receiving that the first time I went there I thought its sails would be rotating gently in the breeze coming off the Mersey. It was a warehouse and factory, processing material from West Africa, sisal and copra and palm oil and groundnuts, and my part in maintaining this process was to hand over a sack of letters, then saunter back. What I relished was the freedom from any responsibility except not losing the bag; to one who had been taught that complete personal involvement was the minimum requirement for every boy, and that this commitment would be tested regularly and without warning, the release was delicious.

Especially so when I took the second and more extensive walk with its greater sense of enlarged freedom. Leaving from the main entrance of the United Africa Company with my haversack and a careless air of knowing my bona fides were unassailable, buying a ticket at St James's Street station to go under the Mersey to the Wirral (or to be accurate, showing my colleague Jeff's season ticket at the barrier and later splitting the fare with him) and with no other obligation in the whole wide world but to arrive at the little wishing-well at Port Sunlight and hand over my sack to a nice girl who would hand me another in exchange, this was heart's delight. No wonder I whistled as I pulled a slab of Nestlés from the slot-machine on the platform coming back, and even deferred to an old sourpuss who looked up at me and said 'Nobody wants to hear you whistle'. I apologised, knowing that unlike the old codger who'd complained, I was a duke who had great estates on which he could whistle as freely as he pleased.

It was the fact of doing nothing without any risk of retribution that was so appealing. Mr Jones, an ancient recidivist of the office world, a lifer, was spending his last years in paid employment superintending the mail department. I looked at him as he approached, a stooped figure, his frozen neck bent forward parallel with the floor, and watched as he eased himself into an effortful tilt that began at the hips so that his head came slowly back with the movement of his spine and his eyes entered the moderately horizontal. He lived for the day his son would return from the war. Gleeful at the very thought, he'd give a couple of feeble hops. 'That'll be the day I'll dance all night.' The stationery cupboard was his kingdom and, leaving a few minutes before us at the end of the day, he would give us the key so we could lock up after we'd put the mail through the franking machine. Mr Jones's unquestioning loyalty to office life was at odds with my own idle acceptance of the prevailing inertia. I think I may have looked at him from time to time with a faint tremor of curiosity, as a tourist might acknowledge the cultural deprivations of the natives and suppose that they didn't mind. When I took one of the girls who was older than me to the pictures, Mr Jones happened to see us as we swaggered into the Palais de Luxe and reported back to Jeff and Norman that he hadn't thought I was that sort of a lad. She was a buxom lass and free with her favours, which in those innocent days simply meant she'd let you kiss her goodnight. Even worse, I hid the outgoing mail in a filing cabinet one evening when I couldn't be bothered to take it to the post, planning to do it in the morning when I set off for the Phoenix Mill. Mr Jones got to the cabinet before I did. I had no more than the faintest sensation of wrongdoing, I was embarrassed that the stratagem had been discovered in all its lowliness, yet I could see it troubled, even disturbed him. The office had grown like ivy over Mr Jones, and you couldn't tug at the one without dislodging the other. In turning my back on the office so casually, I'd turned my back on him. I apologised in a red-faced sort of way. But for the first time since I'd arrived I found myself thinking thank Christ I'm not here for ever.

Liverpool had been a place of myth to me, a book of fairy-stories about my mother's childhood. Her grandmother, Jane Hemming, had painted the numerals on clock faces in the county of Worcestershire and had once walked out with a clergyman. One day in the country he had spread his cloak on the grass and invited her to sit down. She looked him in the eye. 'Henceforth,' she rebuked him, 'you may go your way and I shall go mine.' She had then married a Mr William Jones, a distributor of mineral water in Liverpool. In very late old age she would ask her elderly son to give her a shilling; the son would reply solemnly 'You great big doll', and shaking her head she'd say, 'Shabby fellow, shabby fellow.' They once owned the land on which the Imperial Tobacco Company built its headquarters, but all families have such castles in Spain. They lived in Maria Road which was not exactly Park Lane and women in shawls would hurl abuse at each other: 'If I couldn't do you a good turn I wouldn't do you a bad, but the next time you come past our house I'll cut the eye out of yous with the fender.' Street vendors cried 'Shirt buttons, shirt buttons, any mugs!' The mugs had names on them and a child came back to return one on the grounds that her mother said she wasn't called Daisy. The man brushed the complaint aside with a great roar. 'Is it my business that your mother can't spell? Away with you to the pig market.'

Then, when most of the eight children were working and could make their contribution, they moved to a solid family house in Breeze Hill, and this was a place and time that my mother always spoke of as though it were the transformation scene in a pantomime. Never was there such an idyllic family, it seems, for there was now no father and like the March sisters in another story they felt at ease in his absence, looking after each other in characteristic ways, and clustering round a smiling cheerful mother. How primary were the colours, as my mother turned the pages. Bill cleaning the family shoes, spitting on the toe-caps and warning the girls as they teased him 'I'm just in the humour for you!' Marie looking after the younger ones when their mother was out, making them sit under the table and banging them on the head with the tea-cosy if they so much as peeped out. Tom getting the dog to lick the cake he was keeping for him so nobody would steal it. Joe telling the little maid she must call him Mr Hogan, and the little maid falling about laughing.

And the darker scenes, with the bad fairy in attendance. There was a stolen gold watch and Rose was suspected. Rose was the youngest of the family, but the man she thought was her brother – Bill, the eldest of the children – was her father. Her natural mother had died in her bed with Rose as a baby in her arms, and Rose had been taken in by my grandmother and brought up as her own. She didn't know her true relationship to Bill, who'd married again. 'Listen Rose, if you took it to swank with in front of the lads at the corner and you've broken it, just tell me and I'll have it mended and I won't tell a soul,' said Harry Hunter, who was courting Jean, one of the other girls. 'But I haven't had it, Harry,' said Rose, 'why would anyone think I'd take it?' Bill's wife urged Rose to own up. 'If they find out before you admit it, Rose, you'll be sent to a reformatory.' But it was Bill's wife who had stolen the watch. A true fairy-story, for of course she was Rose's stepmother.

My mother's brother Peter took special care of her, for she was the timid one, and stayed at home. In the bosom of the family she was safe. From what? I suppose what we are all frightened of, other people. With a mixture of humour and delicacy which I came to know was the essence of the man, Peter coaxed her to go with him to see about a job at the main post office. I think it was the proudest moment of my mother's life when she plucked up courage and started work there, and for the rest of her life spoke of it as though she had once been Chancellor of the Exchequer.

This was when she first knew my father, who would meet her outside and walk her to the tram. She told me the one thing he couldn't bear was for her to be standing waiting for him and carrying a handbag. He didn't tell her why for a long time. What she didn't know was that the handbag was the badge of the street-walker, though when he finally told her she took the handbag in both hands and hit him over the head with it. I know exactly how she would be standing, for when she was a widow living once more in Liverpool, I would see her waiting for me across the concourse at Euston, standing as close to the pillar as she could get without actually touching it, her handbag held on a long strap in front of her. When she saw me, her face lit up with relief, and though she was an old lady of eighty, she grinned like a young girl.

Tales my mother taught me, rose-tinted pictures from a family album I carried in my imagination. But now I was in the place itself it was different: Liverpool was drab. I don't suppose I took into account that a place and its fantasy share a common root but it doesn't make them the same: you probably wouldn't enjoy Black Forest gateau in the Black Forest, whatever you felt about it anywhere else. A prickle of disaffection for the city began to stir, I noticed its unfavourable aspects and didn't feel at home.

The little sooty redbrick terraces ran off at right-angles to the tramlines, with names like Pansy Street and Harebell Street and Woodbine Street – 'old property' as my mother always called it, a category which invoked a dignity that wasn't there any more, if it ever had been. Men in mufflers wearing the battered cast-off clothes of others stood at street corners. I stared down from the top deck of the tramcar as it swayed along Scotland Road, and saw these old fellows in the uniform of their dereliction leaning against the walls of pubs that had nothing to do with pleasure. The random relationship between themselves and the garments they wore looked, in its ugly disproportion, like part of a plan to ensure their degradation.

The trams had exotic-sounding destinations – St Domingo Grove, Old Swan, Everton Valley, Cabbage Hall, Litherland, Fazakerley – but it was dark outside as I returned from Mersey Street so who could tell? The tram ground its way out of the ruined city to enter an endless wasteland of concrete ringroads, and scattered across this featureless savannah my mother's brothers and sisters now lived.

Aunt Marie ran a sweet-and-tobacconist's shop which included a post office, at the corner of Stanley Park Avenue, and ran it to drill-sergeant standards. Prowling up and down the early-morning queue of hangdog men who were waiting for cigarettes (it was wartime and nothing was easily come by) she would suddenly bark in a voice loaded with menace 'I don't know your face!', and some luckless supplicant who had hoped to pass as a regular customer would stumble away to the guard-room. All she needed was a pace-stick.

Uncle Chris her husband wore leather gloves when driving his Rover at an unfailing 28mph, and he was the postmaster. He combined this function with his job as an accountant at a factory which made floor polish. Uncle Chris's proximity to the product had caused him to absorb a quantity into his system, and his face was a positive advertisement for Shinio, since it gleamed with crinkly smiles. These only faded when his dignity came under threat, as when other motorists presumed to pass him while he was observing his own special speed limit. The Shinio would drain out of his cheeks and its high gloss would be replaced by unsmiling disapproval as Aunt Marie, riding shotgun, gripped her handbag and turned to the other passengers to utter the dread word 'Overtaking!', receiving a murmur of indignant assent from the rear seat whose non-car-owning occupants had actually come to believe over the years that this was a serious breach of the Highway Code.

There was a terrible moment when the Shinio all but turned matt permanently, when at three o'clock one winter's morning Uncle Chris was summoned from his bed over the shop by a ring at the bell. He came down the steep stairs in his pyjamas and opened the side door. 'Have you got a penny for two ha'pennies,' said the figure in the murk, 'I want a packet of Woodbines from the slot-machine.' This incident reverberated down the years in the annals of the tribe, but most members felt that if such an affront were to be offered to anybody, Uncle Chris was about the right candidate.

What with the shop and the Shinio, Uncle Chris and Aunt Marie made dollops of money, and later lived in a substantial house they'd had built for them in Childwall. Both were the soul of generosity to me as long as I ever knew them, first with fags and sweets and half-crowns when I was a boy and then, when I was buying a house myself and was short of the deposit by a few hundred quid, Aunt Marie had it in an envelope by the next post. At this time of her life her views on society in general were somewhat to the right of the Royal Family, and it was a sight to behold her watching beadily through the french windows to make sure the man she'd hired to cut the grass didn't skimp the edges. She mistrusted the working class but to my astonishment casually revealed in her old age that she had been prime mover in the foundation in Liverpool of the first shop-girls' union.

I was so startled I came back the next day and got it down on tape, and as I play it I hear the severity of her voice, so wonderfully appropriate to the high seriousness of the tale she is telling, and so marvellously at odds with the softness of her heart. She was working at Lewis's the department store – 'Messrs Lewis' as she calls it with a sort of dignified asperity in deference to the tape-recorder – and I suppose she's talking about a time round about 1919. She was 'First Sales' which meant she was a senior hand and was looked on as management material, a reliable employee and the last person the Cohen family, who owned the place, would ever expect to rock the boat.

I thought a lot of the girls in the shop were very much underpaid. I was getting the handsome sum of eight shillings a week, and I was First Sales, and others beneath me were getting six shillings and four shillings. So about half a dozen of us got together and we thought, well, we'll start the union. So we went across the road to a little shop to find out what they'd charge us to rent a room over the shop, and see what we could afford, which wouldn't be very much, of course. You know, for somewhere to go and hold meetings. There were just the six of us, including me.

So we decided then, well all right, we'll just start this union among ourselves, and we'll decide that we'll go out on strike on the busiest day, which was Christmas Eve. The firm got to know about this and they called a meeting of all the first hands, to be held in the restaurant of the shop, and of course I was one of the first hands and I was sent to Coventry for having really upheld any part of this business.

And the firm said they were very surprised at me doing such a thing – the Cohen family, I mean. Well, they had this meeting and they asked for the strike to be called off – we'd arranged all the pickets and everything at the doors for the busy time, it would be going back somewhere about sixty or more years ago, this, and they said that if we would give them time they would see there was an improvement, and bear in mind we were getting very indifferent food at that period.

Out of our eight shillings I myself, and others, used to spend on an average, fourpence a day. Twopennyworth of butter and a twopenny cob, for our dinner, because we just couldn't eat the food they supplied. At the end of a week we'd have gone through about two shillings out of our wages.

Well, the strike was called off. They had a meeting then and it was decided that we should be paid the next week an increase from eight shillings to two pounds ten.

At the start of it all one of the Cohens had called me in and said Well, Miss Hogan, we're very surprised at you who are one of our First Sales should be doing this. And I said Well I don't think I get a living wage, I can't live on what I'm getting, so what must the second and third sales be like? So he said, Really you could be dismissed for doing a thing like this. And I said Well, that is entirely up to yourself.

I should like to give you some idea of the sharpness and the pride with which my Aunt Marie uttered that last sentence, but I can't see how to do it. She was a dark and handsome young beauty in the days she talks about, the photographs show it, and I think she would walk the floors of a department store as though they were a stage. All my aunts seem to have worked as shop-girls, and as demonstrator of the Little Wizard Patent Darner my Aunt Lil always assumed it *was* a play, in which she had a solo spot. I saw customers buy the Little Wizard from her with the faintly soppy look you see on the faces of people at stage doors getting their autograph books signed. I'd go into Lewis's from Mersey Street during my lunch hour and play straight man – 'The gentleman over there,' she'd say, 'is the darner you bought giving satisfaction?' 'Perfect. I am delighted with it,' I would answer, 'I have come expressly to buy three more, since I believe they would make excellent Christmas presents.' I didn't have her touch.

We'd been living with Lil and her husband Jim who looked like Gary Cooper. Lots of people look like film stars but there is always one thing that makes them different, apart from them not being the film star. In Jim's case his face was identical, lean and sculpted, and he was just as tall, but he was a bit knock-kneed where Cooper was on the whole bandy – not all that bandy, but you remember the way he hobbled on the outside of his boots when he walked down Main Street in Westerns like 'High Noon', his hands hanging over his guns; I took Cooper to lunch in Paris once when it fell to my part later in life to meet such icons, and after he'd chosen fish, offering as the reason for his choice that 'there can't be no evil in haddock,' I asked him to identify what he took to be the central requirement for success in films. 'You got to have good feet,' he'd said. Manifestly he lacked these, so this was no more than modesty, but the way he walked and the way Jim walked, in essence very different, were each mirror images of the other. They were both equally randy, though neither Cooper nor my Uncle Jim ever let on about this, until found out. Jim was doing well as a civil servant in charge of deciding who got how many petrol coupons, but earlier in life had gone to sea and one of the other hands on the ship was a writer of short stories called James Hanley, who pinched Jim's portable gramophone: he also pinched Jim's name which was Crilly, and used it as a title for a book.

I was on the cusp of departure, and the last thing I remember about this time in Liverpool was Aunt Lil suddenly getting it into her head that Jim was playing her false with his secretary. This became a King Charles's Head with her, and people who came to the house were kind to her as people are to those who suffer foolish delusions. She was such a bright amusing woman that to see her sitting with her head slumped on her hands in front of the fire was very depressing to me. In normal circumstances she'd have been telling us about her billeting officer days, earlier in the war, perhaps about the man who came to the door on the arm of a large bear, or the house where the wake was going on and she'd opened the inner door only to find there was a rope tied to the corpse's neck and as she pulled the door open, it sat up.

On the grounds that I was a grammar school lad, Jim recruited me to lecture her from the psychological point of view, and I do believe my chuckle-headed ramblings culled from the latest Penguin and delivered with the fierce solemnity of a teenage autodidact, actually gave her some comfort. Not for long, however, because she hadn't been deluded at all. Jim had been knocking it off with the secretary good-oh. Once the confession had been dragged out of him by his increasing fear that his wife might actually die, he offered to commit suicide. This turned out to be a superfluous gesture, since a few days later Jim died in bed beside his wife, my aunt waking up just in time to hear the rattle in his throat.

I'd already gone. I can't remember leaving Geek and Gooch, or Jeff and Norman, and I don't know if Mr Jones's son came back so his dad could dance all night – I hope so, with all my heart. But the next image I see is a rugby ball curving away down the school hall which is empty except for me. I'm working on my own for both School Certificate and Higher School Certificate and to relieve my feelings I've made a magnificent drop-kick. It soars to the roof-beam, then falls towards the swing doors just as our new headmaster Charles Wrinch opens them. The ball bounces off his head and he ignores it. He looks at me. It's the first time we've met since my return. 'You've been doing all manner of meaningless jobs, I hear,' he says, 'but that's all over now. You're back where you belong.' And he turns round and walks out.

SMIVVO

THE GENERAL KNOWLEDGE Exam was an annual charade consisting of a hundred questions like What is a Wykehamist or Who are Negretti and Zambra, and there was no handicapping. Every boy was given the same paper, juniors and seniors alike, and it was a hundred metres dash with the masters upholding the sporting nature of the occasion by guaranteeing to have First, Second and Third on the notice-board within forty minutes of the papers being handed in. Everyone knew about eighty per cent of the answers, but it was in trading the other twenty per cent covertly from desk to desk that the race was decided. Or it would have been, if a boy called Smithers hadn't always won.

Smithers – or Smivvo as he was condescendingly called – was a preternatural conformist who blew his nose every couple of minutes, hitting the same three notes each time, two honks and a parp. His face was oddly faceted, as though an inexpert draughtsman practising to draw a cow had shoved in planes and angles under a sudden compulsion to qualify as a Cubist. Anything that could be mugged up was Smivvo's domain, so geography and general knowledge were territory that was his by right of occupation, if not of conquest, since you would as soon have used the latter word of Smiv as of a flock of sheep which had possessed itself of a field full of short dry grass that nobody else wanted.

It was just a bit of a joke to see how close you could come to Smithers in the annual steeplechase, without committing the solecism of winning. Nobody took the thing seriously enough to want to turn him out of his arid pastures, so you may imagine how mixed my feelings were when that's what I found I'd done. I believe I am only writing this down now in order to make it clear that there were three marks between us, and I may have come by two of them dishonestly; and I want to make it almost equally clear

43

that there may have been two marks between us, and *three* may have been come by dishonestly.

Smiv lies at the centre of my remembrance of the injustice of schoolboy life. Even if I won the race fair and square it was by accident, whereas he'd made the effort. That he was as much in thrall to the status quo as the Vicar of Bray, and that he blew his nose constantly so he could sniff any change in the wind, is beyond dispute. But while such orthodoxy grates on the nerves of everyone, it's not a crime. Yet Smivvo was crucified, as I shall tell.

Conjured away to live in the land of Geek and Gooch, I'd missed a special turbulence that developed at the school when Garrett recruited women to the staff to replace men who'd been called up. True to his inherent dottiness he made it a school rule that the boys should call the women 'Sir'. They had a lot to put up with, what with Kiddle being able to fart to order and Crump endlessly descanting on the subject of bishoprics: 'But just how large was a bishop's prick, Sir?' he would ask Mrs Jackson who taught history. 'Bishopric, Crump. They varied in size.' 'You mean some bishops' pricks were much bigger than others, Miss?' 'I'm not a Miss I'm a Mrs and the rule is you call me Sir. Some were quite small, some were very big indeed. What does it matter, Crump?' (Crump's line in the witheringly literal was almost infinitely extendable and he would cast it with all the cunning of the fisherman who knows just where the trout is to be had. 'So they didn't mind at that school you were at in Canada when you picked them up, neck and crop, and threw them down the steps, sir?' he would say, twitching the line as Lewis Wharton, translator of Villon who had been called out of retirement to teach mathematics, turned from the blackboard. 'Mind?' Wharton would roar, zooming after the fly, 'Mind? What did I care if they minded? I had no patience with idlers. They were out – neck and crop!' And Wharton would mime the action vigorously. 'And didn't their parents complain, sir?' 'They were far too sensible, Crump.' 'My father says Canadians are far more sensible than we are, sir, etc etc etc.'

What happened to poor Miss Farebrother doesn't bear repeating, except you have to know about it to understand what befell Smithers. She had been headmistress of a girls' school, was long retired, but had turned out to do her bit for the war effort. She could hardly have guessed this would involve facing a class of horrible half-grown Mohocks throwing chairs at each other and imitating the air-raid siren so they could tumble out of the door howling in terror. Her life had been of a sheltered order, and now here was Grampold paying Farley a ha'penny for each belch noisy enough to meet his exacting standards, while a boy called Bircher wiggled his fingers under a handkerchief and pretended he had three white mice. She was a game old bird. 'I must confiscate them, Bircher,' she insisted. 'Oh miss, you will be sure and feed them,' he'd say, before pretending they'd escaped so the whole class could jump up on their chairs.

The most refined of the tortures they inflicted on this innocent old party was a simple one – they regularly threw her finely sharpened pencil out of the window when she wasn't looking. She took to bringing it to school tied round her waist on a piece of string. Bircher brought a pair of scissors and would cut the pencil off with a hand as light as Charlie Bates'. She wrote out a sentence for grammatical analysis on the blackboard but when she got to the end she turned round to find the beginning had been rubbed out. She thought she was losing her mind. When the tumult grew unbearable she cried aloud for quiet, and the malefactors would then fall silent, turning round in their seats to point quivering fingers at the only boy who had been silent throughout. 'Shut up, Smithers!' they shouted in unison.

By the end of term the uproar had become too much for her, and she called on Garrett at last for support. His entry cowed the mob upon the instant. They knew as he stepped inside the door they were all to be hanged, and as he began to describe the vengeance he would exact and some of the feebler spirits began to snivel, he bade Miss Farebrother identify the chief offenders. Smithers' name was first out of the hat. He was blameless, but what appeal could there be? The only innocent member of that crowd of footpads was mercilessly beaten – some got six and some got eight but Smivvo got twelve. It is hard to imagine the feelings of one who has always been a King's man, however humble, when with wild injustice he is treated as leader of the insurrection; I only ever heard the tale at second-hand, but if I'd been Garrett I would have known by Smivvo's face that his involvement just wasn't possible; and would a true mutineer, a genuine Israel Hands, have screamed as disreputably as Garrett notes that Smithers did when Gibb laid it on? Smithers made his way home and showed his bum to his mother, whereupon his dad was summoned back from fire-watching at a moment's notice; a step whose gravity, it was made clear to Garrett, was equivalent to getting a man to abandon his search for the source of the Nile. Smithers' mother, a dwarfish figure who had almost certainly escaped from a canvas by Hieronymous Bosch, arrived in the Head's study the next morning with mustard gas coming down her nostrils. Towards the end of her interview with Garrett she physically assaulted him. 'The woman became incensed and I had to ask the school porter to remove her'(cf the entry in vol. 7 of Garrett's secret notebooks).

It was a brutal, farcical deceit, and I doubt if it was even useful as an example of what was going to happen in the world outside. I wonder what Smithers thinks. But I believe it is important to learn to lie, I think willingness to lie is part of growing up; from the moment you tell the lie, you risk exposure: you are on the spot, they are in a position at last to find out who you are. I mention this because out of a special sort of feebleness I found it very hard not to tell the truth obsessively, contriving circumstances in which I could admit everything and abandon responsibility for my existence to those who licensed it.

For instance, when Bob Russell asked me to write out the coarse verse I'd just recited to him so that he wouldn't forget it, I immediately did so: I see the torn bit of brown envelope I scribbled it on, and the stained glass of the little cupboard in the Welsh dresser where I found the pen. But why did I shove the paper in the library book I was lending him – a compendium of P.G. Wodehouse stories in an orange cover – where someone else might see it? It was sticking out like a bookmark and of course Bob betrayed me the instant his shrill thin-lipped mother found it. When I knocked at his door the next day she was standing behind him as he held out the orange volume with the paper still on view. She said coldly, 'Ask your friend if this is his book.' But I was already assuring her it was mine. She gave Bob strict orders never to play with me again, and the fact that he never did made me stop believing in best friends ever after. Frank Allsop told me he stole pennies from his mother's purse, and I egged him on. Then feeling guilty, I confessed to my mother. When I read *Mr Sammler's Planet* there was a line that caught my eye. Mr Sammler's grotesque nephew tells his uncle he can only gain sexual satisfaction from a woman's elbow, and Mr Sammler groans and says 'Do you have to tell me *everything*?' You must learn to lie in order to be able to choose not to. My George Washington complex was worrying, it was a kind of addiction. But noticing that I had seriously embarrassed my father by forcing on him a discussion of masturbation I began to feel Captain Ferguson was holding me to ransom rather too easily. I plucked up courage, and by the time I was sitting my deferred School Certificate I could boldly scatter the pages I'd torn out of my geography notebook among the sheets of exam paper I'd already covered, and crib from them shamelessly. Admittedly, it was only geography (dear me, I got a Credit!) and I was far too vain to cheat at anything else. But it was a step on the road to manhood, the main feature of that thoroughfare being of course sex.

We thought of little else. We couldn't do much about it for, as the poet later pointed out, it wouldn't be available to the general public for some years yet: you could simulate it in various ways, but it was only sex if you did it with girls, and this was a scarcely less remote possibility than being invited to form a government. Fully clad and even wearing an overcoat you stood away during those protracted embraces which were a feature of the period, in case the girl was accidentally reminded of what was really going on. What was happening in bushes and up against walls among lesser tribes I don't know, but in Malden and Coombe kissing was about as far as you got, great marathon bouts of it, whose chronic inconclusiveness was thought to be the tribute paid by lust to true feeling.

Very infrequently, you might get lucky, but the illicitness of the act, however partially accomplished, was at least as terrifying as it was pleasurable, and for days after you expected the girl's school blazer to have been exchanged for maternity gear; accidental entrapment was a horrific possibility, in a world where marriage appeared to be life turned off at the mains. But these feelings were all part of the free-floating anxiety that suffused the sexual landscape: the universe appeared to be plastered with VD posters and there were boys who feared it was possible to get a girl pregnant through four layers of blue serge. All this was simply a focus for the neurotic dread that one day your wicked animal nature would be abruptly revealed to your parents, in whose sexless habitat it was forbidden to grow up.

Meanwhile, the entertainment quotient of that time of slack water, when school was coming to an end and life hadn't yet begun, was considerable. We roamed the avenues endlessly in the blackout, hooting with laughter at nothing, placing empty milk-bottles in the path of harmless citizens and addressing invisible cats in trees until we had gathered a crowd of concerned onlookers. Look, said my friend David Atfield, as two very short persons approached, Let's insult these *little* people. And we rose up and walked past them on tiptoes.

We serenaded girls who looked out of windows, and ran home in the moonlight, suddenly in love. We patched up an ancient motorbike we bought for a couple of quid and I was caught bang to rights by a policeman called Sergeant Cyril Bellchambers (44) for driving without tax, insurance, licence, audible warning of approach, brakes or lights. Fined ten bob on each count, I naturally expected my father to be annoyed, and so he was, but principally with the magistrate. He accused this man of overcharging. He dug out this home telephone number, and lectured him as though he were a wartime profiteer. 'I thought I was very reasonable,' said the magistrate, sounding a bit shifty, like a shopkeeper caught with his thumb in the scales, but my father pointed out that he wasn't fining me, effectively he was fining *him*, and to my astonishment the man agreed to a discount of thirty shillings.

Joining a church youth club because we despised such institutions, we harangued the vicar on the virtues of atheism when not playing kissing games in the dark, and in a wanton display of naked power forced the committee to change the name of the club from something sensible to *Le Boeuf sur le Toit*: we argued that it was time to make a clean break with the merely literal and the new name would be like a beacon to free spirits who had hitherto felt such groups were not for them. It was bullying of an unforgiveable order and when we saw the new name advertised in the *Wimbledon Borough News* I think we all felt ashamed. The next day, on an errand to the masters' common room I saw my name had been crossed out on a list of prizes to be awarded for the best year's work in English, and that of a boy called Pratchett, who was leaving, substituted. Once upon a time I might have thought God or someone very like him was working me one up the throat in the interests of squaring the books. But now all I could see was Pratchett's red nose, and I boiled with rage.

Undue sensitivity to guilt was dissolving; not a moment too soon, for when innocence becomes a craving and is sought promiscuously, you're importuning the world to let you stay a child for ever. Incidental innocence, on the other hand, can be endearing. There was a lady of Rubensesque proportions who taught country dancing on Wednesdays, much appreciated by the boys as an object of sexual fantasy. Her boyfriend Eric played the recorder on these occasions: he had buck teeth and seemed very weedy. Seen together, they looked like a Donald McGill postcard. Peter Smith, my housemaster and friend, was approached by this lady who asked him, 'Peter, do you know what a cunt is?' When Smith told me this years afterwards he prefaced his narrative with a somewhat moralising proposition, viz., that there must surely come a time in every grown-up's life, male or female, when such a question is felt to be otiose: that after a certain age, ignorance of the merely scatological is something you keep to yourself. But he replied to the lady 'Yes, Penelope, I do. It is a coarse reference to the female pudenda.' 'Oh, how very strange,' the lady replied, 'I can't make out how that would fit the context.' Smith went on, 'There is a secondary usage. If you *call* someone a cunt, it means that you regard him as wilfully stupid.' At this the lady's face lit up. 'So *that's* what the man meant when he shouted at Eric.'

Of course, once you get the hang of deceit, it develops an appeal of its own. My friend Francis now had a scholarship in physics at Cambridge, and to fill in time during the school holidays he was going to get a job at Discovery Laboratories in the nearby suburb of Morden. Fond of a joke – and so powerful was Francis's sense of fantasy that he had once persuaded a passer-by that the shrub he was talking to was in fact a very small man in a waistcoat – he said Why don't you come too? I said What do I know about chemistry? About as much as me, he said, I'm a physicist. We turned up in the boss's office and he drew a sketch of the molecules of testosterone. 'You'll be familiar with this structure, of course.' Then he handed us what looked like a recipe leaflet and showed us into our little personal lab down the corridor. 'If it works, it'll be a more effective way of synthesising the stuff. Good luck, lads.'

You just tipped in whatever the instructions told you came next, and boiled it up. Now and again the boss's deputy, a Mr Cowie, would enter our cosy little nook and picking up a test-tube, hold it over a bunsen burner and croon softly to himself the words 'I wonder if they've ballsed it up again?' He'd give the tube an encouraging shake and walk out. Sometimes the boss came in, screwing up the side of his face as he studied the test-tube so the smoke wouldn't go in his eye even when he didn't have a fag in his mouth. In just over a month our first supply of new and improved synthetic testosterone was bottled and stoppered. What was Discovery going to do with it? Why, ship it to South America, said Cowie, where the shagged-out males of that happy continent were waiting for it with their tongues hanging out. 'When they come to write the history of the fuck,' said Cowie solemnly, 'they'll find your names on the label.'

Then there was nothing. The landscape was suddenly empty. Not the sort of emptiness you were a spectator at, but emptiness you were the main constituent of. I didn't seem able to rationalise it on the obvious grounds that schooldays were over – no exam to prepare for, no play to rehearse, no school magazine to edit, no prefects' room to loll in, no fellow wits to break a lance with, no master at a cricket match saying 'Just look after my wife for a minute, will you, Robinson?' Robinson. This is a pretty primitive instrument for identifying anyone, it's at the lower end of the scale of recognition; most people are at least Robinson, it only just passes as a name, it's only one up from saying You. I didn't feel I was even Robinson any more. I say this easily now, but at the time it gave Captain Ferguson the best chance he ever had, and he brought me down. I thought the world was something I was part of. Now it suddenly became a collection of discrete phenomena which didn't include me. I couldn't look at houses and streets and take them for granted. Everything was recognisable, but nothing felt familiar. The comfort of ordinariness had gone. Perhaps it *was* simply having the structures of school taken away and hanging around doing nothing while waiting for a date to start National Service. But none of that sounds as real as the feeling I had that I'd been turned out of myself.

And with it came an underlying anxiety: now I'd allowed this model of anomie inside me, how was I going to get it out again? And if I got it out, what was to stop it coming back? When I was a child, I'd heard the word suicide and my mother told me what it was. The idea terrified me not because I might do it, but because there was nothing to stop me doing it. It was the same with this free-floating dread: once you know it exists, how do you forget it's an option?

Well, you can't. Events overtake it and it's left behind. The trouble is, you don't know that at the time, do you? On the way back from Kingston the sodium lights on the trolleybus route in the late winter afternoon cast the sort of light in which the best of friends seem strangers. I'd been to buy the Skeat edition of *The Canterbury Tales* and was reading the Nonne's Priest's Tale, pretending the opening lines were part of my own history, and that one day I'd get back to that little farmyard, standing in a dale, where Chanticleer and the fox and the widow's two daughters were waiting for me. I took Chaucer like tranquillisers in those dog days. David and Francis had left for the army and I mooned up Blakes Lane on starry nights, shambled down Grand Drive and Linkway, where the girls – Pauline and Jean and Doreen and Treasure and Joyce – were hospitable. But I couldn't tell them that time had stopped and eternity begun, and that it frightened me (Frank Coventry had given me *Mr Weston's*

Good Wine to read when I was about fourteen and when I'd read it I'd said Yes, but I don't know what it means. He'd said Maybe it means more than 'means'. I said I don't know what *that* means – why don't you tell me? But he either couldn't or wouldn't).

When I reported to the army I wrote to my mother telling the poor woman I was resigned to lifelong melancholia. 'That was your first letter,' she once recalled, 'then the second one came, and you were running the army.' Is there anyone to beat a genuine mother's boy for staying true to type? I wasn't the only one – you could spot them in the barrack room by the way they wore their caps on the top of their heads, horizontally, while the ones who'd forgotten they'd ever had mothers put their caps on vertically, hung over the right ear.

Funny business, that National Service; a huge standing army of youthful incompetents that no one in their senses would dream of sending into battle against the Brownies (all armies are like this, but are transformed by the reality of war: there was no possibility of that save in the mutually dependent fantasies of politicians, East and West). Who thought it up? Maybe the numbskull who invented the idea of planting monkey nuts everywhere to prove that socialism worked, or the goggle-eyed leveller Crossman remembered for nothing save losing his departmental papers while eating oysters at Prunier's. No wonder the superannuated sergeant-majors prised out of donkey sanctuaries had to laugh. As for me, I saw it as a bit of a caper, because after this two years' compulsory postponement – and I was never averse to a touch of procrastination, if the sun was shining – life would start in the most desirable way, at Oxford. That was the essential, having something to look forward to. Many a lad drank his can of Brasso because he couldn't see anything waiting for him.

Oddly enough for a boy who never went on Sunday School treats because he couldn't bring his mother, I took to the company of strangers. First, because there was no choice – National Service (a nasty humbugging politician's coinage) wasn't something mummy or daddy thought was good for you, it was the law of the land, like it or lump it: and second, the strangers weren't strangers very long. Straight away you knew you could call the two Welshmen bastards so long as you never, never called them *Welsh* bastards; that every time Jevons was described as a cunt he would produce his member and say 'Look, I know it's not much, but it proves I'm not'; that at the cradle of a poor chap called Tadd the bad fairy had said When you join the army you will always find your clean rolled-up socks filled with marmalade; and that it was decreed in the dream-time that a tall gangling half-wit called Norris who never washed would be stuck under the showers by a lynch mob and scrubbed down with floor-mops: a wonderful instance of the way persecution can be gloried in when it is undertaken for the common good. But the atmosphere was cordial. Revellers with late passes would wake you up in the middle of the night to ask you (a) did you want to buy a battleship and (b) did you want a pee: if so, would you do one for them?

Len Manley was very resentful of being dragged into the army and given thirty-five shillings a week instead of the fifty quid he'd been making as a hustler in the snooker saloons of Hackney and Bow. Fifty quid: in 1946, that was worth six or seven hundred, and no wonder Len had haunted tribunals like a concert violinist, claiming the rough life of the barrack room would interfere with his playing arm. But they'd rounded him up at last and he took my education in hand. I don't know if you've ever been given a present of the sort the craftsman gives his apprentice in *Grimm's Fairy Tales* – a table that covers itself, perhaps, or a donkey that spits out gold coins. Well, what Len gave me was just as unfailing: he said, when you make a stroke be sure your chin is on the cue, and the cue is as near parallel with the table as you can make it.

Doesn't sound much, but it's everything. Even now that snooker is compulsory, amateurs are still standing above the cue. It's not possible to aim that way. You think it is, but that's why the ball doesn't go into the pocket. When my father came up to Charing Cross to see me off after my first leave and met two or three of the lads from the barrack room on the station, he took us for a drink. He said to Len, nodding at me, 'Is he shaping up?' Len took a suck at his beer. 'He's a good rough player,' he said. That's the sort of compliment you never forget. 'Nice of your dad to treat us,' said one of the others, a member of the mother's boy brigade who was a Wykehamist (I noticed my father called him 'old man'). 'Yeah,' said Len, 'but I was a bit embarrassed the way he was effing and blinding all the time.' I laughed. Len had mistaken my dad for a toff.

I didn't know you weren't allowed to write to the War Office, so I sat down in the NAAFI and dropped them a line. Being anxious to get a posting to the Intelligence Corps for no better reason than that the name appealed to me, and rather concerned that the Captain in charge of arranging where you went hadn't taken me seriously enough when I'd made my wishes known, I set out my qualifications. Hoping there might be a bit of spying to do and knowing this would involve false moustaches, I pointed out I'd been the school's star actor. 'The precise use to which this might be put,' I hinted delicately, 'will be best known to yourselves.' I trust none of my readers have ever suffered, or will ever suffer, the mortification of hearing a reference written by themselves, age seventeen, read aloud among the profane. 'Major wants to see you,' barked the CSM, and marched me off. The OC was a dusty fusty looking gent and there were two subalterns in his office. He had my letter in front of him – it had winged its way back from the War Office, probably by carrier pigeon. He read it out in a gentlemanly mumble like a lawyer reciting the will of a mad relative. 'In my day, we were taught not to boast,' he commented. 'I suppose it's a matter of upbringing.' 'But sir,' I said, 'when applying for a job, does one hide one's light under a bushel?' '*Shaddap!*' screamed the CSM. The two subalterns turned to the window and smothered their smiles.

I fear this shameful episode shows as clearly as anything could that Garrett's doctrine of a world that existed so that high-minded grammar school boys could run it, had taken root. In the barrack room I delivered short but irritating lectures on the necessity of voting Labour, illustrating my theme with copious references drawn from the philosophy section of the *Britain in Pictures* series. Looking back, I think I could have made a living selling snake oil, if I'd turned my mind to it, but I pushed my luck one night when the two Welshmen were trying to get to sleep, and with the assistance of colleagues one of them pulled my trousers off and the other poured a jug of water over my private parts. On the other hand, my imitations of Mr Churchill were much in demand, and the two same Welshmen would bribe me with cake to get me going. Shrewdly combining the most seductive characteristics of William and Little Lord Fauntleroy, I got on in society.

WITH ROBINSON TO THE SAHARA
(OR NEARLY)

Five minutes later, as it seemed, I was Officer Commanding the West African Army Service Corps for Eastern Nigeria and the Cameroons. As a matter of fact, there weren't any members of WAASC in the Cameroons, but make no mistake, if there had been they'd have answered to me. A deep canary-yellow in colour and now eighteen, I looked precociously debauched, as though a combination of bilharzia and whisky and a life spent roistering in the stews of Lagos had taken its grim toll. Actually, the banana shade had been imparted by the mepacrine tablets you chewed daily at breakfast to stave off malaria, and my only worry as I sat in the tiny office in Enugu trying to work out whether my bush hat looked more rakish with one side of the brim buttoned up (the orthodox style) or down all the way round, was that my interesting yellow complexion might wear off during the voyage home.

The grandiose title obscured the fact that I was a Second-Lieutenant in charge of a detachment which was no more than a platoon. When Sergeant Briggs came in I asked him why he hadn't dismissed the men to their daily tasks, and he replied 'They won't dismiss.' There they were, rigidly to attention, in three ranks outside my window. I strode out on to the verandah. 'Men,' I said, throwing the internal switch I always hoped would put me into grown-up mode, 'Sergeant Briggs is your father, your mother. He will now give you the order to dismiss.' Nothing happened. 'Sergeant,' I said, 'will you give the order in all the languages, please?' Briggs did it again, in Ga, Ewe, Twi, Fante, as well as Hausa. No one moved. 'Very well,' I said, in the calm voice teachers had always used to me when they were pretending to be patient, 'Corporal George, will you tell me what's going on?' The African NCO stepped forward from the ranks, and stamping his foot as smartly as his bare feet would allow, said 'Sir, you be we father, we mother. We are Gold Coast men. Gold Coast men no fit chop gari, Gold Coast men chop jura. We tell Lieutenant Wagstaff. He promise.'

Wagstaff had been one of the previous incumbents and he'd filled in the right forms, but the wheels turned very slowly and they still hadn't got the food they were used to. For Gold Coast men – God knows why they were in Nigeria – it must have been like having to eat sausages if you were a vegetarian. 'Right,' I said, as crisp as you please, 'what with me being your father, your mother, I'll see about it. Meanwhile, march them to the Guard Room, Sergeant.' Here I was trying to sell the dummy – would they go? Smart right turn, and they were off. Briggs even got them to double. They scampered away so fast one small soldier who had been tinkering under a lorry in the workshops had to rush out to catch them up. As he later said at the court of enquiry, 'I only just managed to get into the guard-room before they closed the door.'

The Colonel said he'd come and see about it. I put the telephone down and breathed again. But Briggs came back from the guard-room. 'I'm afraid they're starting to jump up and down, sir. We have a mutiny on our hands.' What now? Briggs and I walked down to the mud hut that served as the guard-room and as we approached I could hear them chanting and the thump of feet as they danced around. Briggs looked at me. It was my turn. Wondering if they'd notice a white man who was a bit whiter than usual, I walked inside and stood there while they banged up against me, waving their arms above their heads, and jumping around. I thought If I move, they'll have me. So I stood with my hands on my hips and didn't budge. Then I heard the Colonel's jeep outside. They all sat down muttering. I walked out. The Colonel stood up in his jeep and addressed them through the open door. Guess what he said? Right. 'Lieutenant Robinson is your father, your mother.'

*

Back in England I'd thought I'd better be an officer – I remembered what the old pedlar under the hornbeam had said to me when I was a child: officers had an unfair advantage. So I applied for a War Office Selection Board and went on the three-day course where you were tested to see if you had the right stuff. The great thing about these places was you got sheets on the beds, and there were radiators. It was a fearful winter and our towels were freezing by our beds. A trip to Eaton Hall in Chester was a real treat. And it was like a game.

They put you in charge of the others, each in turn, and you had to lead them in swarming over walls and doing what later became a national pastime under the title 'It's a Knockout.' In my case, they gave me a telegraph pole and some rope and you had to work out how your team were going to lay this across a stream and use it as a bridge. After the log had plunged into the water twice, well short of the opposite bank, I twigged. In the history of this test no one had ever managed it, since the pole was about five inches too short. What they were after was intelligent capitulation. 'Lads,' I said, 'let's paddle.' And we waded across. I saw the light of recognition in the eye of the man who was acting as referee. He'd spotted a fellow bullshit artist.

So I was posted to Mons Barracks, Aldershot, and after the usual humiliations, I was commissioned. The humiliations included standing by your bed and being inspected by a black labrador. This belonged to our OC, a Major Dowlish, who wore tartan trousers and one of those black forage caps with a cravat at the back. He was a plump red-faced fellow with a swagger. I thought swaggering in a barrack room was a bit naff, surely it called for a wider stage. Still, he was the boss, but what was his dog doing there, sniffing our balls? The animal's own balls were so much in evidence it seemed to have three, like a revolving pendulum on the sort of clock you win at a fair, and one morning when Dowlish had strutted past I put my toe up its arse and it ran out of the door like shot off a shovel. If I had to give back all the small satisfactions life has ever afforded me, I wouldn't let them have that one.

I'd put down RASC instead of infantry, knowing they didn't have to walk, and at Thetford where you were sent while they made up their minds what to do with you, I heard I'd be going to Germany along with everyone else. Now it so happened I was not as punctilious as I might have been in the discharge of my duties as Orderly Officer. I'd done all the stuff like rounding up the soldiers after the pubs shut, and even accepted the gift of a Luger from one of them, who though staggering slightly, seemed to hold me in some esteem. 'Please, I would like you to have it, sir, I would, I really would.' 'But why are you giving it to me?' I asked. 'Because,' said the honest fellow, with unaffected simplicity, 'if I get caught with it I'll do ten years in the Glasshouse.' I'd even turned out the guard at midnight, and was willing to do so again at five in the morning when a fried egg might be had in the cookhouse. It was the three a.m. patrol I rather edged away from. The Orderly Sergeant was of the same mind, so we didn't bother. But he was found out, and if he hadn't been there, it was plain I hadn't either. Not long after this I was summoned to the Adjutant's Office and told I wasn't going to Germany after all, I was going to West Africa. So was my pal Peter Dunham. 'You didn't by any chance ever fail to turn out the guard at three a.m., did you?' it occurred to me to ask him as we boarded the *Almanzora* at Southampton. 'As a matter of fact, yes,' he said, 'and I was rumbled.' 'Ah,' said I, 'the pieces begin to fall into place.'

But I was well pleased. After the only just war that has ever been fought, Germany was a poisoned land, while Africa was altogether elsewhere, was beyond all reckoning. It seemed strange I should travel to that distant Coast with which my father had done so much business but which he had never seen. To him it was the White Man's Grave, a description he kindly drew to my attention though he told me not to mention it to my mother. That good woman's chief fear, as it slowly emerged, was that I should come back married to a black lady. Maybe I'll marry two or three, I said, comfortingly.

It was the *Almanzora*'s last voyage. The old hulk chugged and thumped and we were berthed eight to a cabin. But the moon shone on the dark water, and we all flirted with the pretty young wife who was going out to join her District Officer husband. One early morning I awoke and looked out of the porthole. Palm trees! We had tied up at a harbour in the Canary Islands, a landfall unknown to tourist itineraries in those days, a Spanish outpost of parched hillsides under the burning sun, where later the same day in a dark bodega isolated in the high savannah I drank a glass of muscatel from a barrel laid down in 1830. Below in the whitewashed town there were grapes and lobster, melon and oysters, crayfish and passion fruit, and in the hot bright square we found a place for drinks that was cool and rambling, smelling of musk, with long high-ceilinged rooms, and alcoves tiled in soft colours of green and gold. A guitar was playing and the punkas rustled idly overhead. Sailors from the harbour chatted with modest girls who fluttered their fans, and haughty Spaniards in black suits sipped the wine of the islands, at their ease. Goya, in a cheerful mood.

I called for another glass of the sweet brown wine and glowing with the hugeness of my good will towards a world which that day had visited me with pleasures such as I had never known, I turned to the rather formal old party who had earlier spoken to me in English. I say, I said to him, this is a jolly place. My words lacked resonance, partly because of the wine but mainly because I was so

wholly absorbed in this resplendent day that none of me was left over
to think of anything to say. How nice those girls are. So elegant, so
charming. Well-bred. Old families. The wine had made me solemn.
Yes indeed, he nodded, it's quite the nicest brothel on the island.
Since they are kind enough to retain my services as their doctor,
I say that with some assurance. And, he added, at the equivalent
of 17/6, the tariff seems by no means unreasonable. When I got
back to the *Almanzora* I leant over the rail and we put to sea.
Drifting past the islands towards Africa, I had a sudden thought.
For the first time in my life I'd been *abroad*! I'd almost forgotten
to remember.

Africa would rise up out of the oceans, an enormous vertical
cut-out, reaching in all directions beyond the clouds to obscure
the sun. But it emerges as a thin fringe of trees on the horizon.
Boys in canoes swarm under our bows at the port of Takoradi
and cry out for Liverpool ha'pennies and Glasgow sixpences, the
nomenclature unchanged since the eighteen-seventies, and they
dive for the coins we throw them. We reach Accra and I spend the
night in a bare mud hut with a bed and a mosquito net, keeping a
sharp eye on the lizards, sinister and motionless, on the wall. For
no reason that anyone bothers to offer me, I am to be transferred
to Nigeria, and fly up the coast to Lagos in a single-engined plane
powered by a rubber-band. I stay in Lagos long enough to read
that morning's edition of Dr Azikiwe's newspaper, the *West African
Pilot*. Dr Azikiwe – Zik – is the nationalist leader and pressing for
Independence. He is rather uncomplimentary to the British. A short
paragraph down-page on the front announces that 'the Governor's
skinny wife has now returned from her annual leave.' Inside, there
is an obituary of an English bishop: this is the conventional lapidary
thing, except for the last paragraph. It reads 'It is not generally
known that for the last thirteen years of his life the Bishop was a
martyr to gonorrhoea.'

Up-country by train to Kaduna, capital of the Northern territory
where the Hausas live, the Mohammedans who came down from the
Sahara and settled the land. Then I am walking up a narrow path in
the evening through trees and scrub and the mindless screaming of
cicadas, trousers worn over suede mosquito boots that are always
put on at night, and watching in horror as a young man of my own
age who is showing me to the Mess hits the knuckles of the black
guard with his swagger-cane because the man isn't quick enough
opening the door. There are three other subalterns beside myself:

two captains, one of whom never sets foot in the Mess in case he meets the other; and the OC who dines in his bungalow with his missis. The cook is called Elijah and the barman is Audu. Both get shouted at.

After dinner – Elijah is a handy sort of cook and has served what he calls steak-and-kidding, with roast yam, and there is beer from the Lagos brewery to drink – the governor of the prison drops in. He wonders if we would like to watch a hanging tomorrow. Is this some old Coaster's joke? No. He just thought it might amuse us – the Major was coming. He drinks a glass of van der Humm and says cheerio, got to be up early, and the rest of us push off to the pictures in Kaduna township to watch Bob Hope in *The Cat and the Canary*. Waiting in the darkness for the film to start I look up and admire the way they've decorated the ceiling to look like the sky – then realise the stars are the genuine article because in these latitudes you don't need a roof. Then back to Mango Avenue, where the three of us, the junior officers, all on National Service, are quartered. It's a bleak red-brick bungalow, and we have a room apiece. Apart from a bed, a chair and a small table, there isn't any other furniture in these rooms. There's a central light with a QMS-issue parchment shade, and the concrete floors make the place echo.

My servant Isa who lived in a collection of little huts at the bottom of the garden of the bungalow brought in a freshly starched khaki-drill uniform each morning at 6.45 and reached up under the shorts to pull down the tail of the shirt. I was at the office by 7.30 and 'worked' until 8.30, then went back to the Mess for breakfast. How many eggs would I like? Oh, five, I suppose. It was the usual number, they were quite small, brought each morning to the Mess by someone called The Fulani Woman who also supplied the milk; I never met this figure and vaguely wondered who milked her, and how she laid the eggs. Then back to the office by 9.30 until the shutters were put up for the day at 1.30. You had lunch and went to bed until 5. This schedule was perfectly sensible, since the afternoons were too hot to do anything until it was time for hockey after tea. But what was the schedule *for*? I was Station Transport Officer which meant I arranged where all the three-ton lorries were to go each day. But since they always went to the same place, which was the Command Supply Depot, to pick up and distribute to the Fifth Battalion the Nigeria Regiment, and 823 Company WAASC, what they always picked up and distributed, they could have done this without any intervention on my part. At a personal level life is always a series of arrangements for passing the time, and in 1946 I was caught up in someone else's idea of compulsory games, so my own functionless function didn't strike me as unusual. But taking a slightly wider view, what were the Fifth Battalion the Nigeria Regiment, and 823 Company WAASC doing there – apart from giving my lorries a purpose in life? What task had we been left there to perform, and were there enough of us to do it? Invading the Belgian Congo didn't seem to be on, and shambling across the border one weekend to plant the Union Jack in Dahomey wouldn't have been very polite. The truth is, we were redundant. West Africa had always been the arse-end of the Empire, where the army's historic role had been to make the country sit still while the United Africa Company got on with plundering it. But these arrangements were running down like an old clock nobody told the time by any more. Any minute now, Independence. Boom, boom.

Meanwhile, tea and sandwiches. Then if it wasn't a hockey day I might ride a horse round Kaduna racecourse. I was friendly with the King of Kaduna, Mallam Sambo, who lived in a mud palace surrounded by his guards and servants. The Mallam was heavily into the wholesale yam and mango business, so kept on the right side of army folk, the army being his best customer. His inner apartments were furnished with deck-chairs, and one morning after the usual repetitive Hausa greetings – Health. Health to you. Health to you. Salutations in your work. Salutations. Yes indeed. Yes indeed. Yes indeed – he asked me to sit down and have a chat. Did I think it was worth taking pills? He had some chronic ailment but wasn't sure medicine ever did you any good. If you were to die, it was written. Well, I egged the old chap on. Take them, you never know. Wonderful thing science, kept coming up with brilliant ideas. Won't do you any harm.

After that, one of his retainers in turban and burnous used to bring a horse over and I'd take the beast out on the empty racecourse and I'd have a bit of a canter. Cantering seemed easier than trotting – I'd never ridden before – though one time the girth came loose and I was fizzing along sticking out horizontally like a rodeo rider. I think it was even more fun than the motorbike on which I zoomed out along the dust roads, going nowhere as fast as I could. Or we might go hunting. I'd take a rifle and a man who Isa explained was a noted hunter, and with a friend from the Fifth Battalion we'd set off in a jeep for the bush.

We were after leopard. I was never too sure this was quite the good idea the little brown hunter seemed to think it was, but since we saw where the leopard slept, saw where it ate and drank, and even where it enjoyed sexual congress, without ever seeing the leopard itself, my reservations were academic. What we mostly did was cut down saplings using a bren gun. In fact only once did we come across anything you could describe as wild life. It gave us a bit of a shock. With an expression of the utmost alarm on his face, the hunter froze. Ahead through the trees, and down in a small dip, were a bunch of evil-looking baboons. They had a look of pharoahs without a sense of humour, and when my companion made to let off his rifle in the air just to stir them up a bit the hunter knocked the gun out of his hands. Under his direction, we crept away as quiet as mice, for as he explained baboons are quite as nasty as they look and there were enough of them to have torn us to pieces.

We consoled ourselves by briefly abducting a solitary bushman who was wandering in the depths of the bush with a spear, a bow and some poisoned arrows, looking for a dyker to kill for his dinner. His face deeply slashed with ritual scars, clad in a loin-cloth and covered in what looked like second-hand talcum powder, the Munchi man sat in the back of the jeep, smiling seraphically and making noises like a factory whistle in celebration of his first encounter with the internal combustion engine. He knew about money, though, because he beat me up from five bob to ten shillings for his spear and the bow and arrows, before trotting back into the bush to tell his chums dinner would have to be a take-out that night.

I turned down the front seat at the hanging, offered by the prison governor, but I had a good view of the consecration of the Bishop of Onitsha. The RC padre said as I was supplying him with the transport why didn't I go with him. He was a man in long shorts who always seemed to be in a tearing hurry, permanently overdue for the next appointment. But what was he doing in Africa, promoting superstition in a continent that already had buckets of the stuff? The Africans had let flyposting missionaries paste labels on them – Methodist, RC, Anglican, Plymouth Brother – but this was only because they were easily frightened. The padre was as meaninglessly employed in Africa as I was. Perhaps it was to keep this thought away that he rushed, or perhaps he rushed because he'd already thought it. But he didn't rush *past* anyone. He knew the young men felt their separation from their real lives and he had a natural bent for cheering people up. In fact, like Pope John XXIII, he didn't really need to be a Roman Catholic at all.

It was a bit of a Sunday School treat, and although sex didn't exactly rear its head, worse luck, on the way to Onitsha we stopped in the bush at a convent, and in the guest room I was brought a cup of tea by a young nun dressed in white, and God knows the way we looked at each other wasn't spiritual, but she knew and I knew it was tender and kind. When we got to the cathedral I was seated next to the wife of a Spanish grandee, and she sat close to me in a way that distracted my attention from the goings-on down the aisle, and if anyone thinks I was just being eighteen they've forgotten that at eighteen you're never mistaken about such things, though turning them to account is another matter.

There was a party in the garden with plates of sandwiches and cut-glass dishes filled with a mixture of mangoes, tinned peaches and bananas, which was the staple dessert of West Africa and known as jungle-juice. An ancient priest who was an old pal of the new man was getting down on his knees with some difficulty to kiss the Bishop's ring, and the Bishop yanked him up and said Ah, James, don't be showing off now, you can do it standing just as well, it'll be easier for both of us. I looked at my friend the padre, and he said Go on, Robbie, for God's sake kiss the ring, I can see you're palpitating to do it, you won't go to hell for it. So I did. What it was good for, I don't know, but it was nice not being left out. And the padre knew that.

*

Isa came in one day and said his father had died and would I give him ten shillings for the fare to go to his funeral. I looked at him hard: ten bob was quite a slice out of the five pounds a week I was paid. And there was no reason to suppose Isa told more of the truth than any other servant round the place: every Thursday he'd come in grinning and say, 'Tonight be biggy palaver. Tonight be cilema.' And I'd give him the shilling for himself and one of his wives. They all lived with him in his *gidda* – I was never clear who was who in his household, tucked away as it was in a corner of the compound. He had one little baby he sometimes carried in on his hip to show me: his picin. It was then permissible to use that word, and I'd squeeze the child's fat cheeks and pat-pat him on his naked black head and take his photograph to send home to my mum.

So I said no. He went out, no expression on his face. I felt uneasy. On Sunday Isa always changed into his best clothes – his best cloth, he called it, white trousers, white smock, embroidered white skull-cap – to go to the mosque. That Sunday he was in working gear. What's the matter, I asked, no church today? He shook his head. He couldn't go. He'd pawned his best cloth to the tailor-man to raise the ten bob he had to have to go to his father's funeral. He came and sat on the floor next to my chair, and wept. This man had great dignity, and it was clear I had none. I gave him the ten shillings and I put my arm round his shoulders and tried to stumble through some words about the deaths of fathers, but I couldn't get them out properly because I was all choked up myself. So we sat silent for a bit, and then he went out and bought his clothes back, and went to his father's funeral.

He might have been about thirty. A wiry man with a bald head and a thin face whose expression reflected amusement and irony – an unlikely combination of humours in a poor black man who answered to the word 'boy' and called white men 'Master'. He was dependent, as though he were an orphan, on the army which fed and housed him in return for his work as a servant; this was far from hard labour, but there was little or nothing in his environment on which his spirit could nourish itself – yet it was sustained. It was clear that his world of the bungalow and the *gidda* offered him the deepest satisfaction, in which the fact that he was the 'boy' and I was the boy was like comic seasoning: his pleasure in this situation was as immediate and distinct as that taken by a man eating a sandwich made out of crisp bacon. He had no words to tell me any of this, it was something that was entirely apparent in his face and in his bearing. When he shoved his hands into his pockets and strutted about, pretending to be me in the bright green corduroys I'd got the tailor-man to make, he was guying my pretensions. 'Big man! Big man!' And at the same time he was claiming the world of swank for himself by proxy. He was a source of energy.

Corporal Shanks, too. He was a gloomy Thersites who smacked the African drivers familiarly over their heads and when they couldn't find the starting-handle for their Dennis Tippers would ask them ritually if they expected him to start the lorries with his prick. He had a way of droning when he spoke which lent a touch of plain chant to everything he said, and he would ask liturgically in his flat northern accent, 'Now then, Abafemi, what are you on?', a meaningless enquiry which preceded his own antiphonal response, 'Five and seven and a third of it done.' He always called me Rob. 'Look, Shanks,' I'd say from time to time, 'couldn't you call me sir once in a way?' But he never seemed to hear. He urged me to take the wheel of the 15cwt – you weren't supposed to do your own driving if you were an officer – and when I put it in a ditch his satisfaction ran deep. He had a melancholy philosopher's air, and when sending an African driver about his business would often start what sounded as though it were to be a solemn adjuration: 'I am only a fucking small cog in a fucking big wheel –' he would intone weightily, but at this very preliminary stage he petered out as though overwhelmed by the mournfulness of the message he had been about to deliver, and would smack the man over the head and warn him not to go with bad women.

Shanks was uninfluenced by his present circumstances; I suspect he didn't notice them. Where on earth was he coming from? As with Isa, his style, in essence, was unrelated to the prevailing styles. Africans on parade blinked eagerly with the effort of showing him he had their undivided attention. 'You black men, when I was first in the army we didn't have numbers, we knew each other by our first names. What did we know each other by?' 'Your first names, sah,' they yelled delightedly. His gnomic utterances were of course founded in an ancient army demotic, and he commanded the platoon to march off in columns of threes, taking its time from the Town Hall clock – January, February, *March*! But he reinvented all he said. Shanks had a long banana-like face and his dazed smile seemed to arrive on it from a great distance.

Isa and Shanks had peculiar powers, like the chaps the traveller meets as he passes through the forest in a fairy-tale. This was a dull part of Africa and the year I spent there was like a succession of sweltering overcast days in an unfamiliar suburb. But the presence of these two men had the effect of re-tuning the apparatus: the defunctive harmonies of this set-aside life faded away, and I could hear the sprightly chords of the future. Such magi were a true blessing, for the OC and his second-in-command were sour domineering men, working out their time and not best pleased to find themselves landed with those of us who had been press-ganged into playing at soldiers. It was a monotonous environment, the day's work repetitive, lunch and dinner in the Mess with its four or five members a sluggish business, and billiards at the Club an occasional event, since we had no money to drink on equal terms with our betters. Not a chance with the nurses at the hospital, though they didn't mind being sisterly at the swimming pool, and none of the civilians such as the bank manager or the United

Africa rep thought it worth their while to ask such junior fry to dine.

*

I was sent down to Lagos by train to collect some new lorries. The fan whirred in the carriage I had to myself, and there were saucers of small-chop and bowls of jungle-juice, and bottled beer, served by a man in a fez. On arrival I made obeisance to my seniors, one of whom was called the West African Herbert. 'Care for a gin pickle?' He pushed a jar of pickled onions and a spoon across the desk and watched while I tried to get one out. 'No place for a woman, this,' he said. I'd got one of the onions up the side of the jar with the spoon and was working it carefully to the top. 'I brought my wife out and she ran away with a friend of mine.' The onion skidded back into the gin. 'It wasn't as bad as you might think. He was a regular officer.'

We set out up-country with the convoy of trucks which had to be run in at fourteen miles an hour, slow progress made slower by my touch of dysentery. Just past Jebba the bridge was down and we had to float the lorries one by one across the Niger on make-shift rafts. Pretty grown-up stuff, I thought complacently as the last one rolled off on the other side, up the planks borrowed from the village headman. Wedgy Spooner the Staff-Sergeant, a disputatious man with what looked like a false moustache, stood with his hands on his hips and watched as the drivers climbed in again. I knew he deeply regretted I hadn't lost a truck or two in the Niger. 'We done it the hard way, Mr Robinson,' he said, shaking his head. 'I know what you're going to tell me, Wedge,' I replied, 'I should have made the waters part.'

We rambled round with the lorries late at night looking for the government rest-house at Zungeru, and Wedgy got fed up and said he'd sleep in one of the trucks alongside the Africans. I took the 15cwt and found the rest-house at last, hard by the grave of an incestuous brother and sister who had done away with themselves. A storm blew up, thunder and lightning, and I was the only guest in the enormous ramshackle empty building. The caretaker laughed like the maniac in a horror movie as he served me fried egg and yam, and all night as the doors and windows banged in the storm his lunatic cackle echoed down the empty corridors. 'How was it?' asked Wedgy, next morning. 'Fine. Just me and Boris Karloff. Of course, he'd blacked up.'

On the heights of the Jos plateau we stopped for lunch at the rest-camp Mess. Cool and breezy, it was a haven for the temporarily deranged – you were given leave in Jos if you'd gone a bit 'Coasty', and many a Major who had taken to peppering his neighbours with a blow-pipe wandered in its pleasant grounds. One of them invited me to have a go at the squirrels with his bow and arrow after lunch, while he sang a verse I'd never heard: 'Aunty Mary had a canary, Up the leg of her drawers. He wadna come doon for half-a-croon, So I gied him a kick in the baws.' The Major went in for what he called a lay down and we pressed on to Zaria.

This was where we were to drop off a couple of the lorries. Then we were to turn south, back to Kaduna. But just round the next bend of the road was the Sahara. 'Do you want to have a look at it before we head back for the ranch, Wedge? Say you've seen it?' Wedgy's piles were playing up. 'Nah,' he said, lying full length in the back of one of the trucks for his greater ease (he claimed the only thing that did his condition any good was Brylcreem, and told me he'd once sent them an unsolicited testimonial to this effect). 'OK,' I said, 'if we get off now we'll be back at base by dinner-time.' So not wanting to miss dinner, we missed the Sahara. But if I'd known what lay in wait, I wouldn't have hurried.

*

Captain Ferguson hovered. His spirit was malignly abroad. Conditions in West Africa were just his cup of tea. But I'd arranged the novelty of my surroundings round me like a stockade, and perhaps because I was so far away from mother, both my feet were off the bottom: I'd broken the circuit. So it wasn't me he got. There were three of us in the bungalow in Mango Avenue and each evening we took our baths in rotation, he who was third going first the following night. Our 'boys' laid out our clothes, Mess kit on Fridays – monkey-jackets and yellow cummerbunds – the rest of the time long-sleeved khaki-drill shirts with ties, and long khaki-drill trousers over our mosquito boots (it was a mark of the novice to tuck the trousers into the boots, since that way the cunning little fellows were able to walk over the rim and climb down to bite your feet). We would make our way up the narrow sandy path that wound round the small hill to the Mess, and each night I anticipated what it would feel like when a green mamba dropped from the branches overhead to wrap itself round my neck and kill me stone dead.

The two chaps I was sharing this out-of-life experience with were pleasant fellows – I hadn't forgotten the way Fergus had banged the fingers of the doorkeeper on my first night, but I'd long stopped thinking about it. And Lewis was a mild and thoughtful boy who was due to take up a scholarship in Oriental Languages at University College, Swansea. We took each other's photographs continuously and in various poses: now pledging eternal friendship with exaggerated handshakes, now bargaining with the trader-men who sold us crocodile handbags and ebony walking-sticks, now having our hair cut *en plein air* by the visiting barber. Lewis sometimes spoke of his escapades with girls in Aberystwyth in tones of infinite regret, as though his sexual nature was something he should have resisted, and had not. Perhaps he'd put one of them in pod and left her stuck with it. He didn't say and I didn't ask, and neither did Fergus. Living at such close quarters, we only gossiped about our elders: how Mel's long bad-tempered face was due to it having been his wife's signature on the Spot-the-Ball competition which netted the fifty thousand, and how the two Captains were not on speaking terms because the birds one of them had picked off with his .22 as they congregated on the roofs of the Command Supply Depot were said by the man who had shot them to have been pigeons and by the man who had not shot them to have been doves; either way, Elijah casseroled them.

The evening I was back from Zaria the three of us sat over our beers after dinner and Lewis spoke again of a plan he had to redecorate the Mess. It was looking shabby and he'd do it at the weekends. Who cared what the Mess looked like? No one ever noticed it, as far as I could judge, and Lewis had plenty to do during the week at his own platoon; he'd somehow got on the wrong side of one of his seniors who would saddle him with extra duties and telephone the Staff-Sergeant to find out the exact time Lewis reported for duty in the mornings. The man was a bully who having once been a sergeant-major couldn't get out of the habit. And indeed Lewis's oft-referred-to scheme of refurbishment sounded like a penance he was planning for himself in expiation of unspecified errors and omissions.

Next morning we took our customary way down Mango Avenue, then along the main road to the Company offices. Lewis was sitting on a court of enquiry at the Command Supply Depot. I said ta-ta, see you at breakfast. But I never saw him again, for by breakfast-time Lewis had gone mad. I looked up from the eggs when Fergus came into the Mess. His face was a nasty grey colour.

The court of enquiry had convened as usual, and Lewis proposed he should be scribe and take the notes. The Captain in charge – a man from another battalion, down south – said he thought it better if the man who had been doing it from the beginning carried on. Lewis repeated the request, but the officer running the session – it was something to do with a corporal who had allegedly gone absent without leave – said they'd let it rest the way it was. Then Lewis got up and seemed to insist. The Captain told him to forget it. Lewis said if he couldn't do the scribe's job, he'd leave. The Captain asked him what was the matter. Lewis got up, saluted, walked out, walked back in, saluted, walked out again, came back, saluted, and went on doing it. He said to the Captain that the scribe's job was rightfully his, because of his rank. 'And what is that?' asked the Captain who by now had told the African clerk to ring the hospital for an ambulance. 'I am second-in-command, the organisation of the world,' said poor Lewis.

Fergus and I looked at each other. It wasn't one of those little fits of stress that got you a month or so at Jos. Something massive had gone wrong. Lewis was now unreachable. Fergus and I went on looking at each other. The night Lewis began his journey home the train sat steaming under the orange electric light of Kaduna station. Lewis was already on board, under restraint. 'No,' said Shanks, 'don't go in, sir. You shouldn't go in.' Shanks had been one of the escorts in the ambulance. I couldn't remember him calling me sir before. Lewis's 'boy' was crying. The Colonel of the hospital stood about looking vague, but he wouldn't let anyone get on the train to say goodbye. He was a psychiatrist and when we asked him, he said 'Manic depressive psychosis', which didn't sound too good. The train pulled out and when Lewis got to England they cut a chunk out of his brain – pre-frontal leucotomy, something the ju-ju men in the bush would have loved to get the hang of, if only their knives had been sharp enough; it was a comprehensive form of gelding, it quietened you down so you were no trouble at all. Back home, a year or so after, I got a letter from Lewis. He apologised for 'letting everyone down'. They'd managed to cut out quite a lot of him, but not the guilt – the fantasy that had caused it all in the first place was perfectly intact.

*

So when I got to Enugu, the mutiny was just light relief. I messed with the First Battalion, and since there were more of them there, things were a bit livelier. On Mess Nights, being the youngest, I was Mr Vice and gave the loyal toast. You had to say 'Gentlemen, our commander-in-chief, the King!', and I lived in dread of getting the words in the wrong order. After dinner we'd pick up sides for a version of billiards that was played on the run, rushing round and round the table, and once I partnered the Colonel at darts. 'I say,' he said, as I managed to stick a lamp bracket adjacent to the board, but about three feet away from it, 'you *are* a rabbit!' One of the Mess boys had a ju-ju against scorpions: he'd come in with two or three of them in his hand and stuff them down his shirt. He offered to sell the secret for five shillings, and one of the Company commanders, rather a fusspot who was known to the Hausas in his Company as 'man who walks as though he had a green banana stuck up his arse', handed over the cash one evening and was given a bottle containing an infusion of leaves. You were supposed to rub it on, but I never caught him putting it to the test.

Now I began to pore over Kennedy's *Latin Primer* – my demob number would come up any day, and my place at Oxford was contingent on getting Latin to Responsions standard. Not having got beyond *amo, amas, amat* before I dropped the subject, I wrote on the paper in the Exeter entrance exam, 'Sorry, will have to come back and see to this some other time'; School Certificate Latin was a tattoo you had to be able to produce in those days, and though they sportingly gave me the place, they said I'd have to do the Latin after the army. If I started now and kept at it while I was on the boat I reckoned I'd have about five days off when I got back home, and then I'd be grinding away till the exam in the summer. Bit of a chore. Meanwhile, did the PSBO's wife know her glossy black pubic hair was vividly on show as she sat in her floppy tennis shorts drinking gin in the Mess on Sunday mornings? I think she was just absent-minded, but adultery was in the air.

Adultery. Something for adults. One cocky little shit was doing it with the wife of someone senior down Port Harcourt way. Went over twice a week, came back bragging. Did the husband know? Would he find out? A man twice my age, a civilian from the town, came to my office and broke down as he told me his wife had confessed to adultery with a man under my command. He wept as he told me of his misery, and I sat there mortified by my youth, my lack of any resource, as this sexual storm broke in great waves about my head. You could call it a learning process for me, but at the price this man was paying, offering his privacy in desperation to an unfledged boy, it was bought by him, on my behalf, too dear. What could I give back to him? I meant nothing to him, of course, being a stranger. But I was eighteen. When the tempest subsided, he would never forgive me for that.

When I was sent away to the Dark Continent I assumed without actually forming the thought that events at home would stop happening until I got back. I opened a copy of the *News of the World* a fortnight old and browsed through the headlines: 'Farmer lived in stable with other woman', 'False moustache was made by married man living next door', 'Menace of gentleman strangler', 'Sold piano to pay for divorce'. Bread was still rationed, the Gay Gibson murder trial was running, magistrates were calling for the return of the 'cat', and the word 'bloody' was represented by a dash. It all sounded like fiction to me. I turned a page and something jumped out at me. In the solemn know-all, no-smoke-without-fire house-style of the sheet, the spirit of prurient respectability peeping from behind a lace curtain, there was a report of a coroner's inquest on a member of my own family. It was Clarice. Her dream of being dressed in bride clothes and lying in a coffin had come true. She had blown her brains out with a single cartridge from a double-barrelled shot-gun.

Clarice had known that the millionaire foreigner she'd been romanced by, the one Aunt Rose had described as 'swahthy' – the central European so ridiculously called 'John' – was married, and I'd often heard the aunts discussing the divorce which was always about to happen, but didn't. Clarice had killed herself in one of his houses – he had many – by the seaside in Sussex. She lay on the bed and pulled the trigger. The gardener found her. The wife may have been in the dark about the affair because she had her own counsel at the inquest wanting to know when 'John' had first come to know Clarice. But the magistrate said 'John' didn't have to reply if he didn't want to, and he didn't want to. Clarice's doctor gave evidence. He said his patient thought she was going mad – insane was the word he used. The coroner's verdict was suicide while the balance of her mind was disturbed.

Adultery, suicide, money – oh, money: 'John' bought Clarice's mother a house. He said he'd sell the jewellery he'd given Clarice, on her behalf. Beatty gave it to him and could never remember if she got the cash. Adultery and mistresses were novelties in our family, so what happened was odd. If I knew more about the timber merchant – or found my father was in love with Clarice – it might lead me somewhere. The flats where Clarice lived in Hampton Court look flyblown now. What happened to the cocktail cabinet? I wonder if the Sussex love-nest is still to be seen, houses get changed round, perhaps people watch television in the room where Clarice killed herself. But the four dull walls of the anecdote don't seem to have a door. The flatness of the event has no resonance, I can't feel it means a thing. Maybe I'm missing something.

★

The *Empire Bure* edged out of the harbour at Lagos into the roads, and a chap in the Nigeria Regiment with a straggly moustache, standing at the rail, took off his boots and holding them aloft momentarily, dropped them into the sea. When we played poker on the way back he called me Mungo, because he'd seen me walk up the gang plank with the spear and the bow and arrows I'd bought from the bushman. In between the poker, I ground away at the Latin primer, reciting the verbs, declining the nouns, and trying to work up some sort of vocabulary. A morning came when we all put on our battle-dress which we hadn't worn for so long. Under a cool sky we saw a bit of land that had hedges dividing the fields. We had turned the corner of England. We sailed up the west coast past Wales to Liverpool. At the Pier Head, I got the nicest little present I ever was given in all my life.

The ship docked and I walked to the rail just after lunch and looked down at the landing-stage and saw my mother and Aunt Lil waving up at me. They'd known the *Empire Bure* was due some time that day, and had been over at New Brighton sitting on the sands when they'd seen the ship coming slowly up the Mersey with its tugs. They'd hurried to catch the ferry – the *Royal Daffodil* or the *Royal Iris* – and there they were.

My mother shouted up to me as I leant over the rail. 'We've just heard. The tutors say you don't have to do the Latin!' I shied Kennedy into all the water that lay between me and Africa, and went up to Oxford.

GOING TO THE MAT WITH
EDITH SITWELL

THE SESAME CLUB was full of Edith-clones dressed exactly like
her in flowing subfusc relieved by brightly coloured pebbles. They
came up to Edith with an air of great confidentiality as though
they too wrote poems but wouldn't dream of mentioning it. After
these casual genuflections they retired to glitter behind their scones
while we stood around awkwardly, waiting for chairs to be placed,
and minding our manners. I was wearing my Montague Burton
matriculation suit and hoping its lack of style, or to be more precise
the way it didn't quite fit, would suggest unworldliness rather than
penury. We were being entertained by Edith because we were the
performers in a proposed concert version of *Façade* that was to be
staged by the Oxford University Opera Club.

Tea was brought and we sailed into the sandwiches, then Edith
handed each of us a poem. At the time I didn't know what this
was the signal for, and I'm pleased to say it hasn't happened to
me very often since; once, later in life, I was on the receiving end
of it at the Writer's Club in Moscow when a Mr Noneshvili thrust
an English translation of one of his works into my hand and staring
into my eyes said 'Read it.' Detaching myself from his gaze I looked
down at the text, nodding appreciatively. 'No,' he said, 'aloud.' And
this is what Edith meant. I was mortified, dropping my voice to a
whisper hoping this would indicate reverence for the text rather
than desperate shyness at being overheard by the waitress. She
got us to do it one by one and then she read them back to us
herself, pausing only to give the title between each. After the recital
everyone made a deeply respectful sussuration which sounded like
tourists in a cathedral going on tip-toe during a service which didn't
really involve them. As we went out I was thinking that if you could
turn the poems into soft furnishings they wouldn't look bad in the
front-room.

And it was sitting in the front-room that I concocted the paragraphs that were going to get me into trouble. Next term I was editor of the *Isis* and I was desperately afraid there wasn't going to be enough stuff to fill it; I liked the idea of the status which went with the job, but a sort of Captain Ferguson panic touched me whenever I thought of all those blank pages. I knew that my deputies on the *Isis* staff were concealing anything good that came into the office and stowing it under their beds against their own future preferment, an event for which they were constantly lobbying; and there wasn't much hope of padding the back of the mag with reviews of books that came in during the vacation, since members of the staff would already have sold these at Blackwell's, having gone up early for that express purpose.

So I thought I'd better have something in hand, even if I had to write it myself. In those days I was a fan of Timothy Shy (real name: D.B. Wyndham Lewis) who wrote a humorous column of great knowingness in the *News Chronicle*. So first of all I borrowed one of the names he often used and made up a couple of pars for the gossip-column about this character called Rapson. Why I thought the name funny I don't know, but I knew I could say anything I liked about Rapson since no one in real life had ever been called this. I cast him as a Proctors' man, a university policeman, one of those chaps in bowlers who ran after undergraduates who were being a nuisance, and I devised some lack-lustre fantasy in which he featured. After the first issue of the *Isis* came out a letter arrived from the Proctors, delivered by hand, telling me Rapson was the name of their most respected officer and would I make it convenient to call on them. Huge coincidence, really, but I think there's something in my temperament that's polarised to disaster. The worst bit was having to admit to them that I'd copied the name from a professional humorist. They thought I was feeble-minded, and I think they felt sorry for me.

Thus, having carefully concealed a rake where I could be sure of treading on it, I next found myself digging a neat little hole so that I could fall down it and be eaten by Edith Sitwell. I thought I'd write a report of the Sesame Club visit; something that really happened, genuine journalism, just the thing for the gossip-column which was called *Oxford Circus* (each editor changed the name of the gossip-column thinking he was the first to think up such a good title, but it always turned out to have been used dozens of times before). The item would be first-rate publicity for the *Façade* affair and show the producer what powers of patronage I had. I concocted a couple of paragraphs which ran as follows:

> The social event of the term will undoubtedly be the Opera Club's production of *Façade*, a piece of confectionery whipped-up by Edith Sitwell and William Walton for the sweeter tooth. John Catlin is producing and the programmes, printed on handmade vellum and autographed by the speakers, will be auctioned in aid of the Distressed Gentlewomen's Association.
>
> During the vacation the performers were received by Miss Sitwell at the Sesame Club where the doyenne of drawing-room letters gave them tips on elocution. Tea was served, and John Lehmann dropped in with a naval friend to supplicate a manuscript from this gracious lady of good family. The members of the Club had good-naturedly blacked-up and jived contentedly as records of *Gold Coast Customs* were played. The proceedings were rounded off with a call for three cheers for Sir Osbert who had very decently hopped off a No. 19 bus on his way to a monthly meeting of the Rotarians.

Who would have thought that Edith Sitwell read the *Isis?* You could just as easily have imagined her reading *The Magnet*. But John Catlin came round to my digs with a sombre face. 'It's all off,' he said, 'she read that stuff you put in the *Isis* and wants to know the name of your tutor.' 'Why does she want to know that?' I asked. 'So she can have you sent down,' he said. 'But you can't be sent down for making fun of Edith Sitwell, can you?' Catlin looked gloomy. 'She thinks you can. It's a hanging offence.' She'd fired off letters to her publisher Macmillan, to Catlin's mum who was Vera Brittain, and to the Vice-Chancellor.

'As I feared would happen,' wrote Lovat Dickson from Macmillan, 'Edith Sitwell has seen the note in *Isis* which, while no doubt amusing to that magazine's readers, is somewhat lacking in respect to a poetess of her standing –' (*poetess*? If she'd seen that, Dickson would have been on jankers) – 'She has sent me a clipping and a letter which shows that she is very much upset . . . I don't know whether you have any influence over the author of the piece, and if you can make him aware that what he has written here is not in the best of taste . . . if not, then I think you must regard the intended performance of *Façade* as being in extreme jeopardy.'

Catlin quoted me a line or two from the letter she'd sent Dickson, and seemed rather pleased than otherwise to report that she'd spoken of 'the brayings of this lout'. I told him I thought this was rather crude stuff for an old lady of gentle breeding, especially when I was doing my best to get people to turn up to listen to her sixpenny poems. But what made it very clear she thought I ought to be transported for life was the line she added when she'd run out of steam. 'I can only say,' she ended, breathing hard, 'that Sir Osbert was as shocked as I was.'

I was blackmailed into apologising. If I didn't do it, the show wouldn't go on, and what a terrible deprivation that would be. So I gave her the best of three falls and a submission, but mulling it over afterwards I wondered if the old girl hadn't overlooked the built-in consolation prize: that in singling him out, if only to chuck a bucket of horse manure at him, she'd made an anonymous undergraduate feel rather special.

*

The raw November night I'd travelled up from school to try for a place at Exeter hangs framed in my memory as a still-life. In one corner of the canvas there is a segment of mottled veal-and-ham pie eaten at the Ross cafe close to the crossroads called Carfax; I wasn't clear that the three shillings included pudding, and had said I wouldn't bother, but when the waitress explained the price was inclusive I frowned importantly and changed my mind. Adjacent to the pie, the heads of the emperors round the Sheldonian, seen through the bedroom-window in Exeter in the lamplit night; in the morning the scout said, 'Your shaving-water, sir,' and a faint blush warmed my cheek which was as smooth as a baby's. A group of figures playing pontoon: one of the other candidates asked me what I was hoping to read and when I said English he exclaimed, 'Oh, I thought I could do that in the evenings.' Two baronial fires blazing in Exeter hall. Dons at the viva in the Senior Common Room, lolling in their chairs as though they gave their gowns the status, not the other way round. A promenade along the high wall of the Fellows' Garden. Then wheeling about, in the wintry evening and walking through the arch beneath Bishop Kennicott's fig tree, whose capillaries crawled above me among the mullions. The picture in which I am a stranger to my surroundings jumps into my head unmodified by later familiarity: the light falling across the pavement from the College lodge, a narrow lane under a long grey wall, the silhouettes of citadels against the sky, an unrevealed topography which stays unrevealed, as though the place I later became part of was not the same as the place I didn't know.

When I came up I found I was sharing rooms. The other chap had unpacked. A plaster-cast of *L'Inconnue de la Seine* was lying unwrapped on the table. Dear oh dear, I thought. When he came in he said, 'Oh, I remember you. We were playing pontoon and someone asked you what you were going to do, and you said –' he started to chuckle '– you said "I'm going to write".' Then he really did laugh. I looked at him moodily. 'It was three years ago,' I said, 'and I repent. Meanwhile, I reckon it's tit for tat, what with you going round with that horrible death-mask.' So Young and I went across to the College bar and were joined by a solemn ginger-haired youth called Davies whose spectacles were tinted yellow at the bottom – this was because he smoked Ringer's A1, and rolled his own. He was a parson's son and liked to drink beer. The three of us became firm friends, and when funds were low Len the barman would draw us pints, saying solemnly, 'This one is on the Rector.'

My guess that Oxford was the true fount of anxiety and competition was a perfect bullseye and it exactly met the demands of a temperament that had been permanently warped by a mad headmaster. I fell upon the place and tried to consume it: there was something cormorant-like about the way I dived into the opportunities presented, my style was not that of a starving man, so much as a greedy one, and it cannot have been a pretty sight. The miasma of activity I generated concealed the place from me, and I hardly remember ever stopping to turn round and *look* at anything; when I did, I thought something had gone wrong, and wondered why I was not at an audition, rehearsal, play, party, *Isis*, lecture, tutorial. When marooned in College I chafed, believing there must always be something more interesting going on somewhere else. In these moods I would nag Young into abandoning the contemplative life and get him to come and stir things up with me. Let's go to the *Peer Gynt* party at the Playhouse, I said, dammit I'm invited, I'll show you the high life.

So we went and stood around on the stage in a big circle, glugging our glasses of Dry Fly, with me standing next to the leading lady of Oxford drama who'd played Solveig in a horrible pair of flaxen plaits that could not conceal either her talent or her beauty. I'd taken the role of the Strange Passenger, one of a series of meaningless cameos with which the eccentric Norwegian had larded the action, if action it can be called: but winsomely as I played my hand with the lady that evening, my hour with her had yet to chime. I saw Young across the circle chatting to an exquisite person wearing a spotted scarf round his shoulders, and later in the evening I saw the stage manager trying to haul Young down a ladder which led perilously up into the flies. As we stumbled back to College I said there, you had a bloody good time what with the booze and the ladder. Young looked baleful and said I don't think much of the company you keep. I said why's that? He said The bloke in the shawl was touching me up. Good God, I said, Why didn't you edge away? Young staggered slightly but spoke severely. Why do you think I was bolting up that bloody ladder, he said.

Edith unknowingly made me feel special, but perhaps I should say a bit more special, since feeling special was something everyone at Oxford seemed to go in for. We were indefatigable in putting ourselves forward, soliciting attention in the form of our poems, our politics or our coloured waistcoats. When all else failed you could write something fancy in the College suggestion book. Some people specialised in this and turned the suggestion-book into a form of scrimshaw. Associating this with men who bought College scarves in their first term, or even worse, with those who wore University ties, I read the entries with a pitying smile, but one night after I'd just got the *Isis* job I thought I'd have a go myself and tell them what I thought of the horrible swede and cold mutton we'd been given for dinner. A touch of Swift, a hint of Christopher Fry. Next morning someone had written at the bottom of my entry 'Sorry, can't use this: Editor, *Cherwell*', and someone else had added 'Could I see the original German from which this crabby translation has been taken?'

In spite of only ever having handled an oar on the pond in Battersea Park, I got a notion that I should stroke the Exeter College boat to victory in next year's Bump Races. I joined the Boat Club and was put in a tank, a craft moored immoveably to the bank of the river and looking as though it had been hollowed out of a tree-trunk (in 1950 at the Scala cinema in Walton Street – an art house specialising in the antique – they were still shouting 'Well rowed Balliol!' whenever a boatful of Africans paddled by in *Sanders of the River*).

I sat in the tank tugging at an oar, learning to rotate the thing after I'd pulled it through the water – you don't notice this awkward little aspect of the process when you're watching the Boat Race, because they do it so cleverly, but it's the bit that separates the men from the boys. It was such hard work that like many an apprentice in many a sphere I had a feeling that it was something they just threw in while you were learning in order to toughen you up and make it harder, and once you graduated you wouldn't have to do it any more. The Captain of Boats with his neck swathed in scarves would sometimes stop on the towpath and stare broodingly at me as I pulled at the oar and then move on without saying anything. One morning I was crossing the quad and he was coming towards me cocooned in the same scarves and I was wearing a brown velvet bow-tie with which I was hoping to keep my end up with the smart set, and he stopped and said 'Did the Boat Club give you permission to wear that bow-tie?' He was a humourless bastard otherwise I'd have thought it was a joke, so I said 'Not the sort of question I expect from a man who sleeps in his scarves' and he said 'I do no such thing. You're in a pair this afternoon.' A pair is a boat with two people and a cox at the back. I felt rather pleased to be promoted to something that moved and biked down to the river in good spirits. I saw my partner was to be the senior classical scholar, a chap who cunningly knotted his tie so that it would end up under his left ear. He climbed into the boat the wrong way round and we sat facing each other. I gave up rowing after that.

Acting was much easier. You just turned up to auditions in the calm certainty that you were as good at acting as the producer was at producing. Once I was given the lead in something or other even though the producer said my vowels were impure. When he opened the door to let me out he patted me on the back encouragingly: 'I'm sure those vowers of yours will come along sprendidry.' But if talent scarcely came into it, it would have been heresy even to have formed the thought. People were perfectly sincere, and took the stage with as much assurance as Donald Wolfit. I played Mephistopheles, Face, Sweeney, Cassio, Perkin Warbeck and never had the slightest suspicion that I was no good. I don't think this was ignorance, I believe it was innocence. Looking back, I have an idea that's what made the place so agreeable: everyone was coming on like Tolstoy or King Arthur because they hadn't learnt to be frightened yet; there was plenty of derisive laughter, but it wasn't at all dissonant since the people laughing at the Tolstoys were only doing it because they thought *they* were the Bernard Shaws.

A climate of innocence. Only in Arcadia would a girl poet compose a masque for a chum's birthday and arrange for the speeches to be delivered from punts, heedless of the effect of the current on these arrangements. The audience had assembled on one of the College barges, and three times the punts bore down upon it, three times they were swept away. With green scales painted all over me to reinforce my impersonation of the River God I was obliged to declaim from a punt that was rotating on its axis. Pennies were thrown, and oh, how the poet cried. Such a convive, such a farce, such a rout. South African sherry was the only drink then known and under its influence men laughed as never before or since, while one who has for long been a monk in holy orders was embracing one who has long been a distinguished producer, with me thinking each must have taken a great deal of the sherry so to confuse the sexes.

The damsel who had played Solveig was in the audience on this occasion because it was only decent that as the leading lady of Oxford theatre she took no part in parochial entertainments. She was squired on each side by hobbledehoys, each of whom had his arm round her waist and believed that he was caressing the wrist of the lady when he was tickling that of his rival. As I helped a don from Lincoln over the locked gate of the tow-path I was hailed by a man in an open tourer who invited my assistance in returning Enid Starkie, Reader in French, to her cottage near Somerville. She looked about a hundred-and-twelve to me, but the effect of the South African sherry was such that as we both perched on the lowered hood of the MG my inflamed eye suggested to the lady – 'a half-baked maenad' as Professor Helen Gardner liked to call her – that I was about to make a trial of her virtue, and as I wavered up her garden path to see her safely indoors she nipped inside quick and slammed the door in my face.

Tony Richardson invited a girl he saw on the top of a bus to play Juliet, and she said OK, she didn't mind; when the scenery fell over during the performance she laughed heartily as though she'd never guessed acting could be so much fun. Richardson said I should be Tybalt because Basil Rathbone had played it in the film and we were both Liverpudlians. Seemed reasonable. Then he did *Dr Faustus* and dressed me up as Mephistopheles in a sort of gauleiter's uniform, but the impression I made (as friends hastened to point out) was more on the order of a car park attendant. Richardson told me to sit in the audience until it was Mephistopheles' turn to speak. I couldn't help thinking that bounding up in the middle of the action and bellowing 'This is hell!' sounded awfully like forthright criticism from a dissatisfied customer.

Richardson wasn't above obliging in the tiny silent role of Lambert Simnel in *Perkin Warbeck* by John Ford. All he had to do, in this joint production by Exeter and Wadham, was to pass across the stage mysteriously, his tentative lope marvellously recalling the gait of an ostrich, a flightless bird he much resembled. It was nice of him to do it because the play hadn't been performed for 400 years, and after the first night we realised why. When a play's as bad as this it not only seems long, it actually gets longer – the production seemed to go into slow motion as Ford's fustian choked the life out of everyone. It was after midnight in Wadham garden before I took my final bow as Perkin, and only a skeleton audience remained. Even chaps' parents who'd come up specially had vanished, later tendering the excuse that they'd feared the Eastgate had no porter and they'd be locked out.

*

I sent off a poem to the man editing *Poetry from Oxford*, which was published each year by the Fortune Press. To my amazement and delight, he accepted it. His name was Dennis Williamson and one of his own poems in the anthology was about a pop musician –

> 'Perfumed his breath was,
> And his hair like tinsel
> Shone in the arc lights.
> He was a seedy minstrel.'

These lines come into my head quite often, like a tune. I sent him a card – at Oxford you dropped a card into the letter-rack at the lodge and a messenger from each College delivered them all round the University several times a day – suggesting I might be next year's editor. Williamson and I met and he seemed astonished I wanted the job: 'You mean, you wouldn't mind doing it next year? Yes, of course, I'll tell him. I was only dreading he'd ask me to do it again.' The Fortune Press lived off the sales of Dylan Thomas's first book, *Eighteen Poems*, whose copyright the poet had sold outright for nothing and which he was always trying to get back. But the scaly old creep who owned the imprint, a man called Caton, knew when he was well off, and hung on to Thomas while continuing to print slim volumes of verse from other people in the hope of striking oil a second time. He worked out of a mouldy basement in Belgrave Road, Victoria, and in addition to poems did a line in mild pederastic fantasy which was much featured in the bookshops of Charing Cross

Road (printed on what looked like cheap lavatory paper, *The Diary of a Boy* chronicled the life of a schoolboy year by year until the youth wanked himself to a standstill round about his eighteenth birthday; it was published anonymously, as clear a case of automatic writing as you could wish to see. It sold so well, Caton asked the automaton who composed the stuff to stick in another volume entitled *Sixteen and a Half*. Caton knew his market and put a wrapper round the volumes inscribed 'A Book for All Schoolmasters').

'Will this flutter the literary dovecotes, Robert?' asked my fellow Collegian Raymond Simson, respectfully, when I told him of the coup. 'Oh, Raymond, I sincerely hope so,' I replied. I had notices printed, soliciting contributions, and distributed them round the Colleges. During the vacation I visited the dungeon in which the Fortune Press was located more than once, but the man Caton never seemed to be there when I rang the bell. An old lady in carpet slippers answered and I proudly described my credentials. But she said Mr Caton was only interested in seeing anyone who wanted to buy books, not publish them. 'But he's asked me to edit *Poetry from Oxford*,' I cried, as one uttering a mantra against whose power nothing could prevail. 'Call again,' she said, 'he doesn't want any trouble with the police.'

There was of course no question of money for either the editor or the contributors, I just wanted to get enough petty cash out of the man to pay for the stamps for sending back the stuff I wasn't going to use. When I finally cornered him he turned out to be a tramp, with a funny eye and wearing three waistcoats. 'Is anyone going to buy it?' he asked, the funny eye darting off at all angles like the reflections from the glass ball in a palais-de-dance. I said he could rely on the poets each buying one for themselves, and another copy for their mothers; the rest would go to those with a nose for quality. With enormous reluctance he wrote out a cheque for £1.10s to cover all expenses.

I wouldn't wish the book to fall into the hands of anyone who was not of a wholly charitable disposition, and even supposing such a reader, and the allowances he would naturally make for the solemn effrontery of the young in supposing a poem is whatever they choose to write down on a piece of paper, I should like to rob him of the satisfaction of being the first to point out that my own contributions are the most distinctively trumpery: they bear the same relationship to poems as an inexpertly forged bank draft does to money; I shall also hope to pre-empt him by acknowledging that my introduction to the collection appears to have been assembled from a fretwork-set by someone who has neither read the instructions nor is in possession of the right sort of glue.

But assuming such an indulgent reader, I can assure him that whatever he thinks of the stuff I included, it was streets ahead of the stuff I sent back. Nonetheless, as an editor I fell short – at least, in the opinion of one of my contributors. This was Francis George Steiner who wrote to me in high dudgeon after the book came out. 'Dear Robinson,' he wrote from Balliol College, 'Right in the first line glares the most unpardonable printing error –' (the word 'knowledge' appeared without the 'd') – 'Makes it impossible to send the thing to anyone; reduces the otherwise not inelegant little volume to the class of typical undergraduate trash which is not proof-read . . . The Fortune Press is at best a quasi-pornographic outfit. The least that could have been done was to spell words rightly . . . Sorry to be so cheerless on the whole point but it is deeply depressing . . . Otherwise, congratulations.'

The last sentence has a touch of humour not always evident in his later work – he ditched the Francis, when he turned author, opting for plain George – but the fact that the rebuke was entirely deserved did nothing to dispose me to accept its tone. So I rang him up. I huffed and puffed, as only a man will who knows he is in the wrong, but feels his error has put him at the mercy of a fathead who should have been delirious with joy at having his poem selected, rather than picking a quarrel over a literal. Steiner's response hit that note of unforgiving solemnity which was later to become the trade-mark of his highly serious linguistic analyses, but to me, at that moment at the other end of the telephone, it sounded fatuously narcissistic. Wild with annoyance at being held to account for messing up Steiner's first line, I remembered his stuff about the Fortune Press being 'quasi-pornographic', and assuming the grave tones of some old legal hand said of course I couldn't answer for how Caton would view this slur on his reputation, but he might feel an action for libel was his only recourse. I don't ever remember being reduced to such music-hall tactics in a row before, but my own sense of guilt, and Steiner's self-importance, combined to produce this mindless response – how on earth could Caton take any action, not knowing about it? I rather hoped Steiner wouldn't laugh at me, after he put the phone down.

Fifteen years passed. Steiner and I were in a television studio for a discussion of books and censorship. After the programme, Steiner

said, 'Do you remember that row we had about the poem?' I said,
'You bet.' He said, 'Do you remember saying Caton might sue me?'
'Oh God,' I groaned, 'I hoped you might have forgotten that.'
'Well,' said Steiner, 'I was so terrified by what you said, I couldn't
sleep, and I went to the chap who was Professor of Jurisprudence
and asked him what he thought.' 'But,' I said, 'it was codswallop.
You can't be sued by someone who has no idea there's any reason
to sue you.' 'No,' said Steiner, 'strange, though, isn't it?'

*

Nevill Coghill picked a nosegay of flowers in the Fellows' Garden
and Professor Dawkins (who'd known Swinburne and lent money
to Rolfe and kept fourteen Greek dialects alive single-handed by
being the only man who could speak them) tottered forward on
his two sticks: 'Oh, thank you, Nevill,' he bleated. 'No, professor
dear,' said Nevill, 'these aren't for you,' and he handed them to
the girl I was with, before picking Dawkins another bunch. He had
a great big late-eighteenth-century Irish face and if you think this is
a little airy in the way of description, you have only to glance at a
Gillray print featuring Irish bog-trotters and you've got him: a chin
like Desperate Dan and that long upper lip with a conduit running
down the centre, and a giant smile. He was a tall loosely assembled
man, about fifty, who wore hairy suits, and between the turnups of
his trousers and his scuffed suede shoes he showed inches of thick
ribbed sock. On the Home Service he read the Somerville and Ross
stories which had been written by his aunt Edith, and on the Third
Programme he spoke Chaucer in the Middle English pronunciation
he'd been researching; he was still at work on his Penguin translation
of the Canterbury Tales, and as he knocked one off he would read it
aloud to his pupils. Later, he was to become Merton Professor of
English Literature.

His splendid rooms had a theatrical air, by which I mean they
could have been translated untouched to the stage for the opening
scene of a play about an Oxford don who had married a beautiful
Swedish woman, fathered a daughter, then discovered that his
homosexual inclinations were not to be suppressed; the Regency
chaise-longue under the window, raised on a dais, and overlooking
the Fellows' Garden, stage centre, was sometimes the subject of
ribald anecdote: an actor from the Playhouse (which Coghill had
done so much to support as a drama centre for both the city and

the University) had supposedly gone into an antique shop in Ship Street, anxious to buy it: 'Where is the chaise-longue you had in your window yesterday?' 'Oh,' replies the shopkeeper, 'it's been bought by Mr Coghill.' 'Hey-ho,' says the thespian, 'then I shall be on it soon enough.'

There was a seasoned disorder about the rooms which suggested the play's action was about to begin, and you might walk in to discover a servant dusting the furniture as though the curtain had just gone up, and your entry was designed to help him (Cantwell was his name) put the audience in the picture. 'Good morning, Cantwell, I'm having a tutorial with Mr Coghill.' And Cantwell would plump the cushions of the big square armchairs and say, 'Good morning, sir, Mr Coghill won't be long, he's just been called to the telephone by Mr Gielgud, Miss Ashcroft, Mr Richard Burton, Mr Noel Coward, etc' – for the range of Coghill's West End chums was both extensive and distinguished, and his writing table was always scattered with recently opened letters from the famous; twenty-five years before, Auden had strolled in for his tutorial hour, and finding himself alone began to read the correspondence. Enter Coghill, stage left. Auden, peremptorily: 'Where have you hidden the last page of this letter – I've only got the first bit.' And the play is off to a promising start.

In the summer term we might have the tutorial outside, on a little square of flagstones under the tall sunlit flank of Duke Humphrey which stood sentinel to the Fellows' Garden. Once he read me *The Phoenix and the Turtle* and when he ended, a tear stole down his cheek. He was kind and gentle with the young and obscure, never subverting them, though the provocation of callow and assertive essays each week must (in my own case) have been severe. He was proud of his daughter Carole, and sometimes when she visited he invited me to lunch alone with them. I wondered if he was match-making. Somehow I felt sure of his unlimited attention, and even after I went down would breeze in on him unannounced, knowing he would drop whatever he was doing, pour a glass of sherry for me and a glass of milk for himself, and listen to my self-absorbed prattle. Once he took me by the shoulders and turned my face to the light – 'Just to see if you've been working too hard,' he said, as though he would always look after me. I took it for granted that I was a charge on him for life.

Nevill told me how he had tried to get the Rector to tell him something about his favourite Greek poet. Rector Barber was one of the editors of the *Greek Anthology*, and his style was not effusive (he had a dread of the generalisation, and as he passed an undergraduate being sick in the quadrangle on Guy Fawkes night, he said, 'We are none of us quite ourselves this evening, Mr Brown.' But was constrained to add, 'On the whole.'). Who the poet was I've forgotten, but Nevill said to the Rector What sort of a poet is he? And the Rector replied A very good sort of poet indeed. Yes, said Nevill, I should have thought so – but what *sort* of poet was he? Surprisingly careless about genders, said the Rector. Was he, said Nevill, but what sort of a *poet* was he? Very few manuscripts extant, said the Rector. Ah, said Nevill, but as a poet –. There are many constructions in his work which are seen nowhere else, said the Rector. Yes, yes, cried Nevill, but the poet, the poet – what sort of a poet *was* he! Oh, said the Rector, you mean the *gush* side of criticism. The conversation then declining, Nevill asked him who his favourite English poet was. 'Crabbe,' said the Rector, 'he goes so well into Latin.'

Coghill relished people when they were being characteristic – a bias shared with his aunt Edith – and spoke of the Englishman who had gone to hunt with him in Skibbereen (the peninsula in the south-west of Ireland that's home turf to the Coghills and the Somervilles) and so enjoyed himself that he said Compared to this, hunting in Leicestershire is like chasing a mouse round a pisspot. And Nevill would let out his great crackling corncrake laugh. Onions, one of the great editors of the *Oxford English Dictionary* had been his tutor, and when the edition that Onions had superintended was published, Nevill stopped him in the High to offer his respectful congratulations. But as soon as he mentioned the OED, Onions cried, 'Oh, I know it's a bad book. *Don't* rub it in!' Nevill's laugh was protective, what charmed him was the great man's instinctive humility. He had a taste for the particular in people, and much enjoyed the irascibility of his pal Hugo Dyson, an English don at Merton. He would imitate Dyson hopping up and down with wrath as he harangued his pupils about the Shakespeare critics they must at all costs avoid – 'And why do you think Lear was going to Dover, hey? Why, to *get* Dover Wilson!'

You read your essays aloud at tutorials, and Nevill said of one of mine, If they were all like that, you'd get a First. With a sigh, I relaxed – this was as close to a badge of merit as I was ever going to get, and the flimsy status of one who in a mile race showed form over the first hundred yards before dropping out to buy an ice-cream was endorsed, for at the end of our first year there was a preliminary

University examination. You did a section of the syllabus as though it were a slice of your final Schools. The subject was Shakespeare, and lo, two Distinctions – the equivalent of a First – were awarded, and one was mine. But – but – and oh, how the memory of Smivvo returns – a night or two before the exam, finding my notes on the playwright's vocabulary somewhat threadbare, I borrowed those of Fred Bleasdale, an elderly undergraduate of a charming and industrious disposition, who had attended all the relevant lectures, had taken copious notes, and having punctiliously memorised the lot, generously lent them to me. Fred was the soul of courtesy, and on hearing the results congratulated me. 'I am honoured,' said this selfless man, who later became a distinguished headmaster, 'to have contributed to such a meritorious result.' His words were the more heroic in that his own notes had not brought him the same reward. Ever afterwards I wondered: in taking advantage of Fred's industry, I improved my own chances – but had I, like the vampire, diminished his?

Pondering this at tea-time in the Junior Common Room I saw Raymond Simson enter with the tight curls of his springy hair plastered flat to his head, and parted strenuously down the middle. He was wearing a white jacket such as College servants changed into at dinner-time, and he was carrying out a tray of tea. I greeted him, and reflected that everyone's style of dress was open to sudden and eccentric variations of style; perhaps on an impulse he had fallen out of humour with his hair, and marinaded it in solid brilliantine. I watched him cross the quad with the tray held before him and I thought he cut a more than ordinarily impressive figure – Raymond had a stately tread, and had played an excellent Sir Toby Belch for the OUDS.

He was rallying to the cause of Alf Dale. Alf was entertaining a lady from the pantomime at the New Theatre – she flew in on the end of a wire during the Flying Ballet, bearing a wand – and Raymond had offered to dress up as his butler. Now Alf was an undergraduate from the North and wore flares long before the world was ready for them. He was working on his accent, and had got it about as far as Wilmslow. There was an inherent unlikelihood in anyone called Alf having a butler, but he may have told the lady he was Gerald or even Nigel (though if ever an Alf was an Alf all through, it was Alf). They'd decided 'Jonathan' was a good name for a butler (though Bill Gaskill, who wore an ear-ring and went to parties dressed as Nijinsky, had met Lady Redgrave in the vacation and after she'd said to her butler 'Butler, would you bring Mr Gaskill a glass of fruit juice,' Bill had asked her if this was the correct way of addressing butlers, and she replied 'certainly, if their name is Butler.').

According to Alf, Raymond's performance was modelled on that of the late Bransby Williams in a touring version of *East Lynne*, complete with rolling eyes. Fearing that the lady, pea-brained as on all the evidence she must have been, would smell a rat, Alf dismissed Raymond with a lofty wave as soon as he'd laid the tray on the table, saying That will do, Jonathan, and Raymond staggered back, feigning astonishment, and before stumbling from the room, cried 'You mean – you will pour – *yourself* – sir?'

Young and I bought a car for £25. To be exact, he paid up and I owed him my half. It was a very old car – a 1929 Rover, a 'Sportsman's Coupé', built on the order of a nightwatchman's hut, perhaps for travelling to tennis in the days when it was called sphairistiki. We bought it from a man called Cheetham, and when we'd got it as far as the end of Cheetham's road in North Oxford, something we learned was called the half-shaft sheared, and we rolled to a standstill before we had turned the corner. In spite of his unfortunate name, Cheetham paid for the repair, but finding a replacement half-shaft for something that was all but a sedan-chair had us scouring the breakers' yards of three counties like crazed antiquaries.

Sometimes we tried to go to London in the thing, and we'd get halfway up the hill on the far side of Henley before it started rolling backwards, and we would have to return to base, roped to the back of a coal wagon. One of the wheels on our coupé – why coupé, since there was no chance of lowering the black bombazine which covered the rear section without it crumbling like a mummy's sere cloth? – went permanently out of true, after we managed to run the vehicle over a traffic island we hadn't noticed. Neither of us was much good behind the wheel, though I was able to take the high moral ground here, flourishing a piece of lined paper bearing my own signature, that gave me permission to drive Dennis Tippers on specified roads in Nigeria. We finally recognised that we were not serious motorists when we took one of the wheels to have a puncture mended – there was no spare, we had to carry it. After it was done, we got on a bus and put the wheel in the cubbyhole under the stairs by the conductor, but after we got off and were walking down the Turl, Young said, 'Where's the wheel?' We'd left it on the bus and had to pick it up from the lost-property office. In the vacation, the car stood in our driveway at home, motionless, as though it had a hermit inside. One day when I was out my father gave the dustmen five shillings to tow it away.

We sound a bit like the chums of St Jim's, and I suppose the enclosing world of the College promoted this. Some people seemed never to venture out. The charm of College life was the sense of continuity it conferred, the feeling that this was the way things had been done for a very long time. I was specially comfortable in a place that had been there since the fourteenth century, for tradition shares out responsibility for the way things are so that most of it is borne by the past; without tradition, everyone would have to be reinventing everything continuously, instead of just lending a hand, now and again. At the purely sentimental level my enjoyment of the environment grew from early experiences of the antique, such as Liberty's soft furnishings department, and the Tudorbethan gabling of the Ace of Spades, a 1930s roadhouse on the Kingston By-pass.

Standing in the hall of Exeter College, I couldn't say the real thing seemed all that different, though the portraits of rectors long gone lacked the Gainsborough Lady effect, their faces anything but ingratiating, looming out of the crepuscule at dinner, permanently unenthusiastic. Tolkien read from *Gawain and the Green Knight* – shouted it out in a high sharp-edged voice during his Middle English lectures – and it occurred to me that the line about the battlements being 'payred out of papure' exactly hit off the scissored stone on the top of the walls of St Mary the Virgin and All Souls. I was too feverish to look at anything for very long, so if the view became clearer it must have reached me by photosynthesis. But you couldn't miss the fact that Exeter College chapel was too big, and that the gothic interior was incomplete without a hunchback (Betjeman gave me a Piper lithograph of it because he knew how fond I was of what he called 'the old Coll'. It hangs on my stairs and is much nicer than the actual building). By happenstance I was at the top of the tower in New College when Warden Smith was showing some people the parapets and chamfers made by the masons who were currently repairing the structure. Epstein had admired them, the Warden said, and had cried, 'Show old Dobbie these!' – Frank Dobson, a sculptor of the war memorial school, wouldn't have cared for the Lazarus by Epstein which now stood in New College chapel, and I'm not sure Warden Smith did either; but I think he was saying that though Epstein wasn't Michelangelo, he knew where it all came from, while Dobbie was catering to lovers of repro.

The factitious mists generated by the mullions and fumed oak of old-fashioned detective stories began to lift from my eyes, though my view remained romantic; the profound reserve of the faces in the Exeter portraits seemed to counter speculation, but there was a word in the Latin inscriptions under each sitter which seemed to invite it. *Olim*. 'Once upon a time . . .'

*

The *Isis* was owned by the Hollywell Press whose Managing Director was a little man with crinkly hair called Sidney Kelly. He treated the staff to lunches at the Bear at Woodstock or the Trout at Godstowe, and after rounding off the meal with what he called one of his 'specials' – four coloured liqueurs poured one on top of the other like a rainbow, in a single glass – he would allow us, radiant with drink, to drive him home; many an *Isis* hand got the hang of the gear lever and the clutch from Sidney's car on these journeys, though falling asleep on arrival, had forgotten the lesson by the next morning. Sidney had a brother called Hector, a man who wrote sexy novels under the bewitching alias of Darcy Glinto. Sidney kept this dark, but I for one thought the others were pulling my leg when they spoke of such titles as *Lady Don't Turn Over* or *You Found Me, Now Keep Me*, until years later at an antiquarian book sale, there they were.

The most dispiriting chore attaching to the editorship of the *Isis* was thinking up subjects for editorials. As Alan Brien pointed out to me during his tenure of office, you could ring the changes on a single meaningless phrase, and say Oxford was like a lecherous mistress bought for a song, and the next week try Oxford was a lecherous song bought for a mistress – or (I had to shout, because he was a difficult man to dislodge, once he got going) what about an out-of-tune Morris Oxford bought to get lecherous in? He wasn't listening. But leaders were a burden, and I remember one editor threw in the towel and simply wrote HURRAH FOR THE HOLS and got them to set it in 30-point Bodoni.

In retrospect, my editorial style is reminiscent of a man straining his thoughts through muslin without getting the lumps out. I did the one about the Oxford pose ('O pose, though art sick' – 'a pose by any other name'), had a go at television ('the glistening horns announce another house has been cuckolded'), told the tourists to stay away (why?), and said there were 7000 undergraduates but only

700 who mattered. This last produced a letter which accused me of reaching beyond my Ken (Tynan had gone down the year before), but my only purpose had been to provoke, and since I didn't know 700 undergraduates, let alone 7000, the proposition was based on a handful of show-offs who happened to be friends of mine – each had a different story they were anxious to tell the world, but all shared the same innocent desire: to be the centre of attention while they were telling it.

Josée Richard for instance, whose nervy high-strung presence in many a play had made her the reigning queen of Oxford theatre – working my way ever closer to this strange girl, I made sure I held the pen when the time came for her to be featured in the *Isis* as an Idol (an Idol was just that, one who was idolised in the form of a profile). There was John Schlesinger, who was looking forward to a career as a character actor, particularly as a pantomime Dame – 'You will understand if I can't get to the stage-door when you call,' he once said very seriously, 'it won't be because I don't remember you'; he makes films, of course, and he won an Oscar, but after his appearance as the chef in the Chef Sauce commercial, this was overdue. Robin Day was President of the Union the term I was editor of the *Isis* – 'We'll never be as famous again,' he told me, and of course he was right – being well-known isn't the same; Michael Codron and I were detailed off to write the OUDS Smoker together, but he did it all because every time I suggested something he said very primly 'Too broad!' (as he pondered what rôle I should have in the actual performance, he enquired 'Do you like drag?' and I thought it was something to do with fox-hunting).

Tony Richardson arranged an audition at the BBC and arrived with a macaw on his shoulder, specially hired for the occasion; and Bill Gaskill, with his hair curiously brushing one shoulder, did one of his Nijinsky leaps at a party in Worcester garden and Hermione Gingold who was the guest of honour remarked quite meaninglessly 'You get a lot of that in the industrial North.' Shirley Catlin (later Shirley Williams) of the Labour Club had a genius for friendship, everybody felt they were her best friend (she very decently wrote my Idol – every editor was given one, it was a perk); Norman Painting who was to become Phil Archer lent me a quid and I didn't return it until he was the subject of *This Is Your Life* forty years later; Ron Eyre acted everyone else off the stage; Tom Chitty was meditating *Mr Nicholas*, his first novel, while Sue Hopkinson – later Lady Chitty – and Martin Seymour-Smith were turning their attention to the possibilities of biography; Alan Brien, Jack Waterman, Godfrey Smith, John Thompson, Brian Tesler, Paul Vaughan and Derek Cooper were preparing their assault on Fleet Street and the media, and Nigel Davenport, David William, Charles Hodgson, Jack May, Michael Malnick, Hugh Dickson, Peter Dewes and John Wood were planning their acting careers on stage, screen and radio. Ann Broadbent's elegant and distinctive style would make her the great hostess she has become. Anthony Besch was to produce opera, Peter Parker was looking to industry, and Bryan Magee would opt for television and philosophy. Anthony Blond was to be a publisher (he was ever hopeful that his father, the very rich Tootal tie manufacturer, Nevill Blond, would make a substantial investment in the venture. One day the telephone rang and Blond senior said 'Come round. I've got something for you.' Anthony set out with high hopes, but it turned out to be an old dressing-gown).

It may well have been one of this colourful throng who suggested OUDS should tour a couple of plays round the universities of the American mid-west in the Long Vacation. In 1950, going to America wasn't something anyone did as a matter of course, because it didn't feel like a place you could get to by simply buying a ticket. Cinema had made it not so much somewhere else as another dimension, and deciding to go there was like planning a trip to the end of the rainbow. So that when we made landfall at Valparaiso, Indiana, the prosaic ordinariness of the little town was quite invisible to our wondering eyes since we felt we had fallen asleep and woken up in an Andy Hardy film.

We trundled from campus to campus in our station-wagon and battered convertible and ladled out *The Alchemist* and *King Lear* to kindly but bewildered Americans at universities that specialised in engineering or agriculture. 'Johnson was one of Shakespeare's cronies,' wrote a helpful correspondent in a student magazine, 'and many a friendly wrangle over the mead would they have in the famous Cheshyre Cheese Tavern, while Captain James Boswell recorded their words prior to his historical voyage to Australia.' The writer seemed to be in as much of a dream as the rest of us, sitting out as we did on stoops and verandahs after the performance listening to the cicadas while Judge Hardy and Spring Byington served us non-alcoholic fruit punch and Bonita Granville came in with Mickey Rooney to tell us how much they'd enjoyed the show. Ron Eyre who played Abel Drugger plucked a blade of grass from the front garden of a white clapboard house on the shores of Lake

Michigan and handed it to me. 'Fancy that blade of grass always being here, and me not knowing,' he said.

We hitchhiked the 150 miles from the town of Normal, Illinois to see the Mississippi one weekend when there were a couple of days to spare, and people stopped and gave us lifts in a free and easy way even at dead of night. There were three of us, Dick Evans and me, and the girl who played Regan who was fed up with having to share a bed with Cordelia. The free-and-easiness may have had something to do with the drivers being drunk, and one of them pulled up abruptly as Dick fumbled in the bag where he kept his tobacco. 'Tell me frankly,' he said, 'have you got a gun in there?' Reassured when Dick produced his pipe, he insisted we make a detour with him to his farm where he was going to show us the biggest steam shovel in Burlington County. When we arrived he poured whisky for all of us but fell asleep before he could unveil the monster, and we got back on the road to be picked up by a bunch of sports from a car factory in Peoria. These merry ruffians drove up close to any vehicle that was in front of them and nudged the bumper before overtaking it with whoops of delight. When they dropped us off, their leader, a swarthy youth played by Ben Gazzara, offered us a pack of fifty Camels if we left the girl behind.

We leaned over some municipal railings on a bridge at Burlington, Ohio, and looked at the Mississippi. It was night-time and the dark stream reflected the moon. I didn't say anything to the others but it didn't look much different from Beverley Brook, being rather narrow at the point we were observing it. Still, anyway, it was the real thing and you couldn't beat the real thing. Of course, you could only tell people you'd seen it. But we had. We went to a motel and paid five dollars room-rate in advance because we didn't have any luggage. Then we went back.

First we got a ride with a tall black man who was delivering a new car to somewhere, and 90mph was very fast in those days, and that's the speed he cruised at. I doubt if any of us had ever been in a car that big, that new, that fast. But it was quotidian to the black man. That's what he said. He scarcely spoke, he was somewhat aloof, delivering new cars was but part of the way he spent his time, but he offered no explanation, went into no detail. The girl had said of his car delivery function, 'You're doing this all the time, I suppose,' and he replied, 'Yes indeed. It's quotidian to me.' There it was, the word lodged in my mind. I've used it ever since, and when I do, I get a whiff of the inside of that untouched brand-new car, plus a remembrance of the envy, even resentment I felt for the aura of competence and command that surrounded the man who was driving it. Of course, he might not have been competent at all.

Then we thumbed a truck, and we told the driver who we were and what we were doing, and as we drove along he explained that Shakespeare was something he'd never felt the need of. The way I pounced on this must have resembled the tone used in later days by correspondents reporting on traffic conditions for commercial radio stations: self-important, callowly assertive, and based on a conviction that this was a topic nobody dare overlook. I was of course wholly sincere, but the childish absolutism with which I delivered the lecture would have made uninvolved onlookers bring back their elevenses. But the driver was a decent man with an open mind, and besides he was captive. Gazing ahead as through a door that had been opened for him, he said as we bundled down the turnpike, 'You bring it all back to me. It was just my English teacher was so attractive, I paid her the wrong sort of attention.' When we got down and waved him goodbye our girl companion shot me a glance of a kind she hadn't been handing out in my direction before. 'I'm really impressed,' she said. I felt a sense of incredulity mingled with pride, or maybe the other way round.

That night after the show we went to a party at the house of the Vice-Chancellor and were given large tumblers of pink ice-cream in ginger-beer. The wife of the Vice-Chancellor had been chosen off-plan by her husband who saw she was soundly constructed from the same blueprint they use for duchesses in England. She complained loudly that the people of Illinois had spent the entire war sending Bundles for Britain and had never received a single word of thanks. 'And we were over only last Fall and Martha and I tried to buy a *banana* in Oxford Street and they wouldn't sell us one because we had no *coupons*, and after all those parcels we sent *throughout* the war and they wouldn't even let Martha and me have *one* banana.' Little we could do but cluck sympathetically and say How awful, but she did go on saying the same thing over and over again, and it got harder and harder to make the responses.

Now there was a chap called Ralph Hallett whose father was in biscuits – and when I think of it, Hallett was the man who had the MG sports car in which we returned Enid Starkie unopened to Somerville – who was probably the quietest, most civil member of the company: the others shared a sweetness of character that endeared them to all, but none of them, as far as I remember, ever stopped talking, mostly about themselves. Hallett on the other hand had a reposeful, musing air, a tall languid figure quietly smoking a fag, more or less continuously trailing about back-stage in one pair of underpants, while the wardrobe mistress, Ann Lever, devotedly darned his others.

The Vice-Chancellor's lady returned to her theme for the umpteenth time and Hallett, who had been smoking one of his endless fags and nodding in an understanding if faintly distracted way, suddenly fell forward. 'He's ill!' cried the Vice-Chancellor's wife, and there was a hush. Hallett, who was now on his knees, slumped lower, his arms outstretched until his forehead was touching the parquet floor. 'Call a doctor,' screamed the lady. But Hallett was salaaming. 'Madam,' he said, 'on behalf of the entire British nation I offer you our profoundest thanks.' Only one thing was absent from Hallett's superb gesture. 'I don't really have to tell you what it is,' I said afterwards as I finished congratulating him, 'but wouldn't it have been wonderful if you could have done it wearing your underpants?' Hallett smiled. 'Well in a very real sense I was, of course. But I know what you mean.'

If you had a big part in one of the plays you had a smaller one in the other. I was playing Face in *The Alchemist* and the Duke of Burgundy in *Lear*. We'd done *The Alchemist* in Long Island to a silent and bemused audience, and New York was our final stop. That night it was *Lear*. Sorting out my costume I found the crown had come apart so I stuck it together with elastoplast and popped it on. Not a lot for Burgundy to do while Lear is giving Cordelia the office, you just stand about looking haughty. New York was very hot, and it was hotter yet in the theatre. Adopting a ducal stance, hand on hip, I felt my crown starting to move. The heat was melting the gum on the elastoplast and the crown was creeping down towards my ears. Had it been a trilby I could have taken it off and stared quizzically at it or flicked a bit of dust off the brim as though us dukes were always at our ease. But you can't take a crown off and fan yourself with it. I contemplated putting my hand up to one side of the thing as though this was what Burgundians did when they were much struck by something, but concluded this might look as though I'd suddenly been attacked by neuralgia. I ground my teeth together in the hope of making the veins in my temples swell. If I could just keep it on until I was off-stage! 'Come, noble Burgundy,' thundered Lear, grabbing me round the shoulders and the crown slid past my ears, twirling round my neck like a well-thrown horse-shoe.

The Korean war was declared on and the ancient plane we were going to fly home in was commandeered. We were stuck in a sweltering New York and went to air-conditioned cinemas to enjoy the cold. I began writing up our trip for the *Isis* and after the piece appeared it was given a much wider circulation than I was expecting. 'How does it feel to be famous?' asked a man I'd known at school, pulling up on his bike outside the Sheldonian. 'What do you mean?' I said. '*Time* – don't you read it?' I slid across the road to Blackwell's and saw *Time* had reprinted the *Isis* article and added a photograph they'd got from someone. It showed me putting a great deal of effort into smoking a cigarette, so that I looked like a dwarf caught in the middle of a fire-eating act. *Time*'s style was immutable, and the picture was captioned 'Oxford's Robinson'.

It was robust stuff. 'The majority of Americans I met socially were agreeably childlike. They did not seem to be very good at thinking, largely, I suppose, through lack of practice. The American student inclines to statements that are dogmatic and unoriginal. He has an implicit and almost mediaeval trust in Authority. I raise a mug of foaming pink ice-cream in ginger-beer – the national beverage – to their formidable hospitality: but a Bronx cheer for the neons, the nylons and the nut-melbas . . .'

My tutor seemed a bit put out. 'It's going to be such a pity if you go on mistaking brashness for something it isn't,' Nevill remarked rather tartly as we met crossing the quadrangle in Exeter. 'Quite apart from the fact that some of us are hoping to be lecturing there in the vacation.' This was a week later, and *Time* had printed a column of letters from furious citizens across America.

'Sir, The boorish, pompous, patronizing and ill-considered remarks of Freshman Robinson should be excused, if not condoned, on the grounds of his patent youth and immaturity. Brian E. Webster, Cornwall, Ontario.' 'Sir, I hope Robert Robinson will come back to the US after he has grown up. Eugene Gieringer, Marblehead, Mass.' 'Sir, What, again? I'm getting darned tired of seeing that type of hogwash being given undeserved circulation in *Time*. Ted Powers, Waterbury, Vermont.' 'Sir, Bit Player Robinson had best revise some of his sweeping generalities on the calibre of American intellectuality if he ever hopes to graduate as a truly educated man. Jack Nealon, Columbus, Ohio.'

I suspect it was the pink ice-cream stuff that was the combustible particle, the central irritant. But that line about 'Bit Player

Robinson' gets marks. I received a pile of similar mail at Exeter College.

'You imply Americans are inferior because they smell better than the British . . . You have a certain rustic bluntness and stupid honesty which recalls Bottom the Weaver. Philip Sullivan, NYU.' 'What may have confused you is that Americans when they think don't *look* like Oxonians look when they think. Gilbert Harrison, Paris.' 'Please send me a foaming mug of pink ice-cream so that stock piles may be built up. Philip. B. Thresher, McGill University.' 'We are now quite immune to such accounts – anyway Charles Dickens, Matthew Arnold and Fanny Trollope did it better. H. Shuman, USA.'

I'll bet they did. Anyway, the letters that came to me were addressed rather generally to 'Robert Robinson, Oxford University'. It was an awkward coincidence that this happened also to be the name of the President of the Royal Society who was Waynflete Professor of Chemistry. 'Not SIR Robert Robinson' was scrawled angrily across many a re-sealed envelope that reached me after the Professor had discovered over the toast and marmalade that he was an object of scorn and vilification to Americans everywhere. Many years later I read a letter in *The Times* sandbagging the then Director General of the BBC, signed by four disaffected broadcasters, one of whom appeared to be me. But I hadn't received any such round-robin and wouldn't have signed it anyway since I didn't believe the cause was just. Won't do me any good, I thought, better ask *The Times* what's going on. It turned out the signature was that of Sir Robert Robinson, PRS. He'd got the letter by mistake, and (I like to think) after many a year had taken his revenge.

*

So at last the entrance fee was exacted as we traipsed into the Schools for our Finals. Men suffered blackouts halfway through a question on *Havelock the Dane*, others were carted off to the Warnford psychiatric unit babbling of green fields, and one man contrived to get a passing builder who was carrying a plank over his shoulder to clonk him on the head just as he was turning across the pavement to enter the Schools, and was given an *aegrotat*; the builder was very apologetic, but the victim sent him a letter of thanks from his hospital bed. The rest of us paid our dues. During the thirteenth and final paper – I think it was the nineteenth-century Romantics (the English syllabus still stopped dead at 1830) – I found I was writing diagonally across the sheet and feeling that things were getting very big and very small as they did during childhood fevers. But Captain Ferguson was too late. I came away with the respectable Second I was counting on, and Oxford was over. Some people couldn't believe it. They hung about the Stowaway or the Town and Gown as though it was a continuous performance and you could go on sitting it round. But most of us made a beeline for the exits: after all, everything had so far been preliminary and now we were going to see what it was all about – I was really quite curious.

GOMER'S MISSIS OR SCENES
FROM FLEET STREET LIFE

My FIRST JOB as a paid journalist was to rig the crossword competition in *The Weekly Telegraph*, then fake the readers' letters – or at least this is how I interpreted it. It wasn't quite the image of the work as it had been sold to me.

The man who hired me had a personable enough face, but you wondered how people had been sure of recognising him before he grew his moustache: the moustache was not a boss's moustache (it would have been more at home on the lip of a man in a stiff felt hat, collecting insurance premiums on a doorstep) but it was an indispensable landmark. He was very quietly spoken, when he spoke at all, but actual silence was his chosen instrument: to an uncanny degree he had the capacity to stay silent when an ordinary person would have felt himself unable to – colleagues who waited for his comment on a point they had made, waited in vain, and in their confusion talked on, until they fell off the edge of the world. No doubt it was his strategy, and this eerie command of his tongue allowed him to survive the whims of one proprietor, and then another. It was an unappealing faculty, but it lent his silences a sort of energy, as though he was constantly in pursuit of some unnamed goal with enormous firmness and intent. But I think Gomer rumbled him in the end – this was the thickest Berry of them all, Lord Kemsley, who sold his fusty dusty empire of newsprint to Roy Thomson at a firesale price, but banked the money under the impression he'd got the better of the Canadian miser. As a goodbye present, Gomer presented his lieutenant with a photocopy of the cheque; he had never before been known to make a joke.

Interviewed for the job, I sat in front of the man and his familiar – a scaly-faced Scotsman who filled his inkwells – fresh from the University, wearing a bow tie and carrying a walking-stick. The oddity of this regalia was matched by my off-hand manner – I behaved as if I was doing these men a favour by hearing them out on the subject of their dim provincial newspapers (what a comment it is on the psychology of the free man as compared to the man he becomes once he is hired, that within a month of accepting the job I wouldn't have dreamed of addressing either of them except in terms of the profoundest respect).

Perhaps he found this free and easy air provoking, since he rather defensively said he wasn't ashamed of the *Empire News* – his 'servants' read it. This flourish made me feel faintly uncomfortable, which I suppose is why I remember it: he managed to sound as though he'd come no closer to servants than Old Hethers on the lemon barley water bottle. (The *Empire News* was an ineffectual Sunday broadsheet whose similarity to the *News of the World* was confined to the way the ink came off on your fingers, since Gomer's missis had the dummy delivered to Dropmore in Buckinghamshire – a jerry-built 1830s pile whose library she had furnished with unopened books from a wholesale warehouse – and there on a Saturday afternoon she scanned the proofs of the Sunday editions in case the word 'sex' had slipped past the subs who had standing orders to replace it with the word 'glamour'.)

But the Editorial Director spoke more freely than I remember him ever afterwards doing, and explained the *Weekly Telegraph* was about to be re-launched as a big-time glossy and advertised on the eye-pieces of buses. I was to add my champagne to the editor's brandy – had he heard this phrase used in a film? – a combination which in the event turned out to be more or less Tizer. The woebegone mag was printed on thin blotting paper and sold for threepence to readers I imagined to be comprehensively deprived. It was a satellite of the *Sheffield Telegraph* and if the derelict organ was to be transformed into something like *Picture Post* then it called for the magic wand of a Sugar Plum fairy: nothing in the Kemsleys' frowzy empire looked capable of anything but lining a cat litter, and shortly after I started forging the letters no more was heard about advertising or glossiness.

And it wasn't even Fleet Street, it was only Gray's Inn Road. Kemsley House was a heap of red brick in the wastes between Clerkenwell and King's Cross, and had the dejected air of a building site where the money had run out and the owners had decided to let the building project go to hell and make do with the Portakabins. This rookery of temporary cubicles which were continually being partitioned and re-partitioned was serviced by two lifts, one manned by a Strict Baptist with evil-smelling feet who wouldn't stop at the first floor on the way up, but only on the way down, to teach you a lesson (I always meant to tell him this was a short-sighted policy for a lift attendant who should spread smiles and good will against the day the world tumbled to the fact that passengers could work the lift themselves; but I was too busy holding my breath). The other one was in the command of a bow-legged corporal who kept the doors chained back until someone of field rank showed up.

There's a touch of resentment in what I'm saying – I hear it, somewhat to my surprise, since I had no such feeling at the time. I'd passed out of the preliminary Arcadias of life where, as everyone is, I was known, and into the world, where I was a total stranger; the tumble-down ant-hill in which I worked was the image of this, and while I wondered why they didn't invite me to write a column for the leader-page of the *Sunday Times*, what I hacked out on ancient typewriters with two fingers filled the *Weekly Telegraph* to overflowing, and the ramshackle arrangements of paid work, where no one gives a damn about you so long as you get the job done, gave me a sense of knockabout competence.

At the same time, there was an assumption I couldn't leave behind or abandon, since it was so much part of me I didn't know it was there – it was unexamined because unacknowledged. Children are taught about the world in terms of certainties and part of growing up is being able to pass from these primary colours to the ambiguous shades of the way things really are. But if you are of a fanciful or romantic temperament you may go on believing, long after there is evidence to the contrary, that what happens in fiction is as literal a guide to human nature as Wainwright is to the Lake District. Sooner or later, most people make the necessary accommodations, though some are slower in making them than others, and some few never make them at all. Well, there's a lot to be said for innocence, because it will occasionally let you spot what custom and usage otherwise conceal, but of course it mostly gets in the way. The assumption I refer to came in two parts, the first being slightly less footling than the second, viz. that my seniors were artless and disinterested. I took it for granted that each was his own man, for I knew nothing of hierarchies and what was involved in securing your position in one. But the second bit was not to be extenuated, and ran as follows: that along with my schoolmasters, the dons at Oxford, and my mother, those in authority would always be delighted with my progress. I even fantasised that Gomer, if I ever got to know him, would respond to my own candour and agree to shake off his small-minded corner-shop inheritance, renounce the title which he had bought, and run a campaign in the *Sunday Times* pressing for abolition of the House of Lords. Putting the Seebackroscope to my eye, I focus on these sorry vestiges of an innocence I thought that I'd jettisoned long before, and being forced to recognise them may account for a slightly acid note that creeps in at this point.

We published in London, but I was allowed an occasional jaunt to Sheffield to see how they printed the thing. Behold, on one such trip I saw a man on the platform who actually held a copy of the magazine in his hand. I approached him: was he, I importantly enquired, a regular subscriber? Not really, he replied. And why was that, I asked, giving him to understand that on matters of policy a word from me and the thing was done. 'It's a bit too instrooctional', he said. It didn't occur to me he may have been thinking of an article by a dim cleric which had recommended compulsory church parade for everyone ('if we are completely honest, is it not just a matter of common sense?'), or perhaps a piece about the 'criminal waste of milk' involved in the Japanese habit of bathing in the stuff ('soap and water was good enough for my grandfather – and he was a missionary in the Land of the Midnight Sun'); I simply thought he'd caught a whiff of the intellectual seasoning I was adding to the mix, and was finding it unfamiliar (my debut had been an article entitled 'It's Still a Wild Wild Oxford' in which I spoke of girl undergraduates keeping themselves going during exams with 'pinches of snuff that would make a printer sneeze' – curious fabrication). So I beamed at the chap on the platform, seeing a potential convert. 'Listen,' I said, 'we're trying to get intelligent people like you to come up-market with us.' 'Then where are the pictures of scantily-clad women in bathing costumes?' he asked. 'And the crossword's got too many long words.' It wasn't the length of the words, it was the necessity of having second sight. The crossword prize was a guinea, and the puzzle was rigged. Here and there the answers could be one of three or four words – the clue would be something like 'household item' and the answer could be hat, mat, or cat. Or you might have 'physical movement' and the answer could be fit, sit or hit. My business was to weed out all the entries where the answers were simply wrong, then sift through the rest, all of which were correct (since the various options were equally apt) and find the one reader who'd selected the unique combination of ambiguous answers. Without my gerrymandering, everyone would have won tuppence. As a task, it wasn't quite as shabby as blanking out the racing results in the evening newspaper so that old chaps who'd come into the library for a warm couldn't read them (part of the apprenticeship to a Chair of Sociology served by my old friend Laurie Taylor) but it was comparable.

Having fixed the crossword, I'd knock off two or three features under a variety of pseudonyms – 'Figaro' was the by-line under my weekly profile of ancient monuments like Gilbert Harding, Donald Wolfit, or Jack Solomons – and devise double-page picture spreads on long-time standbys such as the Caledonian Road market, the BBC sound-effects department, and the Hidden Sights of London (of the last, there were only two, and all the journalists in the building had them out of the cuttings on a regular basis – the police station inside a Corinthian pillar and the Tube ventilator dressed up as a summer-house; we had to blow up the pictures extra big that week to fill the space). Then I'd review the books, a practical business which came in two stages: first, scooping out the contents to fill as much space as possible, then turning the books into cash at Simmonds' bookshop in Fleet Street. This process of pocketing half the cover price for each review copy really was like magic, and every time I did it I wondered if it could possibly work again.

Then I was ready for the readers' letters. These I signed with a variety of distinguished names, humanised by more humble addresses: Henry James, Walton Hall Avenue, Liverpool; George Moore, Chingford; J.E. Flecker, Scunthorpe; though I felt Mrs Grendel was entitled to Belgrave Square. But since my improvisations on the why-oh-why school of correspondence were state of the art, I also liked to attach them to names of old acquaintance, as a gesture of esteem.

'Why-oh-why do not Britain's old age pensioners wear a red light fore and aft during the hours of darkness? With schoolchildren careering about on roller skates or bicycles in these winter evenings, it is surely good sense to attach a small cycle lamp to the tail of the coat, while clipping a similar item to tie or scarf – the latter doubling as a tasteful fashion accessory. Yours sincerely, Kenneth Tynan, Accrington.'
'Why-oh-why are new shirts always so full of pins? Surely it is not beyond the wit of the retailer to fold his merchandise into a neat package without causing the customer to impale his fingers on these painful and well-nigh invisible aids. Here's hoping! Yours sincerely, Robin Day, Wells-next-the-Sea.'

The next week I would spare myself the labour of dreaming up further subjects by inventing replies. 'I wonder if Mr Day has any idea of the work that goes into presenting a shirt for display and sale? If he jibs at a few pins, I can only say this is hardly the spirit which has made these islands great. Yours sincerely, Enid Sitwell (Mrs), Grimsby' 'And where does your correspondent think the money is coming from for the purchase of red lights out of a pension of two pounds a week? It is discipline we need, not bicycle lamps. I advise Mr Tynan to think again. Yours sincerely, Old Stager, Brownsea Island.'

Listing heavily to starboard under the weight of the articles I piled into it, the *Weekly Telegraph* slowly foundered, and as the waves closed over its head I was winched off to a newspaper called the *Daily Dispatch*. Little need be said of this sheet, which was printed in Manchester, other than to note the hard work I put into persuading friends in London that it existed: my lack of success reminded me of the undergraduate at Christ Church who bet someone £5 there was no such college as Wadham. Provincial papers are second division, but the Kemsley lot were second rate as well, the issue on sale any day in Sheffield, Manchester or Newcastle as stale in spirit as if it had been pulled at random from one of the musty files in the cuttings library: I imagined men hired years ago by the Berry brothers to bring out papers whose deferential columns would never upset the advertisers wearing jackets with lateral creases deeply incised across the shoulders, stigmata of long days spent snoozing against radiators. Defter ways had been devised to tickle the readers' prejudices, and the *Daily Dispatch* ran aground on the shoals of indifference. I was first into the lifeboats as television correspondent of the *Sunday Chronicle*.

Gomer put his youngest son in charge as editor of this paper, but the poor fellow couldn't get his mind to focus on the job since he was constantly distracted by his real concern. 'He'd do anything he was told,' said one of the subs, reflectively, 'including bringing out the paper printed in Urdu and decorated with arseholes, if only his father would let him have a Bentley instead of a Jag.' The pilotless hulk went down stern first, and clinging to a spar I was hauled aboard a ghost ship called the *Sunday Graphic*. For a while it looked as though the vessel might make port. I wasn't too familiar with the paper myself, and since my dad had once said he thought the *Graphic*'s typical reader would be a middle-aged spinster in a Ladies Only carriage, Hugh Cudlipp's comment that it was 'England's least influential Sunday newspaper' sounded about right. But it was a national. It didn't do much for my prestige, but at least everyone had heard of it. And I had a column. I was to write about film stars.

★

At first nights I noted the same elegant figure was always first up the aisle for the free drinks in the little room off the foyer at the interval: the exquisitely groomed husband of one of the maturer West End actresses, he would rise alertly from his seat the second the tassles at the hem of the curtain began slowly to descend, and as people started to applaud he would break into a graceful trot up the rake between the stalls, not so much running as miming running, turning his knees in with a hint of the feminine, as though he were being specially thoughtful about someone else – perhaps hastening to hold the door open for an elderly companion. It was a wonderfully understated performance, no question of a sprint, but equally no question of anyone beating him to it. What beguiled me about this little display was its ravishing hauteur, as though he *condescended* to hurry. Where the ordinary patron who had actually paid for his seat might have been effusive if the management had offered him a drink, here was a man exercising a *droit de seigneur*. As I stood behind him, matching him glass for glass with the Louis Roederer Crystal, I recognised the great principle that lay behind all this: that in the world of entertainment no one would ever dream of paying a penny for the commodity they sold.

Of course, freeloading is built into the very foundations of journalism – imaginary 'expenses' were concocted and phantom 'sources' were expensively lunched; no one ever felt they could joke about this shifty aspect of the inky trade, and how well I remember the solemn face of a colleague who had just returned from an assignment in Scotland as he entered on his expense sheet the words, 'To being carried across stream by ghillie: £5.' These were backhanded dealings, connived at by editors (when Hugh Cudlipp was hiring a young journalist for the *Daily Mirror* he explained the expenses he would be allowed. 'When claiming them, you can use any names you like. Except the Archbishop of Canterbury. He's mine.' Checking with the Wizard of Fleet Street, he confirmed the accuracy of the story, adding: 'And I used not only the Archbishop but the Dean as well – Hewlett Johnson. It was only when I was invited to some C of E quinquennial celebration that I learned the old bugger had been dead for five years.'). But in these little fictions, money was acknowledged, whereas in the larger fairy-tale, the world of entertainment, where PR men were the courtiers and the journalist was Buttons, money hadn't even a walk-on part: to the thesps I memorialised in the *Sunday Graphic* their hotel suites, chauffeured cars, restaurants, first nights, premieres and booze were experiences that came direct, money did not intervene. It was a PR culture, and it engendered a deliciously prodigal piss-elegance in one and all. I cherish many instances of it.

A tucket sounds, and high up in a riverside suite overlooking the Thames at the Savoy, enter Curt Jurgens, the twelve-foot high German film star with the jumping-bean head, who was so often featured in unremarkable British films of the Fifties. Jurgens wears his shy smile, perhaps wondering where the two pretty girls who seem to be his minders have appeared from. He invites one of them to ring down for a couple of jars of caviare, and Bluff Hal, the PR figure, smiles indulgently as the pots – stone jam-jars of the stuff, £300 a throw – arrive with crystal bowls and silver spoons, and the assembled hacks dig in as though not wanting to be standoffish. Some vote it every bit as good as jellied eels, though one of them, shovelling down another £20 teaspoonful, says it is 'overrated'. When the party-minded Jurgens calls for another couple of jars Bluff Hal's smile notches down very slightly, but for myself, swallowing a bumper of the Montrachet, I grow sulky, knowing that instead of falling into bed with the two girls, like Jurgens, I have to write about the bastard.

Film companies offered huge lunches to journalists before press shows, to which the knowledge that the more lavish the entertainment the more determined you would be to demonstrate your independence and write savagely of the film, was a pleasurable added ingredient. On one such occasion, bizarre even by PR standards, a conjuror had been invited to mystify the hacks as they lowered their faces into the *moules marinières*. His act involved a pigeon who was supposed to disappear up the waistcoat of the critic of the *News of the World*, but whose refusal to go near the man drew roars of approval from the rest of the brotherhood. When the pigeon perched on the chandelier and shat on a tray of petits fours being carried round by a waiter the hacks, now well lubricated, had grown solemn and were all for getting up a petition to the RSPCA, and some of the more deeply sincere were cooing and clucking to the bird to come down and be sent to a home of rest. The conjuror had been sidelined, and turned from being Mr Mystery into an ordinary irritable human being who cried pettishly, 'Leave him alone, he'll come down when he's ready.'

Once we were flown out to Monte Carlo – dozens of us – to meet Frank Sinatra. But the one thing that didn't happen was meeting the man. We were given dinners and taken on coach trips and even saw the potato-faced songster do his stuff at the Winter Gardens. But no one managed to meet him. All we were there for was to supply a chorus to augment the myth. Bluff Hal was in attendance, and when I asked him when I was going to have my interview he said 'I'll keep on top of that one. Are you getting enough to drink?' More than enough. On the way back to the airport I sat next to an elderly hack whose face was a mass of cuts where he'd tried to shave himself. How are you feeling, I asked him? 'Oh dreadful, old boy,' he answered with simple sincerity.

When we flew to Dublin for the first night of Noël Coward's terrible play *Nude with Violin* our main object – after we'd made sure we had collared the best rooms at the Shelbourne Hotel (one hack who lived in Pinner – 'The West End Is His Backyard' boasted the strapline above his column – was concerned about the water. 'Is it safe to drink?', he worriedly asked the ancient waiter. 'Put a drop of whisky in it, it's better altogether,' replied the Boniface) – was to get the Master of the Shiny Dressing Gowns to say something witty. Very hard on him, really. He allowed me to interview him in bed after he'd had his afternoon nap, but anything he said had to compete with that morning's story in the *Irish Times* reporting a grand piano floating upside down in the Liffey. How do you get this out of your mind, even when Noël Coward is sitting up in bed eating crumpets and asking you if you think he looks Chinese? Thoughts of the piano may have made me seem abstracted as he pulled his eyes ever more slantwise with his fingers and asked my candid opinion. I was wondering whether I'd have been sure it was a grand piano – legs sticking upright, but how many did they have? 'Yes,' I said, 'yes, I think you do,' (five – but the configuration?) 'Do you always use a grand piano when you compose, Mr Coward – the five-legged sort?' 'Aren't you thinking of giraffes?' 'But the position of the legs – doesn't it affect the acoustic?' 'One doesn't compose from beneath the instrument and so long as the keyboard is within easy reach I assume the legs are where nature intended.' I concluded my interrogation by asking him what he did when he met a bore.

'Run like a stag,' he replied, and jumping out of bed, fled into the bathroom.

Moving on to the Cork Film Festival I encountered room service of a very Irish order, for when I rang down for some ice it was brought to the room on a dinner plate, by a nun. No explanation of this phenomenon was ever forthcoming, and it was clear that the flim-flam with which we were hoping to fill our pages would find itself in competition with the genuinely odd. The occasion was hijacked by a local politician called Leary, whose slogan was 'Leary for the Weary' though those who cared little for rime and less for scansion said it was 'Leary for the Legless', what with him being a publican.

This unreconstructed human being sucked attention away from the J. Arthur Lunch Brigade who had been flown in from Pinewood for no other reason than to be noticed, and Leary contrived without effort to absorb the light at all the press parties. After one of these genteel orgies he offered us further hospitality at his pub. It was three in the morning and there was a placard in the window which read 'The softest beds in town. Why not telephone from here and cancel your earlier arrangements. You will not regret it.' Leary dragged his toothless sister out of bed to bring us drink. When we had thanked her for her kindness and were sipping our brandies, Leary handed us a bill. 'Seventeen and ninepence,' he said, 'but tis the old price.'

My friend Philip Oakes, then of the *Daily Express*, turned the event into a splendid short story in which under the thinnest of aliases he characterised me as an amateur of the Irish folk song. My light baritone with its range of three and a half notes cultivated during competitive hymn singing in the school hall, seemed to affect him strangely, for just as the sun was coming up and Leary's sister was making tea – Leary had given her orders that he didn't want it so weak he'd be able to spear a shark through fifty fathoms of it – and I was letting go with 'Oh the Brown and the Yellow Ale', I saw Oakes suddenly strip to the waist as though my performance had brought him out in a muck sweat, and as I got to about the fourth verse he removed his spectacles, cast them to the floor and ground them with considerable feeling into the floorboards.

Not being of brochure quality, such incidental felicities wouldn't do for the show page of the *Sunday Graphic*, in whose service I seemed to be in a permanent state of riding in from the airport with someone like Robert Mitchum. This great man sat in the back of the limo like a silent Indian in a suit as big as a wigwam while

I plied him with ingenuous questions. We had got off to a flying start during the introductions. 'This is Robert Robinson,' said the flack. 'Does he suck?' asked Mitchum courteously. Responding to his sense of fun, I asked him who it was who gave him the idea he could act. 'Me mother,' said the great man. He'd arrived to play in a film called *The Grass is Greener* with Cary Grant, but as we trundled down the Great West Road in the Vanden Plas it was gruelling work trying to get him to leave his tent, and the pauses were long.

Minutes after I'd asked him how he dodged the autograph hunters he said 'I am swift and devious'. Then later, emerging from a deep coma, he volunteered, 'Cary comes round straightening your tie for you.' He added, 'Cary only likes clean people in his films.' He told me his children thought he was a pickpocket, and if they found out he was an actor they would disown him. He suffered from insomnia – it was only when he got to work he fell asleep. 'It's not the work I mind, it's the attendance. It's a pity you can't phone it in.' The car pulled up and Mitchum stalked off into the Dorchester, his silence clinging to him like fog on high ground.

During a similar convoy, the cargo was Zsa Zsa Gabor and a gentleman friend with a name so lacking in vowels he had changed it to John Mills: perhaps he hankered after the Austin Reed style of his diminutive namesake who turned up freshly ironed in so many films flattering the Island Race. But since he could have passed for a bouncer outside his own club – he ran a Park Lane gambling house called Les Ambassadeurs – the name sat uneasily with the pencil-slim moustache and the enormous chest which, as he breathed, caused his boiled shirt to click like a metronome. With coquettish zeal I asked the bulky Romeo if he were about to marry the lady. He removed his cigar and without looking either at me or at Zsa Zsa replied without relish, 'Are you crrrazy?'

The Dorchester was the favoured billet for such visiting celebs, and there was something about Joan Crawford which made me think of ectoplasm. Was this an interview or a seance, I wondered, as the apparition force-fed me the home-brewed vinaigrette which she always carried with her – she actually used a tablespoon as though she were a reincarnation of Mrs Squeers dosing the boys with brimstone and treacle. Her hubby, Alfred, the elderly Pepsi Cola king, entered with bottles of the beverage so we might refresh ourselves. It was eight o'clock in the morning, and I wondered if it wasn't a little early. '*Any* time is Pepsi time,' announced the Medusa grimly.

Under the same glittering roof, which soared aloft on columns belonging to the sixth order of classical architecture, the expense-sheet, Anita Ekberg the muscular Snow Queen from Scandinavia held me enthralled as she told me how happy she was in her choice of husband. She had married a handsome slob from Elstree called Anthony Steele. 'And believe me, Mr Roberts,' she insisted, 'every time we climb into bed it is like tearing the brown paper off a wonderful Christmas present.' I thought this was rather a nice way of putting it, but I knew it wouldn't do for the *Graphic* – the idea of removing the wrapping paper from Gomer would not have appealed to Gomer's missis, and I had to bowdlerise. (It was about this time that the *Graphic* ran a front page picture of the Smithfield winner, a massive bull whose organs hung down like bagpipes. Gomer's missis had his balls painted out after the first edition, and the owner won massive damages.)

I interviewed Peter Finch in the presence of his mother, which as impossible tasks go beats the labours of Hercules. I met him at her house in Bury Walk, Chelsea, and she stared unblinkingly at me as I got out my notebook and tried to strike up. She was a solidly built gentlewoman of some breeding, and I just couldn't get round to asking Finch about falling asleep drunk with ladies of the town – his principal pastime. Indeed, so delicate was my questioning under the maternal eye that the dissolute Finch came out in the paper sounding like St John the Divine. Afterwards I wondered – had he hired this woman for the evening? No question of performance in the case of Ralph Richardson – what he did on stage was but a muted version of his genuine eccentricity. We lunched at his club where the member would write on a slip of paper the dishes he and his guest had chosen. But Richardson wanted tongue and had difficulty spelling it. He knew there was a 'u' in it somewhere but couldn't quite place it. After making a few boss shots, in which the 'u' appeared before the 'g' and which he tested out aloud – 'Too – UNGE – no, no, doesn't sound right' – he finally got the letters more or less in the right order, and turning to me, said confidentially, 'We should have been in a pretty pickle had it been vol-au-vent.'

Perhaps it wasn't surprising that when the subject was an actor of real distinction, I found it difficult combining him with *Sunday Graphic* requirements. These were vague, but certainly excluded serious consideration of what acting was all about, unless you could come at it sideways with chirpy quotes. I was constitutionally unable to keep irony out, but fortunately it wasn't on Gomer's missis's proscribed list – she wouldn't have been able to identify it, but she'd sense the sceptical bias, and I had to be pretty careful not to land her with too much of it in case she felt challenged.

But giving the readers an idea of Paul Scofield's quality in tabloid form defeated me: I had to apologise to the man for wasting his time. If I'd been a real Sunday journalist I'd have been too busy doorstepping the then Marquess of Milford Haven about when he was going to walk up the aisle with the film star Eva Bartok to have bothered Scofield, but I was too squeamish to go nosing up even the mild degree of scandal Gomer's missis might have allowed through her cheese-bag. I couldn't bring myself to ask questions I wouldn't have asked in real life – I didn't even have the courage to ask Mitchum if the report was true that he'd been to a fancy-dress party as a hamburger, naked and covered in tomato sauce, with a bun fore and aft. There was a measure of vanity in all this, because I still thought I could beguile the readers in a way that was approximately my own, even though I had to pretend I was using the sort of mug's patois the paper went in for, and remained inextricably entangled in the bone-corset of Gomer's missis's prejudice.

Against the charge that I was a cissy, I can only offer in mitigation the fact that I did once ask Rita Hayworth to jog my memory as to which husband belonged to which child, and was dragged away by a minder; and I had Vivien Leigh sharing a paragraph with Peter Finch, which the lady felt was tantamount to being exhibited as an attraction at a bawdy house: ever after when anyone from the paper tried to solicit a quote from her she wouldn't come to the phone, her fixer announcing Miss Leigh was 'permanently too busy to talk to the *Sunday Graphic*.' (In later years, when I hoped my *Graphic* days had been purged by my association with *The Sunday Times*, I discovered Laurence Olivier was sharing the house next door with Joan Plowright. The great man sported a small Pooterish moustache at the time; it might have been for a play he was in, but when he gave me the time of day in the street I always suspected he felt himself to be in full disguise. And oh, how I lied to the journalists as they tumbled down my area steps to ask me if I could mark their cards and put them on the right track! I had become respectable, and lived in dread that when it all came out I should be blamed as the source. We must have remained on good terms, however, since one day my wife locked herself out and plucky Joan Plowright, the tomboy of the school, sportingly clambered through our front window and let her in.)

So it is the grotesques that stay with me – perhaps because they could always be relied on to collude. The immemorial George Sanders stands amid the linenfold and escutcheon in the great hall of that costume-piece hotel in Egham, and raises his dry martini in solemn greeting. I hear his voice echoing down the years like the mewing of seabirds in one of the Anglo Saxon poems as he utters the haunting cry of the desperate celebrity – 'Shift ho!' The words have as melancholy a power to invoke the landscape of those freeloading days as the ones with which Errol Flynn would rally the party if it seemed to flag – 'Let's put out the lights and get naked!' Such were the capering figures at the centre of the film industry's promotional revels, devised to sell its products to those who paid, via those who didn't.

Did it work? Did the endless press parties and interviews make a ha'porth of difference to the way the product was presented in the papers? Well, it reinforced what was going to be written anyway. The journos who were too proud to be bought liked the idea of someone trying to buy them, and those who could be bought didn't need to be, since their view of the icons they were invited to celebrate was as endorsing as that of the industry which manufactured them. So everyone had a good time. Especially the Osrics, the PR men who got a living presiding over the cakes and ale. These mercenaries of schmooze could hardly be memorable figures, but as anthropological curios they were collectable.

One of them smoked a pipe stuck into a clean-cut jaw and vigorously shot out his hand in greeting, crying keenly, 'How are ye?' An opening gambit which signalled great firmness of character – as of a tea-planter played by Gregory Peck, a surgeon, Lord Peter Wimsey – but when you looked, the air had been let out of him, and suddenly he appeared to be draped over the back of his chair rather than sitting in it; another, superintending a lunch with Charlton Heston announced, 'I'll just have something light,' and ordered ravioli and chips, laughing only after Heston (Chuck) laughed, not knowing why a laugh was toward; while a lady member of the craft, somewhat over the cusp of middle age, would raise a large whisky to her lips after the long day's work was done and say very gravely, 'It isn't the first today, but it's the best,' hinting at unstinting service that would not be fully recognised until after her death.

Advertising tells gaudy lies, but public relations is a muzzier affair altogether and settles for the benefit of the doubt – its practitioners have only very general skills, infusing ambiguities of mood into situations where a little scotch mist might help. They laughed with you, nodding amusedly, seriously, solemnly, watching the door, looking over your shoulder, were never ever found agreeing or disagreeing. But they were not evidently sly or devious, and the only situation in which they might have caused you unease was if you were in the dock, unjustly accused, and you were relying on their testimony. They were easy to be with – not just because they were the fount of hospitality, the point at which it was delivered, but because they aroused in no one the remotest sense of obligation. They were holograms. They were walked through.

My life with the Osrics left me permanently skewed – I still feel a touch of surprise when the waiter presents me with a bill for the oysters, the confit, the Beaune. How freely such fare came to my table at Quags or Ricky Dajou's where one always brought a companion to the feast, and when the waiter at the Café de Paris asked her whether she would take six oysters or twelve, how delicately she twiddled her fingers and charmingly dithered, until even the waiter thought he must be an old retainer as she quizzically opted for *nine*. When I look at the plane tickets and they're not first class, or am offered a single room rather than a double, or collect my tickets at the box-office and am asked for cash, I feel for a moment bewildered. I thought nobody paid.

*

I dropped in on Godfrey Smith for a chat. He was on the top floor, at the Mahogany End – so called because it was the posh bit where the directors did whatever directors do. 'Mahogany' was overstating it, since the doors were from the same job lot that hung throughout the building, but they'd been veneered. Godfrey had a small room across the corridor from Gomer's eldest son, Mr Lionel, and while waiting for a suitable editorial posting, was treading water as Mr Lionel's PA. This meant phoning down and ordering his lunch, and while the other hacks not long out of the University – Ken Pearson, Peter Chambers and me – laughed about it, so did Godfrey, since nothing about our early days in journalism seemed to matter very much.

'Well,' said Godfrey, scanning the menu for Mr Lionel as I lolled across his desk and asked him if he had to taste the stuff in case it was poisoned, 'it's better than being snubbed by Diana Dors because you said you preferred her real name.' True enough – she'd flounced out when I'd said Fluck had a certain ring to it. 'And you in your bowler and the overcoat with the velvet collar, eh?' I dressed like a prat in those days, and it was nice of Godfrey not to mention the cuffs on the sleeves of my jackets, and the revers on the waistcoats: the bowler hat seems to have been a special error, and I remember the man in Scott's of Piccadilly handing it down beneath the counter to his colleague in the basement who steamed the brims, saying 'Set this one up very smart, Mr Phipps.' Then Godfrey said, 'Oh by the way, I've just had my first novel accepted by Gollancz.'

Laugh that off! The one incorrupt achievement, something to be dreamed of, and here was Godfrey and he'd done it. It was to have climbed Everest. I shook the man by the hand, admiration and envy compounded with the certain knowledge that as soon as I got home that night I'd stick the first page into the typewriter and catch him up.

When I say dream, I mean it literally. Some mornings I'd wake up and the book had been a Penguin with an orange cover, sometimes it had been a green one. Once I dreamt I'd written a book and forgotten about it halfway to publication and there it was on a shelf in page proof form, covered in dust. I also dreamt I'd written a *second* book without being able to remember the first. It's true that being employed to interview film stars irked me a bit, like something down my back I couldn't scratch, but I wasn't just trying to improve my street cred; it went deeper than that, or anyway, the book dream had lasted a much longer time. As a child I'd thought writing a book which told a story must be a magic act – any book whose content was invented or imagined was an inexplicable event. Which meant only special people could do it. You might think in constructing such an exclusion zone I was cunningly devising an alibi for not trying it myself. But the truth is less seemly: it had been permanently on my mind for as long as I could remember that I would turn out to be one of these special people myself.

Only without making the effort, so to speak. Actually writing the story that Godfrey's quiet revelation had forced me to begin put me into a continuous ill-humour. Dreaming about it was so much more relaxing than squaring up to the bloody typewriter in the evenings after a hard day knocking out stuff about Julie Andrews and her homely red nose or Cary Grant sending back the Rolls Royce the film company had given him as a present, Cary claiming the car had fifty-eight delivery miles on the clock and so was second-hand. Irritating to be punching the keys voluntarily and after hours, in order to get sixty thousand words on paper which no one had asked me for. I thought I'd write an old-fashioned detective story, because if the motivation of all first novels is the author's sense of his own specialness then it's important to avoid making this conviction the substance of the work – if you set your hand to a genre of fiction that is a humble public utility there's less chance of committing this solecism. A detective story's structure was unambiguous, it had to have a beginning, a middle and an end, and it was a test of competence which either succeeded or failed. And once you'd started, you had to go on. It was like papering a room: once you'd got the first chapter neatly done it was like having hung the first roll of paper, you were committed to going on to the end, or there was nothing to show. Don't think I'm grabbing similes out of the air, because I did once paper a room (my mother could scarcely believe it: 'You'd think it had been done by a practical man,' she said) and this sense of having to keep going round all four walls until you got back to the door was peculiarly annoying in just the same way as getting to the last full stop. I realised then that what I liked about writing was having done it.

Much of the book was written at 23 South Terrace, a handsome mid-Victorian house near South Kensington, a *garçonnière* I shared with three friends: Peter Chambers my fellow hack, Tom Milne a theatre historian, and Colin Jackson a barrister and Labour MP. At this time, Chambers had moved on to the *Evening Standard* as editor of the column 'London Last Night', and employed a variety of legmen. One of these seemed particularly anxious to please – Michael Winner, who reminded me of someone I couldn't quite put my finger on, and it was only years later it suddenly came to me that it was Liberace's aunty. Tom Milne, later a film critic, spent his time with a collaborator compiling an index of all the plays that had ever been produced in London, while Jackson shuttled back and forth between America and Britain, going to America to lecture about Britain, and coming back to Britain to lecture about America – this conserved energy in classic perpetual-motion style, and was a nice little earner.

Our chatelaine was 'Madame Minnie Richard', to quote the card she presented to everyone; I think she may have been the widow of someone French, but then again this may just have been her fancy. She had a round face and a cherry nose and was secretive in manner, though what she was concealing, if indeed she was concealing anything, never appeared. Minnie gave little tea-parties at the Rembrandt hotel just round the corner in Knightsbridge, and her circle consisted of genteel ladies well past middle age who lived in the neighbourhood – perhaps in the sort of tall stuccoed hotels further along the Old Brompton Road to which the novelist Elizabeth Taylor consigned Mrs Palfrey. Minnie would summon us to pow-wows in her quarters on the ground floor to speak of her lease, and with a finger raised to her lips would say we were to claim to be her nephews should anyone enquire. She had an elderly admirer who seemed of retirement age, though when you bumped into him he was always at pains to make it clear that he was active as a Civil Servant. These casual encounters were usually on the stairs where he seemed to be in a state of slight bewilderment as to whether he was going up or coming down; but as you passed him he relaxed, Minnie evidently having rehearsed him in the relevant formula, and he would announce 'I'm just taking a few days off my annual leave to tile the top floor bathroom.'

This was a time when the Edwardian 'look' for men had been revived, and I was fully committed to it as I have already hinted – 'a symphony in blue,' Godfrey had murmured respectfully as he saw me in my latest suit, a rather waisted affair from Hector Powe. Minnie let on to be much impressed by my wardrobe and having fired our daily for being, as she put it, *au dessus de sa gare*, hired a man called Graves to do the housework. 'He has also worked as a valet, Mr Robinson, and will know just how to look after your lovely clothes.' This was said entirely without irony. Graves looked like a horse who had been systematically starved, a tall stooping man with long lank hair. Minnie had marked his card on the subject of me being the dressy one, and he not only ironed my trousers, he pressed creases down the sleeves of my jackets. Only he never got the crease in the same place twice – I could easily have started a new trend as I swaggered down South Terrace, multiply creased all over. Graves seemed vague, and grew vaguer, and one evening, having donned his white jacket to serve drinks at a party, joined animatedly in a discussion of apartheid, hooking his arms round the shoulders of the guests and calling them 'babes and sucklings,' before lying down on the hearthrug and falling asleep.

An occasional visitor was Peter Chambers' mother, a small and very formidable lady who wore a flat black straw hat. She took an instant dislike to Minnie whom she suspected of profiteering, and she was always trying to prise out of her son what he paid in the way of rent. Peter's accomplishments as a journalist, and his fluent French and German were a tribute to this forceful widow, who had 'educated him up', as they say in Scotland, single-handed. But like the shopkeepers who referred to her somewhat fearfully as 'the little old lady in black', Peter was slightly in awe of her, and thought it diplomatic to prevaricate. 'Two pounds fifteen', he would say of the rent, telling her it was a bargain. She looked at him narrowly, and on her next visit would enquire again. In fact together we paid £11 a week, and it was the global figure she wanted. One morning she crept into Peter's bedroom before he was awake, shook him by the shoulder, and said 'What's the rent?' 'Eleven pounds,' mumbled her son. 'I knew it,' his mother cried triumphantly. 'The old rat!'

One evening we were in the Harrington Arms in Gloucester Road, one of the few pubs in 1950s London to feature a snooker room. Peter had just chalked his cue and Monty the Liverpool barman who looked like Arthur Askey brought in fresh drinks for Peter, David Atfield, Philip Purser and myself – Guinness and bitter, a nourishing mixture that I felt was the equivalent of a pint of meat. As we waited for Chambers to take his stroke he froze, then turned towards us. The expression on his face was of sudden dismay, as though the ball he had been addressing were made of crystal and he had seen something disturbing. In a voice scarcely above a whisper he said, 'I forgot to turn it over!' He laid down his cue and dragged on his jacket. 'There's just a chance –.' And he was gone. We carried on with the game, well knowing what was on his mind – hanging on the wall of the communal sitting-room where his mother did her crochet work when she came to stay was a reproduction of Van Gogh's 'Sunflowers'. But on the reverse was a print from an eighteenth-century edition of *Fanny Hill*, a party scene that was the distilled essence of the work, in that it combined total licence with complete formality: Chambers had had it blown up in the *Evening Standard* photographic department, and the picture was held in reserve to startle country cousins who were so deceived by the studied elegance of the design that for a couple of seconds they didn't realise what they were looking at. We turned from the green baize as Chambers re-entered ten minutes later. He seemed relieved. 'She'd left her distance glasses at home,' he said.

When a member of the household was doing something that didn't look like work but which actually was, he would wear the Viewing Hat: this was a summer-weight canvas trilby which I'd brought back from America as an undergraduate, and it was ritually worn when the book being read or the television programme being watched was for the purpose of review. In between, we played squash and Scrabble, and carried on a protracted feud with Fanny Cradock, the bibulous television cook who lived next door with the geezer in the monocle. She devoted herself to trying to stop Chambers parking his car outside her house: 'You're not living in Peabody Buildings now, young man,' she'd say as she swept inside, a crash rattling down the hall as she tripped over the empty bottles. Chambers' car had once belonged to Mussolini, though it had passed through several hands since. It was the size of an American locomotive, a resemblance enhanced by the enormous cow-catcher on the front – presumably for pushing peasants out of the way. It was an open vehicle, since Musso liked being looked at, and as we drove away with Fanny and Johnny staring out of their front window, each shaking the fist that wasn't holding a glass, we would all stand up and I would raise my bowler.

And we entertained girls, in my case one girl in particular – following her triumphs at Oxford, Josée Richard was now at the Royal Court with John Osborne and Tony Richardson and George Devine, and I followed her around like a lapdog: years after, Helen Gardner (her tutor, who had sat with the ends of her *directoire* knickers gripping her knees, knitting grimly as her favourite pupil read out an essay she'd cobbled together in the early hours, muttering 'Rubbish!' at the end with the unalleviated abruptness of the blade thudding into the block), said to me at our house, 'I thought you were just an attendant lord. Sorry.'

But now with the Viewing Hat pulled well down over my ears, I gave the typewriter a seeing-to. My tale was of murders at Oxford, a Chaucer manuscript newly discovered, of pornography stored in the Bodleian (Caton of the Fortune Press coming in nicely here), and high jinks that included a rout of naked dons scampering out of Parson's Pleasure as they chase the murderer down South Parks Road. Plenty of plot, lots of jokes and some fancy dialogue – glittery as a Christmas tree, really, and I sincerely regret the silly names I gave the characters (though the butler was quite properly called Dimbleby). Some cod Chaucer was needed for the fly-leaf, and having composed it I sent it to Nevill Coghill and asked him to check it for anything truly fatheaded. He sent me back a superior version of his own. But my pastiche was required for purposes of guile; he hadn't spotted it.

The magic that fiction does is unrelated to merit – Barbara Cartland is the equal of James Joyce, because the magic is in the act, not the quality of the act. This act is the transformation of the author and the reader, who become all that belongs to the story: they become all the characters, they become the narrative itself, they are the decor and the scenery, the days and the hours, the rooms and the furniture. The story is not anywhere until it is written. But once it is out, it cannot be denied. I finished mine, then went back to the beginning and wrote it through again. 'Folie de perfection', cried Chambers, but Tom Milne who'd approved the draft said, 'You've left something out – after the murders are done, wouldn't the others be frightened they might be next?' I thanked him and shoved in a bit to this effect, and sent the MS to Graham Watson of the literary agents Curtis Brown. I'd tried out all sorts of titles, but decided on *Landscape with Dead Dons*. Inside a week, Hilary Rubinstein of Gollancz said they'd do it. Then Rinehart in New York (they made me change the names because they said they were too strange for their readers. I wrote back and asked why, since Americans were famous for having funny names, and the lady editor said tartly Quite right, that's why they don't want any more). Then it was bought by Penguin. I was glad, but naïve as ever, I was expecting it; Mummy never says No.

When the book was given the lead review in the *New York Times* – a couple of thousand words, and they were usually too snooty to do detective stories like that – there was a certain amount of chagrin· among the Oxford alumni who were working in the States. Alan Brien in New York for the *Evening Standard* said he was looked at as though he were a plagiarist when he retailed some Oxford anecdote at parties and people said Oh you've been reading that detective story: I'd scattered them all over the text. But plagiarism – that's a strange business. Marghanita Laski reviewed the book and said, 'The plot probably derives from Kipling's *Dayspring Mishandled*.' *What?* The style was certainly left over from the schoolboy crush I'd had on Michael Innes and Edmund Crispin (both of whom decently gave the book a puff on the dust jacket) but the fantasy, the tale, had come out of my head like – well, I was going to say, ectoplasm. But if it was ectoplasm, it would mean it was the spirit of someone else! *Dayspring Mishandled* – something was coming full circle, because there it was, in the volume of Kipling's short stories that Clarice had had expensively re-bound for my dad. I opened it and came to what I'd long ago forgotten – the Chaucer manuscript, the uses to which it was put, the revenge; I'd read the tale as a child, wiped it from memory, but had not dispossessed it. My story was a different story, and I'd turned the theme of revenge round (even there, though, it was an exact inversion of the *Dayspring* theme); but the names of some of the characters were like a planchette board trying to remember the originals – Kipling had Manallace, I had Manchip, he had Castorley and I had Carsonby, and the rest of my names were quite as queer as his, which is saying something. Kipling specialised in arcane names, and they invoke the quiddity of the story itself, but I went in for them as though hoping they might bestow it. Big difference. There was another odd touch. After Nevill Coghill read the story he wrote and said I had a trick of acting-out or miming specialist knowledge about subjects of which I really knew nothing – the game of bowls, or the way libraries were organised – 'just like Kipling convincing you he knew all about ships' boilers.' After forty years, the thing is still in print – Viking in the USA, Werner Soderstrom in Finland (ideal for those long dark nights) and Dumont have just brought it out in Germany. I seem to hear Kipling, as quoted by Angus Wilson in his biography: the great writer, then a schoolboy, is pounding wrathfully along the pavement, having been affronted by a person of no consequence. He is muttering, 'I am a very angry little Ruddy indeed!'

*

While still breezing round to the Dorchester to maintain contact with the real business of journalism via Raquel Welch and Co, I'd been writing a panel of radio criticism for *The Sunday Times*.

One breakfast time I received word from a place far beyond the lead mines of fantasy in which an interviewer of film stars passes his days. For through my letterbox there dropped an envelope from Rapallo. I opened it and at the bottom of the page read the words 'cordially yours, Ezra Pound.' This seemed wholly unlikely. You simply don't associate figures of myth with ordinary channels of communication. Pound fired off letters all the time, but I couldn't imagine them arriving via a real post office – you might just as well expect a telegram from the Ancient Mariner or a change of address card from Ulysses. But there the thing was. I'd been writing about the strange cadences of Pound's voice – the Third Programme had dug out a recording he'd made of the Usura verses from the Cantos – wondering in my radio column whether this wasn't the style they used on Mount Olympus (though keeping to myself the thought that Pound would have picked it up as he scoured the pots for Joyce and Eliot).

'Thanks for friendly utterance in unexpected quarter . . . Heaven

knows we need writers who do NOT like the blackout of history
. . . Wd/ cert/ send you review copies of the Sq $, if any chance
of reviewing american publication in *The Sunday Times* . . .' – each
sentence appearing separately as if it were a verse, with the characteristic abbreviations and upper case emphatics. I wrote back in the
spirit a child writes a note to Father Christmas, not quite believing
it was going to get there. Pound replied. 'Rather exhausted/ Hotel
Italia . . . Dear Robinson . . . Confirming RAGE of N.Y. reviewer
who thought it wd/ WASTE of his work to mention book not
on sale at book stores . . . i.e. reviewing, publishers, advertising
. . . NO provision for communication to intelligent readers/ . . .
indoctrination vs/ education . . . Yrs E. Pound.'

All in the pale blue ink of his ancient typewriter. Which was not
quite Homer's lyre. Pound was free of the Pantheon, though never
a member. He banged the drum for his betters, which might have
embarrassed the more austere, though Eliot showed no signs of it
('*il miglior fabbro*' – can this have been simple politeness?). There are
isolated lines in his work that ring true – 'he fished by obstinate isles'
– but though he said often enough his stuff was out of date when he
began in 1909 there was a touch of the Bohemian Boy about Pound
all through, too much velvet jacket when they'd all stopped doing
that, a faintly bogus whiff of the garret. I feel treacherous saying it,
for in my teens those Provençal songs he 'translated' were a balm
to the cuts and grazes I got from Auden and Joyce and Eliot.

When I was a professional listener to the wireless (which was only
just being spoken of as radio) the world as mediated by it seemed
intriguingly various. Reith's obsession with authenticity had been
a function of his personal manias, but was a gift beyond price to the
rest of us. Listening to the wireless wasn't very high on my list of
ways of passing the time, I shouldn't have turned it on if I hadn't
been paid to; but then I wouldn't have read *Beowulf* if it hadn't been
a set text. And there was one particular series for which I sat in front
of my new Decca radiogram – 'Full Frequency Range Recording'
('ffrr'), its veneers so dark and glossy, the lid closing softly on its
suction pump arm – and felt the same gleeful anticipation that I'd
felt when my grandad would have hurried home from his walk and
we'd be sitting together over our tea, having turned on in good time
for *Toytown*.

A Very Great Man Indeed was a fiction that accumulated round
the figure of an innocent middle-aged literary gent who was trying
to write the biography of a great writer. It was a Third Programme

programme – 'the ever-admirable Third Programme' as Michael Flanders, playing the part of a BBC commentator in the series, described it – and was transmitted in fifty-minute episodes. So intense were its comic flavours, so distinct were its characters, so remarkable was the understanding of the actors for the parts they played, that I became addicted. Henry Reed was the author, whose poem 'Today We Have Naming of Parts' and whose lampoon of the Eliot Quartets, 'Chard Whitlow', are imperishable items in the repertoire of post-war anthologies.

The narratives grew out of Reed's chronic failure to get to grips with a long projected life of Thomas Hardy. The hapless biographer in *A Very Great Man* is called Herbert Reeve, though the people he meets in the course of his researches very often get this wrong and call him Reeves, Treves or even Breve. As in *Toytown* the characters are amiable, grotesque, recognisable, the two principal figures being General Gland, the foot fetishist and bell fancier, who in moments of stress pronounces 'd' as 'b' (e.g. 'Breadful!') and the composeress Hilda Tablet whose 'musique concrete renforcée' is the talk of the avant-garde. The General's portrait, painted in the nude by R. Bunnington Bonningfield ARA hangs in his hall. 'Breadfully realistic, isn't it?' asks the General glumly, as he shows it to Reeve, 'apart from being fourteen feet high, of course.' Hilda's nine-act opera *Emily Butter* is set in a department store and on the first night at Covent Garden the curtain finally comes down in the small hours of the morning.

Reed made these figures, and many others, sound like your own relatives, a gift he shared with S.G. Hulme Beaman, creator of *Toytown*, and with the great Beachcomber, and with Lewis Carroll. Reed was a melancholy recluse, and I would meet him from time to time at the Savile Club where he would listen to my enthusiastic prattle about a work which I still feel is the one wholly original contribution made by radio to the canon of English humorous letters. Reed was pleased enough with this *succès d'estime* and knew how much he owed to the craft of Douglas Cleverdon who was the producer, and to the sensitivity of such actors as Derek Guyler (creator of General Gland, and also of a minor character, Mr Gabriel Hall Pollock, the music critic, whose glottal pronunciation of the word 'beauty' was much prized), Mary O'Farrell (Hilda) and Hugh Burden (Herbert Reeve). But this saturnine figure was never cheerful, and as men left the Club to catch their last train, he would wander off to his bachelor apartment in Montagu Street, expecting

(I always thought) the worst. One night before he left he wrote out a verse for me – a verse he had dreamt:

> Whenever Waterson saw anything of interest or note,
> He sate down at once about it, and to his grandmother wrote:
> 'You should have seen this thing, it is the kind of thing I like.
> I saw it today, from my bike.'

The two Pound letters, and the verse that Henry Reed dreamt, are true relics to me. And like true relics, cannot be reduced or explained.

When the *Graphic* went to Davy Jones with all the others, *The Sunday Times* invited me to be Atticus. This was the fancy pseudonym under which the likes of Sacheverell Sitwell and Ian Fleming had written a gossip column featuring admirals and diplomats and MPs. Though Gomer and his missis had now decamped to a home of rest on the Riviera, the idiom of *The Sunday Times* remained essentially stuffy, though it was at the start of that sectionalising process which is no more than badge-engineering for advertisers; once Roy Thomson started it, it was unstoppable, and now the paper teems with salesman-friendly categories and the journalism is often hard to disentangle from the promotions. When I was Atticus, the paper was just beginning to ogle this scenario, and its emerging tone – deference to a specified trend within an amorphous category more and more loosely described as 'style' – was most clearly heard in the new colour supplement; this was edited by Mark Boxer, in memory of whom someone unkindly suggested an office block be kept empty in perpetuity.

Atticus needed cheering up, and I hoped a touch of the allusive, a spot of irony, might take the curse off its aldermanic bias. Rallying round as members of the team were John Pearson (who later took to biography – the Krays, and Ian Fleming), Bill Foster, and Hunter Davies; I was the editor, and wrote the actual copy. I took my cue from Anthony Sampson who was doing the same sort of column for the *Observer* – as Pendennis, he did a very convincing imitation of the cleverest boy in the school patronising the headmaster. We included figures from the world of art – admittedly from the waxwork end, so that older readers wouldn't feel uneasy. I did Munnings and went down to Suffolk to see him, but as soon as I tentatively suggested there might be something to be said for Picasso he reared up on his chaise-longue and shouted for his wife. 'He's trying to annoy me,' he bellowed as she ran in and mopped his brow. Bill Foster fared little better with Henry Moore. When he came back he said, 'He is a knight, isn't he?' We looked him up. OM, but otherwise Mr. 'Dear, dear,' said Bill, 'I called him Sir Henry throughout.' I said, 'He probably thought you were one of those saloon bar wags who call everyone Sir Henry.'

I borrowed Mayhew as a pseudonym and we interviewed traffic wardens and removal men and even a lady Channel swimmer: 'I just take my passport and a cuddly elephant for luck. I worry awfully about the fish, jellyfish and cuttlefish, the ones they give budgies to sharpen their teeth on. Eating while you're swimming's very hard, I had chicken this time, but it gets salty, I mean too salty. Soup's all right, out of a carton, but you're going up and down all the time.' Mayhew exhibited the inherent tendency of the genre, which is to make everyone sound perky and colourful. 'No, no, no, cab drivers are not bad-tempered, but you don't expect to drive round in all that traffic grinning like Cheshire cheeses, do you? Stupidity and ignorance, no, no, I don't care where I go, I have no preferences, but I don't like Lillie Road, Fulham, I don't like going there, it seems so drab, a funny area.' No journalist of the writing sort can bear to put down what someone says exactly as they say it, he likes to sharpen it up by leaving out the uncharacterful bits; he ends up playing the part. But it was a change from just maundering on about who was going to be the next Governor of the Leeward Islands.

And I preferred Harold Shlupp to David Eccles. There was a circular plaque on the wall of No. 6 Southwick Street, Paddington, which read 'Harold Shlupp, Fat Render and Cyclist, Lived Here.' Knocking on the door I discovered a bicycle standing in the hall which one of the tenants explained was a great inconvenience. 'Beyond the bicycle,' I wrote in the column, 'little is known.' Next week brought further information. A lady describing herself as Harold's aunt pointed out that 'Fat Render' was an error for 'Fat Bounder', his nickname in the family. Another reader recalled Shlupp's ride on a Bagwell Challenger – an early form of unicycle – from the Archway (horse trough) to Islington (slipper baths) in 1929. His daughter Mabel who described her father as 'the common man's Montgolfier' said that he preferred to be known as a 'wheelsmith', though the idea of Shlupp ever being in any real sense a cyclist was scouted by another reader who pointed out that as a child Shlupp used to run errands for Henry James.

'He was undoubtedly fat, James once referring to him as "beauti-fully gross". During the day he worked as a render, that is, one who tears up old clothes for shoddy: in the evenings he would exhibit himself as "the Fattest Man in the World" at long-vanished music halls; he once appeared on the same bill as the great Lottie Collins. This was a comforting memory during the forgotten years in the little Paddington room, adorned with faded affiches and theatrical graffiti. I do not know why he is referred to as a cyclist. This his size alone would have precluded. He was an excellent *typist*, though it is hard to see how such confusion could have arisen: the bicycle in the passage is an irrelevance. That triste plaque is now his only remembrancer, preserving the name he adopted for his music-hall appearances. He was, in fact, a cross-dresser, properly called Henrietta Shlupp, and a close friend of my grandmother.'

But mostly it was Eccles and his kind. He was Minister of Education at the time and schoolteachers were wanting more money than he thought they should get. He gave me a glass of whisky and asked me to tell him frankly would I pay my cook more than the going rate. We were a little more direct in our descriptions than Atticus had been in the past, and in his Henry Moore piece Bill Foster had said the sculptor 'physically resembles garden gnomes you see round West Ewell'. I described Eccles's face as 'meaty', though actually it looked like a whole carcase. Going through the proofs for that week, Harry Hodson the editor said Eccles had telephoned 'just to check your chap had got the politics right,' so it was plain he'd decided I hadn't got a cook. When he got to 'meaty' the editor put a line through the word. 'Can't say it – they're friends of mine.' (When Gomer offered him the editorship of *The Sunday Times*, Hodson hadn't replied for some days: he'd been a Fellow of All Souls and wondered if journalism was really his thing. But he delayed long enough for Gomer's missis to exclaim at one of her *soirées* 'Fancy my Gomer being insulted by this *intellectual*'; yet in tribal matters, their notions of disrespect didn't seem to be all that different.) Public persons were quite often extraordinarily complacent in the presence of journalists in those days, and I remember telephoning Hewlett Johnson, Dean of Canterbury, an old noodle whose Stalinist sympathies had earned him the nickname 'the Red Dean', asking if he would be interviewed. 'All the relevant data is in '*Who Is Who*', he mooed loftily, his refusal of the apostrophe 's' delighting me as much as the father of a childhood friend once did when he spoke of 'Walter Disney'. But Eccles was in a class of his own. 'Think of a really good way of spending a couple of hours,' Eccles said. 'The opera. Making a bit of money on the Stock Exchange. A trip on a gondola in Venice. There's nothing to beat the Cabinet.' As an example of the irredeemably naff, it is of museum quality.

Being interviewed was a feature of the lives of certain sorts of people, who never questioned the arrangement. For politicians, indeed for film stars who were promoting films, the thing served an obvious utilitarian purpose, but I doubted if the interview as an institution would have become as much part of the landscape as cathedrals if it hadn't been rooted in something much more atavistic. For in the interview you were bestowing the most desirable gift of all: attention. Attention, moreover, that your man could *prove* to himself he had received, for when he opened his paper the following morning he would find his words in print. The accuracy of the record would be neither here nor there compared to the fact he had been attended to, concentrated upon, taken into account, and thus he could feel he undeniably existed. Only once did I find the principle queried – I telephoned George Sanders at the Connaught, knowing the old fraud would turn out like the trouper he was. But I got his wife. I asked if her husband would make a date to be interviewed. She said 'Why should he?' This was unique.

As the people I interviewed were spilling enough of the beans to keep my attention, while not spilling too many, I realised they were responding in the liturgical sense. Here was a ritual. Naïve and self-assertive, I tried to startle them with questions that would let them know what a smart cookie I was – but a catechist who tries to score makes his quarry even warier. More cunning hands sat with their mouths innocently agape while their man grew boastful, and when he opened the paper he found he'd hanged himself; I didn't have their confidence. Watching television at South Terrace one evening when there was a newspaper strike on and we were all at a loose end, I mused on the way the chaps who did the interviewing on the screen had all the best of it: where I had to work twice, that is, do the interview, then go away and make something of it, they turned up just once and it was finished. Moreover, they shared the attention given to the people they interviewed, and this did not seem to be displeasing to them: I noticed many found it hard to suppress a smirk. They had an easy cheerful air, which you often find among those who are paid a lot of money for doing not much. Feeling a touch morose at the thought, I heard the telephone ring. It was a friend from Oxford days, a delightful girl called Catherine Dove, later Catherine Freeman. Would you like to turn up tomorrow evening and tell everyone what you'd have been writing in the paper? Turn up? Yes, Lime Grove, a television programme, round about six – they were running a series on the back of the strike, where journalists would do the talking. But, I said, I wouldn't really be writing anything that *mattered* – I didn't do that sort of journalism. That's not the point, she said, I'm trying to find hacks who can speak clearly – most of them seem to have terrible catarrh. OK, I said, yes, OK – right, I'll be there. And I was.

THE OBLONG HALO OR SCENES
FROM TELEVISION LIFE

I TOOK A cab and hastened to my lawyer with the *Daily Express* tucked under my arm, knocking at the door of Pennington's in Lincoln's Inn in a lather of fury and self-righteousness. On Saturday evening I'd been chairing an edition of '*BBC3*', the third and final series of the so-called 'satire programmes' that had begun with *That Was The Week That Was*. On my left that evening at Television Centre was the American writer Mary McCarthy, on my right sat Kenneth Tynan, theatre critic and literary manager of the National Theatre. We were having a discussion of censorship. When Tynan said 'I don't think anyone would mind if they heard the word "fuck" spoken in the theatre' there was a tremendous gasp from the audience, as of a mighty wind blowing through the ruins of a temple that had that moment been brought down before their very eyes. This word had never been heard publicly in institutional circumstances before: it had never been used in a newspaper, never uttered on radio or television; it was not simply a convention, it was a taboo that ran very deep, and when Tynan took it upon himself to shatter it people felt the foundations of their privacy shift.

'Oh well,' said the novelist, her shark-like smile flashing on and off as the credits rolled, 'I suppose it's a historic moment.' 'Then history's made very easily,' I said rather spinsterishly. I was right in one sense, for Tynan, a clever journalist but rather a weed, grabbed at notoriety like a child, and a child could have done it, just as easily. But if I implied the event had no historic status, I was wrong, for it *was* a taboo, and a universal one, and if you defy such a magic prohibition you release the power it conceals which is then free to take on other shapes; one of these turned out to be an even more irritating ju-ju, in which 'fuck' was now to be used as often as possible as an emblem of sincerity. If a historic event is something after which nothing is ever the same, then this one counts – however callowly contrived.

But what I was thinking at the time was 'It's too late for the hacks'. Part of the programme's remit was that it could go on and on, and it was past midnight. I thought the first editions will have gone away and everyone in Fleet Street will be drunk or asleep. I was forgetting it was a show whose 'smartness' spoke direct to the heart of suburbia, the journalist's heimat; those of them who'd gone home would have turned on, and many a bottle of Merrydown would have been knocked over as they dashed for the telephone. It was in the later editions on Sunday, of course, but by Monday the papers were afloat on waves of indignation which were now at high tide.

The *Express* had a headline which read THE BLOODIEST OUTRAGE OF ALL. Their use of an adjective that had itself been impermissible at one time was, in the circumstances, a residual irony, but the paper was obliged to refer to Tynan's word and thus make it clear they knew it existed: in admitting it existed, they were admitting we all knew it existed; thus they reinforced Tynan's fracturing of the taboo, since the operation of a taboo proscribes any reference to what the taboo forbids. I have a feeling this double-bind beefed up the fury of the newspapers and their readers; Tynan had given them no option but to take part, at one remove, in his act of impiety.

The piece had been written by William Barkley who supplied political notes for the *Express* and was also wheeled out to sound a trumpet whenever this seemed necessary. His article had much in common with the vengeful graffiti seen on billboards outside non-conforming chapels: Tynan had uttered the dread word, he said, while Robinson's face had worn 'a lecherous leer'. Reading this on the Monday morning I drove over to Shepherd's Bush to look at the tape: just as I thought, while Tynan was doing his stuff I was sitting there with a face as long as a fiddle: I wasn't too happy about my decision to join the satirical brotherhood, whose idiom I took to be closer to the Hackney Empire than Jonathan Swift, and I think this sometimes showed. If I was doing lecherous leering, I certainly hadn't got the hang of it.

So I was shown into the office of Phil Mabey, an old libel hand at Pennington's, and put my case to him. It didn't take him long to agree that there was a clear ground for action. 'And you'd almost certainly win,' he said. The only thing was, it would take at least two years to come to trial, and the publicity would keep the offending phrase alive. 'Then you'd be standing up in court as the plaintiff who had been unfairly described as The Man with the Lecherous Leer. The jury would award you damages. You'd have won.' Mr Mabey fell silent for a few moments, pondering what this scenario portended. He stared at the desk top. Then he raised his head and looked at me. 'And for the rest of your life, that's what you'd be billed as. The Man with the Lecherous Leer.' Silently, I shook his hand, paid him his guineas, and left. I've never received better advice.

There was a small incidental consolation. It was said that the boneheaded Barkley's daughter had been sitting up with her mother and father as a special treat to watch the show, but after the sacred word had been uttered, Mrs Barkley had turned round and pointing to the door had said to her daughter 'Bed!' This affecting scene, in which the little girl's innocence is seen to have been wickedly abused, would have been marred, said Fleet Street wags, had anyone known that the daughter was twenty-eight.

And there was a further bonus. A week later as I was staring moodily into the window of an antique shop in the King's Road and thinking how things were going from bad to worse, I saw reflected in the glass what looked like a large grisly bear. It said, 'Are you Mr Robinson?' Turning round I saw an elderly lady with a red face and wearing a ginger fur coat. She said she was the wife of the Chairman of the BBC governors, Lord Normanbrook, and that he was not at all well. 'But they've sent him a new wireless with a much bigger picture, and it's cheered him up.' I'd sometimes wondered if Lord Normanbrook who had been Norman Brook thought of himself as Norman Normanbrook, and if this preyed on his mind. Then the lady said, 'You know that word Mr Tynan used?' I said I was afraid I did. 'Well,' she said, 'it doesn't form part of *my* vocabulary.' I said I shouldn't have supposed so. 'But,' she said, 'ever since I heard Mr Tynan say it, I use it all the time.'

As to Tynan, having done it once he did it again, in the form of the entertainment he called *Oh, Calcutta!* By this time the new orthodoxy had taken root and the show in which the actors wore no clothes treated the word as obligatory. The scenario was mostly sixty-nine ways of not quite having it, and brought the fuck into disrepute.

*

'It will cause pain, it will cause great pain.' I remembered Maurice Bowra's comment when he heard a friend had been given a knighthood. There was something in the smiles of old chums when they chaffed me after my first appearance on television during the newspaper strike which told me they were really thinking Why him? 'I wouldn't have guessed you had it in you,' said my barber, as though I'd ridden a motorbike through a wall of fire. He didn't mean it that way, what he meant was You have no obvious qualification. The day after my debut I was rather hoping people would stop me in the street and ask me to touch them for the King's Evil, but I seemed as anonymous as ever. I dropped into the Lyons just up from Gamages in Holborn for a cup of coffee and a chap across the table looked at me and said Hope you don't mind me saying so, but you look like a man I saw on television last night. I glowed with pleasure. It was me, I said, or rather to be exact, it was I. You look just like him, he said. Well, yes, I said, I do, because I am. You are what? he asked. Him, I said. It was you? Oh. And he sounded dubious – disappointed even. If it was me, forget it. Without the oblong halo round your head your manifest lack of distinction was all there was. I shambled out rather cast down.

The strike went on, and I did the talking journalist stuff a couple more times. I was very po-faced because I couldn't risk smiling: if I'd tried it, the way my mouth wobbled would have shown everyone how nervous I was. So I sat there like a man who was unable to get the shirt stiffener out of his upper lip. None of us seemed much at ease, and the large moustachioed sports reporter of the *Mirror* ('The Man They Can't Gag') was so agitated by the experience that he hurried off to a boxing match forgetting to wash the make-up off his face, and when he arrived at the venue he got some odd looks. So that seemed to be that, and I was sinking back into the primeval slime of Gray's Inn Road when someone rang to say would I like to come to a sort of audition. They were trying out some of the hacks who'd lent a hand earlier, just to see if there was any further mileage in them.

I turned up at Lime Grove, a flyblown citadel of terraced cottages that had been knocked together round the film block that had belonged to Gaumont British in the early days of the Gainsborough Lady. The studio I entered was bare, towering up into the murk like the great hall of Gormenghast, ropes and cables hanging down in loops like giant cobwebs. There were a couple of chairs and a monitor in a ring of light, and figures hanging about in the gloom round the edges. The emptiness of the place felt threatening. No doubt the buzz of actual programmes made the surroundings vanish, but now the place was insisting on itself; it had a cold decommissioned air that disclaimed any knowledge of the fantasies they cooked up here – nothing to do with me, mate, you're on your own. Then a voice over the talk-back said assertively that we were going to do some try-out interviews, and a camera trucked in from the darkness where one of the figures hovered like a man wrapped in a dark cloak. Captain Ferguson! There hadn't been sight nor sound of him for – well, long enough. It was actually the absurd Woodrow Wyatt, but I knew Captain Ferguson was on the premises somewhere.

'Before we have the interviews we'll get you all to do a piece to camera,' said the talk-back. What! 'Anything you like, just speak extempore.' I walked through the door marked EXIT, made my way down the fire-escape. I couldn't do it. Being called upon to speak extempore was the final horror in Captain Ferguson-type dreams: to reply on behalf of the guests, the chairman turning to me with a smile and without warning; or just as I was named as speaker, remembering I had agreed to do it but had put off preparing anything. Stand up and be shamed or run away and be shamed. In front of everyone. I was halfway down the fire-escape in the night air, in flight. 'In front of everyone': I seemed to want to be in front of everyone quite badly, yet it was a source of terror; to be unmasked. I went back up and told them about the pleasures of shove ha'penny. 'This is too easy for you,' laughed the talk-back, as I came to the end of my monologue.

The interview with the batty Wyatt was like the first time you knew you could ride a bike – you'd be able to do it over and over again and never fall off. Wyatt himself did interviewing on *Panorama*, a true mystery in that the man's voice slowed everything down like glue on a fly-paper. But he'd been roped in on this occasion to let the candidates try themselves out asking him questions. He was a Labour MP so I asked him if it was true the House of Commons was a form of poor relief for the otherwise unemployable – he had the kind of face that brought out a tendency to contradict anything you imagined it might say. When I walked out of the studio I didn't give a hoot about being on television because anyone could do it; but going back up fire-escapes was what you got medals for. Captain Ferguson had left, I'd seen him off.

The talk-back voice belonged to Donald Baverstock who invented *Tonight*. But sitting behind him, smoothing her stays, was Grace Wyndham Goldie who drove everything and everyone before her. An old boiler with pop-eyes, she had the mother of all bad tempers. You might have assumed her sharp ill-natured style to have been part of her headmistressly crusade against the exploitation of the television audience by down-market forces. And it was. She led the partisans in a war against sloppy thinking. But sloppy drinking also played its part. The top echelons of television were afloat on booze, overlords like Cecil McGivern, Kenneth Adam and Grace herself taking to the bottle as though it were the equivalent of holy water, something you blessed yourself with in the struggle against the philistine. It only seemed to matter now and again, as when President Kennedy died and nobody could get hold of Grace or Kenneth Adam to find out if they should play solemn music and pull the plugs, because they were at a pissup at the Savoy. She was a great one for shouting at her staff. This was the booze, sometimes pink wine, which she drank as though the glass had been put into her hand stealthily from behind without her noticing.

But quarrelling was her instinctive response to almost anything, and I remember sitting next to her at a party at Television Centre for a showing of some specially important documentary. The lights went down, Grace fell instantly asleep, glass in hand, the film was shown, the lights went up, Grace woke from a deep slumber and launched into an entirely accurate, very detailed and wholly vituperative analysis of what she hadn't seen. Nine o'clock in the evening seemed to be the hour at which she was transformed from a moderately offensive Nurse Jekyll to the unconstrained virago that was Mrs Hyde. Michael Hill, a fellow Oxonian involved with the *Tonight* programme, described how Grace had been discussing church matters in the hospitality suite at Lime Grove with a bishop. Though somewhat barbed, her line of conversation was no more than waspish, with the ecclesiastic nodding gravely; but then from some distant church tower nine o'clock was heard to strike and Grace got him by the lapels, head-butted him and told him the Church of England was a hotbed of heresy. Next morning she'd forgotten all about it until one of the bolder members of her team pointed out that she had offended an important member of an outfit whose goodwill the BBC often needed. 'Oh dear,' Grace said, 'but he'll be at the conference I'm going to in Edinburgh next week. I'll make it all right with him.' And so she sought out the cleric and sweet-talked him and smoothed him down, for she did a very good line in molasses when it was required. By this time they were toasting each other glass for glass, but unhappily nine o'clock struck again and Grace kneed him in the groin as though she'd heard the bell for round two.

But she was a goer. She was on the audience's side in the sense described by Peter Black who at that time was the idiosyncratic and highly imaginative TV critic of the *Daily Mail*: he said, 'If it's true people can't tell the difference between butter and margarine, then that's the best possible reason for giving them butter.' She thought a sceptical eye was to the viewers' benefit, and she said she'd taken a fancy to me. I found I was being invited to do odd turns on *Panorama* when Richard Dimbleby or Chris Chataway were too busy. They got the important people and I got the flat-earthers: I interviewed the president of the society that wanted to implement Shaw's mad scheme for reforming the alphabet; and Barbara Cartland and James Laver on the fascinating topic of double-breasted suits. 'Pull your ties straight, boys,' commanded the Queen of Romance before we began, 'sit up straight. Don't slump.' (Here was a woman to go into the jungle with: she told the lighting-director on '*BBC3*' that she wanted a single lamp on the floor so it would shine up under her chin and obliterate the detail. He smiled and said the lighting had been fixed. 'On the floor,' she said, 'just *there*. Run along and fetch it.' A lighting man puts up with the fancies of the director but doesn't stand any old buck from the guests. The stand-off went on all afternoon as we rehearsed, but he was dead in the water from the start. It was her sheer implacability. In the end he brought two lamps and invited her to choose. I said to him afterwards, 'There's no shame in it. It's just you were Hemingway and she was Tolstoy.')

When the arts programme *Monitor* was conceived, Catherine Dove took me along to see Grace. They were looking for an anchor man. Grace seemed testy. 'If Mr Robinson wishes to help, I'm sure his advice will be welcome.' I didn't know I was a candidate, I thought I was just there to say Hullo; I wondered why she was so annoyed. But Huw Wheldon had just been inducted, and Grace thought her decision was being questioned. Wheldon was just the man – we became great friends and he once told me, 'I specialise in admiration.' *Monitor* was the first of the arts programmes – it was the best, perhaps because it *was* the first – and what it needed was Yes. I couldn't have mustered much more than Maybe.

But my contributions were invited. With John Schlesinger directing, I wrote a little lampoon called HI FI FO FUM – men in pullovers staring into the windows of Tottenham Court Road in the early days of the electronic revolution. We conducted a similar exercise at the Cannes film festival, and Schlesinger ensured we should both appear, walking down the grand staircase in our dinner-jackets as though we were Hitchcock. (I made a great coup at the casino: Ian Fleming had said the thing was to win or lose the price of a good dinner – a fiver in those days. I lounged in and won the five pounds in short order. Then broke the Fleming rule by staying on, and won another fifty. Updated, this might have been about five hundred – it had a certain bulk when you tucked it in your wallet. The man at the caisse counted out the money but got the sum wrong. Figure to yourself the satisfaction not only of winning at a casino, but also of correcting the arithmetic of the cashier! His minder who was looking over the man's shoulder stared unbelievingly at me. '*Mais – il a raison, il a raison.*' I sauntered out humming, just like Psmith when he bested the headmaster.)

I interviewed Pinter for *Monitor*, something about the film of his play *The Caretaker*. Before we started he was mildness and smiles, pointing out some aspect of the process I hadn't taken into account when I'd been chatting to him about the techniques involved. 'Ask me again in the interview, if you like,' he said. 'Well,' I said, 'not much point, now you've put me right.' Wheldon laughed. 'I don't mind looking a charlie,' he said. 'He does.' When we did the interview, Pinter became someone else, opaque, uncomprehending, apparently puzzled that anyone was sitting there asking him questions, squinnying at me as though I were speaking Chinese. After the programme which was live I rang my wife (for I had at last persuaded the *Isis* idol to dwindle into one) from the place where we were all having drinks and said 'What a shit.' By now Pinter had changed back into his earlier beaming self. 'What did she think?' he asked, as though he were a human being again. I said 'Think', as though pondering the word. 'Think.' 'Of it,' said Pinter. 'Of *it*'. 'Yeah'. I paused, as though troubled by the question. 'Think of it. *Think* of it.' After a bit he said, 'Didn't she say? You know, whether she liked it. 'She's –' I paused again. 'She's –' He nodded, anxious to find out if his back was going to be patted. 'Look,' I said, lowering my voice, 'best thing is, I'll – get back to her.' I slid over to the telephone. Spoke into it, holding Pinter's eye across the room. I put the phone down and moved over to him. I raised my eyebrows as high as they'd go. Put my finger to my lips. Then left.

But my encounter with T.H. White, author of *The Sword in the Stone*, was truly strange. The book had just been bought in the developed version, *The Once and Future King*, to be turned into the musical *Camelot* with Richard Burton and Julie Andrews. My wife had been lying on the matrimonial bed in the Station Hotel, St Tropez (nice to find the homely and the exotic so neatly juxtaposed, especially on your honeymoon) reading a profile of White in *Time*. Why don't you do him for *Monitor*? White had been a hero since I'd read the book as a small boy, and the prospect of meeting him thrilled me. When I got back Wheldon jumped at the idea, and I flew over to Alderney with Peter Newington as producer, and Humphrey Burton as Best Boy.

White had a bright red face and big white beard, and looked like an actor playing an old salt. It quickly emerged he suffered from chronic and fulminating paranoia. This took both particular and general forms. He'd built a temple to Hadrian in his back garden where he could keep a sharp eye on the universe – 'If I take my eye off it for a second, it's going to collapse.' The Labour government was anathema to him because now that he was going to make a bit of money after a lifetime of penury they would take it all away in tax. He referred to Aneurin Bevan as Urinal Bevan. This wasn't bad, until you'd heard it for the sixth time. As for the working classes, they couldn't write their own names in shit on a lavatory wall. I said I thought they could. That night Newington took a call from White and passed on what he'd said: 'I don't think I'm going to get on with that chap of yours.'

All the time we were with him he was talking about wanting to run away with John Arlott's wife. Apparently she was coming over to the island with one of her sons and he said he'd been in love with her for a long time. As for Arlott, who'd once worked as a copper, 'He was only a bloody policeman.' When we dined in a local pub I looked forward to a bit of literary chat, bandying quotations with White in the way he does in his books. But he was silent throughout the meal, an angry silence. He wasn't drinking, and we were, and that was the trouble – though if he had been drinking we might have had a different sort of trouble, since when he drank he said he only did it to get drunk.

The paranoia then took an odd form. We were sitting out on the rocks with the camera and getting ready to film, and the others were busy scouting out a second location somewhere else on the headland, and White said confidentially, 'I really like little girls.' What the correct response might have been I don't know, but I went on staring out over the cliffs at the sea. 'I wouldn't do anything nasty to them,' said White. 'Just stroke them a bit.' Why was he telling me this? As a matter of fact, I'd noticed three or four paperbacks from the Traveller's Library on his book shelves, their green covers unmistakeable to anyone who'd leafed through them in the porn shops of Pigalle; I hadn't taken in the titles – of course, *Lolita* had first come out under Girodias's imprint.

We did the interview and I trod on his prejudices a bit, just to get him going. A man reviewing the programme in the *Listener* said I was someone he'd never heard of but that it was clear that in talking to White I didn't know I was in the presence of my betters. By one of those emotional inversions that are inexplicable, I was now White's best friend and he wrote to me saying 'I thought you interviewed me *beautifully* and I would 1,000,000 times rather be stood up to and treated as a human being instead of being smarmed to like some frail old "genius".' And then he sent me a copy of his poems which he'd had printed privately, and he inscribed the fly-leaf with a heart and an arrow going through it and 'TW loves RR'.

But what about the little girls? That was a mystery, and remained so until Sylvia Townsend Warner's biography of White was published after his death. Then it became clear that, in true paranoid style, he had gone to the trouble of laying down two false scents to distract me: the first one was that he was in love with Arlott's wife, and the second, which was the 'confession' about the little girls, was linked to this. For White was actually in love with Arlott's son, and far from caring for little girls, he was a pederast.

The BBC wanted to re-launch a series called *Picture Parade*, a mix of clips and interviews that was supposed to give you an idea of the quality of the films on current release. But its sugar content had been high and there was little to distinguish it from advertising that came as a free gift. The BBC was fearful of the film industry, and in its programme output tended to behave as though the product was a rare species it was their duty to protect. But *Picture Parade* had become so much like a sales pitch they were a bit ashamed of themselves and told me they wanted a little perspective – not too much, I was warned, because the show was to be informative not critical. By way of seeing whether I had the popular touch they tried me out on a closed-circuit, interviewing a superannuated stunt man, and when I asked him if he'd graduated from tripping over kerbs to falling off high buildings, they hesitated as though they'd caught a whiff of something subversive. But they couldn't put their finger on it, and I got the job.

After I did the first one, that old trump Gilbert Harding, the TV icon of his day, went to the trouble of getting through to the studio on the telephone and telling me to resist any pressure to jazz up the way I did it, and to stick to my straight face. Well, there was no chance of doing otherwise because no other option was available to me, but the disabling part of the nerves I'd had when I started seemed to have gone and I could have smiled if there'd been anything to smile about; later on I was able to smile when there was nothing to smile about, but that just takes practice.

Gilbert was a very kind man. He had no reason to bother about me. In the days when I wrote about television in the *Sunday Chronicle* I'd give him a ring and ask him what the *on dit* was and he'd say, Oh I can't talk on the phone, come round. So I'd drop in on him at his flat in Cadogan Gardens where there'd often be other stray callers, and we'd all have a glass of champagne while Gilbert gossiped. He liked young men, and I had all my hair, not to mention the suits with cuffs at every corner (once in El Vino's in Fleet Street I went over to talk to him and he said to his cronies, 'Isn't his suit nice – and it's not even his best.'). But he knew my interests and his didn't coincide in this area; once I was at his flat on my own and he materialised in the sitting-room half dressed in baggy underpants and started talking about the masters at school who'd enjoyed beating him. I laughed coarsely and said 'You old fraud, you're talking like a scoutmaster who's trying to seduce a sixer,' and he smiled sheepishly and went back into his bedroom to finish dressing – this was a moment of low comedy, but Gilbert's friendship was entirely disinterested, and his telephone call that first evening came from a man who was a roaring success on television and managed to treat it as the accident it always is.

His moods swung wildly, from the tearful to the irascible. Once at the Savile Club – of which I was now a member – he arrived late in the evening with a diminutive companion, and a large offensive American started talking of 'catamites'. All parties were full of drink and Gilbert closed with his tormentor in a wrestling hold and both fat men fell in slow motion to the floor, with another smaller Savile member who had felt it his duty to interpose his body pinned beneath them. Alarmed by the blood flowing from the arm of the small Savilian who was trapped under the waistcoats of the two champions, and who had cut himself on a brandy glass, Gilbert's friend fled out into the street whinnying with terror, bent upon finding a phone box and calling the police. This he did, reporting agitatedly that there was a fight at the Savage Club, his Freudian slip being altogether understandable. The police raced round in two plain blue vans to the Savage, and found the members homely but unwarlike. Meanwhile, Gilbert's friend had tried to re-enter

the Savile, but found he had locked himself out. *Exeunt omnes.*
Later Gilbert insists his opponent accompany him to a restaurant
in Knightsbridge where he assures him the best salad in the world
is to be had. The salad arrives, but his erstwhile opponent's share
contains half a caterpillar. Gilbert roars at the waiter, 'You insult
my guest by offering him only half a caterpillar!' and both sweep
out. In the cab, they pass the Brompton Grill and Gilbert presses
twenty quid into the other man's hand, bursts into tears and says
'That is where you will get the best dinner in London. I must return
and apologise to the waiter.'

With this fortnightly series, I was appearing on television regularly,
and back at *The Sunday Times* they thought their boy was doing great,
so why not cash in on the publicity? He should write a signed column.
I was hauled off Atticus, which I regretted, since I rather liked the
anonymity of the alias, well aware the chums of Fleet Street knew
who lurked behind it; and I found the directness of the attention
now being turned my way obscurely disturbing. Top bananas in the
office who'd never given me the time of day now hailed me when we
passed in the corridor, people had time to stop for a chat, and I found
myself doing a lot of smiling in the company of strangers. There were
now two of me: the original, and the one on the telly. Everyone liked
the new version, that was quite clear, because they seemed to want
to know him – or rather, they behaved as if they *did* know him, when
they saw him in the street or in the pub; and this meant they took him
to be the same man on and off. Yes, he was; but the television job only
called for him to show certain aspects of himself – all perfectly genuine,
because he had no actorly skills beyond the one which allowed him to
stand up in front of the camera as though that's where he belonged;
and naturally, while he was doing it, he did it the way anyone would
have done it, namely, he gave the best account of himself, not the
worst. But they took the part for the whole.

Meanwhile, the family of the original, together with his friends,
had the same ambiguous feelings about him as ever – he wasn't
clearly a nice man or a nasty one, he was only the man he seemed to
be, which were much the same feelings as he had about them; there's
no summing anyone up. But when the rest of the world treated him
as though in real life he was the duplicate of the image on the screen,
he found himself playing to this, as though it were so; and while
he was thus engaged, the outline of a third version of himself was
apparent, as though each of the first two had been riven more or
less down the middle, and a section of each – never quite half and

half, because the proportions varied – had been stitched together to make the third. For how was he to keep the real man and the image wholly separate? Especially as the combined version came in for lots of what everyone finds irresistible: attention. But as I say, this was also a source of unease.

You had to be visible on the screen before you could perform the functions for which appearing was the pre-condition; this blinding glimpse of the obvious is of interest because the act of 'appearing' seemed to have a power of its own, quite distinct from anything it mediated. It was as though in being the centre of attention you were transformed into all the people who were looking at you; I think this was why when strangers buttonholed me they talked about themselves, as though I accelerated their sense of their own identity; it was pleasing to have your response sought, but it also felt as though you were losing something. I think some people on television lose all of themselves, they become a blank space inside which the audience inscribes its own features; these are the hugely successful ones, for there is nothing of them left over to get in the way – they are everyone and no one, which is a new fate for Narcissus. The rest are subtracted from – some more, some less – and the way this happens is that you are encouraged to see audiences everywhere, and it becomes a way of looking that is a kind of squint, and you can't help feeling it's distorting something that you probably shouldn't have allowed it to. On the other hand, you might always have been like that. Hard to say.

When I did *Picture Parade* I wasn't allowed an autocue, which is the device which unrolls your script invisibly across the lens so that you can read it without looking as though you are reading it – you just have to be careful to take the line in at a glance because if you swivel your eyes it gives the game away and makes you look very shifty. Basically, I think the producer wanted to save the twenty quid it would have cost, but he said it was because he wanted me to be really involved in what I was saying and not just winging it. So I wrote out my introductions to the film clips and memorised them. Since we did it live, this was quite brave, and once I forgot what I wanted to say. So I staged an impromptu performance within a performance and said 'Dammit, there was something good I wanted to say about this film, and I've forgotten what it is. Hold on a minute while I get my notes,' and I got up and walked out of shot and picked up my script which as a matter of honour I always placed out of reach, came back and sat down and said, 'Here it is, it's such an unusual film I didn't want to muff it,' and then having remembered the words, didn't have to consult the sheet of paper, so afterwards people said 'Did you really forget or was it a put-up job just to show how cool you are?' No, but I quite enjoyed doing it. And it would have been a pity to have mumbled just anything, since the film was *Last Year in Marienbad*.

I was only supposed to describe the plots, but there's more than one way of doing this. The BBC was still unworldly enough to believe the Wardour Street flacks who implied they were donating the film clips as an act of charity, when it was obvious that getting the product in front of millions for free was marvellous publicity. Not quite as marvellous as it had been, though. They knew something was going on, and took me out to disciplinary lunches to try and get me to admit what it was. But since all I did was tell the plots, they couldn't get the goods on me; you'd have clips where Frank Sinatra was thrown from the top of the Eiffel Tower and walked away dusting his trousers, and I'd say, 'With one bound, Jack was free,' and though it made them uncomfortable, they weren't sure why.

Round about this time, Captain Ferguson paid me a visit. Sitting in the studio waiting for a clip to finish before I started a live interview, I had an all but overmastering impulse to get up and walk out – a blind and meaningless panic. When I reveal that the interview was with a chimpanzee, the impulse might seem perfectly rational. But I remember clearly when it had last happened: I was a little boy having tea with a friend, and suddenly I had to get up and run home. The monkey was fine, and ran about and wouldn't do what it was told and jolted me out of the claustrophobic fit. But the Captain was reminding me of his power. Claustrophobia – why should it have reappeared? And now it got to me in lifts and tube-trains and I stopped using them. How strange, an overwhelming urge to leave a situation which you can't leave – a train stopped between stations, a lift marooned between floors, a live broadcast. You are in no danger, so where does the panic come from?

Theory: I caught sight of myself in the mirror in the hall of my house one Christmas Eve, and what was revealed to me was my own separateness; I was ten, and the revelation overwhelmed me. I saw I was on my own and it was a profound shock. When the lift door jams, the separateness is undeniable; you hammer to be let out. Of course, you can't be let out, because you're on your own for ever, but some of us can't bear to be confronted with the fact. We like to be out in the open among all the ambiguities which allow us not to think about it; outside the lift we can dissemble our deepest fear:

that we have been abandoned. Mother again, I'm afraid – isn't she the garden from which we are all thrust out? Isn't being born the original separation? I think the claustrophobia reappeared because I now had something else to lose or be lost by, something that echoed the primal condition: a wife, a family. And an identity I could destroy by simply getting up and walking away – I wasn't going to do it, but the fear was the same as it was when my mother told me what suicide was: there was no one to stop me. All of which is my theory, and it's never been the slightest consolation.

And aeroplanes came into it, too – you were trapped between sky and middle-earth. On the three-and-a-half hour flight to Athens for a feature on the making of *The Guns of Navarone* I was co-pilot: I see the logo of Olympic airlines on the bulkhead as I write, for it was only by staring at it all the time that I kept the thing in the air, though this wouldn't have been any good if I hadn't forced the engines to keep turning by revolving with the propellors: when the engine note changed I dropped my legs through the floor of the plane to skip across the atlas below, stretching my hands above my head to bear the machinery through the clouds in its travail. But I didn't mind the little aeroplane which took me from Athens to the island of Rhodes where the film was being made – the closer to a toy the thing was, the more secure I felt.

I was there to interview the nobs: Carl Foreman the director, and a bunch of thesps who included David Niven, Gregory Peck, Anthony Quayle, Stanley Baker and Irene Papas. Quayle wasn't on call that day, so I buttonholed him and started my research. He instantly launched into a diatribe about everything and everyone connected with the enterprise – the food, the flies, the dust, the bathwater, the director, his fellow actors, and roundly condemned his agent for getting him into the thing in the first place. This sounded promising: actors were seldom outspoken when it came to criticising anything connected with their bread and butter – this man Quayle was about to break the mould.

Basil our Greek cameraman set up the Arriflex for the interview and I opened the bowling. Quayle's face assumed the expression I always associated with him when he was doing his acting – a sort of moist, soulful look as of a headmaster in holy orders who'd been let down by his prefects. Aha, I thought, it's going to be more in sorrow than anger. Quayle began with a few feeling remarks about the glory that was Greece and then launched into what sounded like the keynote speech in a campaign to have Carl Foreman canonised

– surely this great artist would top any fair-minded person's list of lay saints. But then such sweetness of temperament appeared to be contagious on this wonderful island of Rhodes, for he had found that the brilliance of his fellow actors was only matched by their abiding unselfishness. Quayle then spoke of a script which would not have disgraced Homer, descanted upon the care with which the production manager had ensured the comfort of all – no expense had been spared. Then, ablaze with sincerity, he summed it up. 'All in all, I think I can truthfully say this has been the most wonderful experience of my life.' I dashed a tear from my eye. 'Thank you,' I said.

Peck was shy about interviews and wanted to keep his mind on the acting, and politely asked if he could be excused. Foreman was wry and sensible about the sheer effort of getting such an unwieldy film made. And Stanley Baker was a cheerful uncomplicated narcissistic actor. Who should I try next? Be careful of Niven, said Schlesinger, who was making his debut in the world of the feature film as director of the second unit. I asked why. Well, he said, don't rub him up the wrong way – he's touchy. Spare him your well-known irony. Thanks, I said huffily, and went off to catch Niven in a spare moment away from the camera. He was hanging around in costume and seemed like a man with a headache coming on.

'Well, what sort of questions do you want to ask?' he said sharply, tilting his ear towards me and staring at the ground as people do when they want to indicate they're expecting something crass. Producing questions for approval wasn't anything I'd been asked to do before. I said it might be interesting to consider the business of acting in this curious natural location, what its advantages and disadvantages might be, when compared with doing the same thing in an artificial setting, the studio. 'Frankly, old boy,' he said, 'I think that's a dull question.'

I paused for a moment. 'No,' I said, 'it isn't. It's just that it's had a lot of dull answers.' He started walking back and forth, flailing the end of his Sam Browne belt, and asked me who else I was interviewing. So I named them all. 'I don't do group interviews,' he said. I explained they would each be single interviews. 'After all,' I pointed out, 'three thousand miles is a long way to come if – well, if you're going to miss the chance of doing the others as well.'

'Now listen, old boy,' he said, 'in this business the only raw material you have is yourself. Put it this way, I don't do interviews with anyone appearing below the title.' I said something like Um.

'Stanley Baker's an awfully nice chap, but I tell you frankly *I've never heard of him.*' This rather stumped me. 'Well,' I said, 'I don't suppose he plays as important a part as you do –' 'That's it!' cried Niven, 'no, no. All off.' And holding up his hand, he stalked away.

On the night the programme went out I thought I'd better explain Niven's absence. 'I'm afraid we fell out,' I said, and after the credits had rolled the continuity announcer said 'I wonder what it was about.' It was about the illusion of the interview. If Niven had been interviewed he'd have been the soul of good humour – the chap on the screen isn't the chap not on the screen. Niven with a sore head would have been the real thing – but why should anyone own up? If Basil had secretly been filming our little run-in, it wouldn't have been transmitted; illusion is too valuable and too perishable a commodity to be outed. We were left with Quayle, and we always are.

*

I sat in the front office of Warner Bros in LA while the head of publicity finished a phone-call. He'd been fixing interviews for us with Harold Lloyd and Edward G. Robinson. It was a hot day and the air was full of iron filings. The PA came in with a Coke and handed it to me. 'That hit the spot?' she said. Her boss was nodding as he discussed over the phone the degree of warmth that should be accorded a visitor not quite of the first rank. 'Show him every conversational kindness,' he finally decided, and as judgements of Solomon go it ranks with the finest.

'Now,' he said, putting down the phone, 'you want to interview Cary Grant. Well, gee, I don't know, but we can try. I have his number in my personal book.' Bravely he picked up the phone, and I thought he flinched a little at the impudence entailed in dialling an immortal. He flushed scarlet as Cary himself answered. No, no interview, but hey, nice to hear from us. Our man couldn't believe this was happening. 'Gee, I wish you'd come back to Warners, Cary,' he blurted moistly, like a little boy in an old movie trying to make Wallace Beery give up drink. He put the phone down and he was breathing fast, and smiling. 'Cary picked up the receiver himself. Hot damn!'

At this point, we were a little late for lunch with Harry Cohn, head of Columbia Pictures. We dived into our giant convertible, and it was my turn to drive. My companion was Christopher Doll, producer of *Picture Parade* and brother of the distinguished scientist, Richard Doll. Christopher's style was motherly, and knowing my fear of flying (he himself had won the DFC in the war) he kept up a stream of quickfire prattle to distract me from my anxieties as we took off from Heathrow. He kept it up *presto fortissimo* until he sounded as if he was reciting the patter song from *Don Pasquale* and fellow passengers were turning round. He certainly succeeded in distracting me because I'd ungratefully begun to worry that people might think I was travelling with a madman. But it was the goodness of the man's heart, and if his concern made him a mite fussy, it was the defect of his virtues. We motored on through Wilshire Boulevard at about twelve miles an hour, falling into the sluggish style of the traffic around us, and Christopher was advising me to slow up, speed up, turn more slowly, turn more quickly, ah-ah-ah, no, faster, brake here, turn left, no *left*, until I pulled into the kerb, stepped out of the vehicle and said, 'Why the fuck don't you fucking shut up and drive the fucking car your fucking self?' You only speak to your friends in these terms, and I know he will not deny that the words set the seal on a friendship that has lasted to this hour.

Cohn, a greatly feared ignoramus, sat at the head of the table reserved for the brass at the commissary at Columbia. You picked your food up from the cafeteria and took it to the table. Cohn spoke no word from the beginning to the end of the meal, and only stared when Doll and I were introduced to him. It became clear that the others present, some eight or nine, reacted for him; Cohn's facial expression never changed, he looked like a tortoise. As we sat down, one of the courtiers, a very short man, rose to his feet, twirled like a dervish, and began to berate Doll and me for arriving three minutes late; Cohn stared at him as blankly as he had stared at us. Either the man was drunk before he arrived as a precaution against the iced water which was the only tipple served, or was acting out some comedy routine for which he was noted. Assuming the latter, while not entirely abandoning the possibility of the former, I laughed appreciatively. Not used to the unedited response, the man stopped revolving and collapsed back into his seat, then after a momentary pause shook me warmly by the hand, as though on impulse he'd decided to take out insurance against the chance he'd made a mistake about my rank.

As the meal which seemed to be an endless salad wore on I began to think Cohn must have died and the figure propped up at the top of the table was a mummy. When we all got up from the table

Cohn's toadies stood huddled so closely round him it looked as though they'd lifted him vertically off the ground and were carrying him back to his pyramid. When Cohn actually did die, all Hollywood turned out for the funeral. 'Give the people what they want, you'll always have a full house,' said someone at the graveside.

By arrangement with Columbia and Fox and Warners, we were assigned a cameraman, an aged party called Vern. He was a pensioner of one of the studios, kept on, as superannuated gamekeepers sometimes are, to help out with the visitors. We entertained this veteran of the celluloid toy-fair at an eatery called Blum's. I have said before that the national dish of America is menus, and Blum's menu was in a class of its own: it read like an opera libretto translated into English by a Rumanian – the famous aria celebrating Blum's Blumderful Patisserie went as follows –

> 'A joy for the palate, a treat for the eye
> Beautiful, luscious yet light as a sigh.
> To eat this cake and have it too,
> Is the delightful dilemma of millions like you.'

Then you get Richard Tauber to come on in his monocle and give us –

> 'Apricots, apples, dates and prunes
> Custards and pastes and filled half moons;
> Raisins and nuts, poppy seed, cheese –
> *Ach Gott, mein herr*! to choose among these!'

The bathos was inspired, the tin ear unequalled, and though I felt Doll was behaving like a tourist when he asked for one of the menus as a souvenir, I slid another under my coat when no one was looking.

So we ordered our Blumburgers ('*Saludos amigos, a vuestra salud!* However you say it, it's everything good !') and while we ate ours in our fingers, Vern picked up his knife and fork. As he did this, they danced a jig against his plate – our cameraman had a tremor in his hands that would have registered on the Richter scale. We were going straight on to Jayne Mansfield's house, and the lady was to give us a guided tour – as soon as Vern picked up the camera to follow us round, the pictures were going to be jumping all over the place. Was this some cunning plan to subvert the limeys?

145

We cruised out on to the freeway, our eyes watering freely from the smog which turned policemen's badges from silver through yellow to purple – temperature inversion held the effluent from cars and oil refineries to ground level so that Los Angeles was a gas-chamber with a blue sky. We turned into Beverly Hills where the houses had been extemporised from gingerbread, and drew up at 1010 Sunset Boulevard which had actually been iced: a special glitter effect caused the walls to sparkle sinisterly in the poisonous sunshine. I'd run into Jayne Mansfield a few months earlier in London when she had been asked to open the Chiswick Flyover: 'What connection do you have with fly-overs, Miss Mansfield?' I asked, but this bewildered her. Losing the point, I asked about the bathroom in her house in Beverly Hills which was said to be covered in shagpile not just on the floor but up the walls and across the ceiling. She'd replied, 'Which bathroom? We have thirteen.'

We announced ourselves at the electric gates and were invited in. The aged Vern extended his autograph book and pen to the chatelaine, as though bending his knee or touching his forelock, for in Hollywood the feudal system was intact. The book and the pen wavered in his fingers as though he were about to perform an act of prestidigitation, and as the lady signed I looked at Doll in alarm. The first bit would be OK because the camera would be on the tripod and Vern would simply keep us in shot as we strolled round the pool. Vern used the zoom but referred to it as 'dollying in' – 'First we do a long shot, then we dolly in', and he would mime the camera moving forward on some long-gone apparatus involving railway lines – I don't think anyone had dollied-in since the days of Mary Pickford. But it was when he lifted the camera off the sticks and followed us round the house that the problem was going to arise.

The pool, like everything else in the house, was heart shaped, for this was Jayne's favoured motif. The words 'I love You Jaynie' were picked out on the bottom of the pool in 22-carat gold mosaic, for much of the construction work in the house had been done by Mickey Hargitay, Jayne's Hungarian weight-lifting hubby. The pool area shone with sand imported from Acapulco: the contractors had unloaded several tons of the ordinary yellow stuff at first, but Jayne didn't like it, so they bent down and picked up every last grain and replaced it with the silver sort.

Then we went into the house itself. You had the impression of entering a temple in the cupid doll style, and this was reinforced when the hostess invited you to leave your shoes at the door of the living-room. It was to protect the floor covering, a lush white pampas about a foot high in which the spoor of the visitor would have been clearly visible long after he had left if the butler hadn't followed guests round with a vacuum pipe that sucked the fronds upright again – 'He has a *jahlly* good time,' laughed the lady of the house. A marble fountain played at one end of the room and the other boasted a spherical clock made of cork. The doors were ten inches thick and heavily carved as in a Vincent Price movie. One of the walls had been constructed out of petrified drift-wood, and Mr Hargitay had not omitted to incorporate vast heart-shaped fireplaces in which, curiously, they held card parties.

The Arriflex rattled like a felon's chains as Vern fumbled with the screws and unclamped it from the tripod. Placing it on his lap he changed lenses, managing to shatter with his trembling elbow a small faun perched on a marble column imported from Mr Hargitay's native Hungary. Vern offered to replace it with something similar he had at home. 'OK,' he said, 'ready to roll.' Miss Mansfield and I sashayed out into the fairy grotto and Vern picked up the camera, and the instant he touched it the tremor vanished: it was the only miracle I ever witnessed, and it was a serial miracle, for it happened every time.

We visited the stars in their homes, or at least in their gardens – Dick Powell explained that he had his wife in the house, somehow making her sound like wood-worm, so we did the interview by the pool. Shooting outside, we had no lighting to bother about, though Tony Curtis refused to be interviewed in full sunlight unless a make-up artist was summoned: we did him in the shade, under a tree. Kirk Douglas invited me to put my finger in the dimple in his chin – 'everyone does,' he said. Janet Leigh noted that Doll and I were wearing the same sort of shoes: 'do you share a bootiay?' she asked, as though this might be the chic-est thing. At the house of Edward G. Robinson, nee Emmanual Goldenberg, we were actually allowed inside, and as he showed me round the art gallery which housed his Matisses he said he didn't admit just anybody – 'but after all, we're both Robinsons. It's a proud name.' Harold Lloyd hadn't made a film for years, but lived quietly on his twenty-nine prime acres, a place he'd bought from Joe Schenck, one of the founding fathers of the industry. The gardens were an exact copy of those at Versailles, and every tree had been imported: 'they say there's a nine hole golf-course somewhere on the property,' said Lloyd, 'and one day I'm going to make a real effort and find it.' He passed wet days in his great drawing-room, listening to music played through the thirty-two hi-fi speakers which had replaced his thirty-two pianolas: he showed me the annexe where the old pianola rolls were still piled up, preserved like the Dead Sea Scrolls.

They seemed symbolic. Hollywood's day was done. Films weren't made that way any more. Fox sucked up the oil which lay beneath the lot and sold off its eighty-six acres for housing. The onion towers of Sid Grauman's Chinese Theater added a touch of the mausoleum and the paving slabs in front, bearing the hand-prints of long gone celebs, were like tombstones from prehistory: 'Thanks Sid, Betty Grable', 'To Sid, sincere appreciation, Jean Harlow', 'May this cement our friendship, Joan Crawford'. Poor old Jayne's candy floss house already seemed antique. It struck me as empty in some absolute way, and as we were leaving it that evening and walking past the giant kitchen I was aware of a faint odour, as of a solitary lamb chop wondering how it had come to be cooked.

WITHOUT THE NET

'AAARGH!' CRIED JACK Lambert, literary editor, 'don't go in!' He had just emerged from the office of the editor of *The Sunday Times* and whirled his hands at me as though trying to make me disappear. He seemed perturbed, but enjoying it, as people do when they are the bearer of ill tidings which affect you not them.

It was a sunny day and I was sauntering down the corridor with the idea of inviting the boss to bestow some sort of title on me – almost everyone else was called assistant editor, so why not me? I was not so intemperate as to suppose I should actually edit, or even assist anyone to edit, anything whatever, but since I had never seen any of the other assistant editors do anything which I could identify as either editing or assisting, I assumed it was a courtesy title, and wondered why I'd been left out. I seemed to be the last of the private soldiers on *The Sunday Times*, and since my column was incontrovertible evidence that I produced something that helped fill the paper, I thought the fact might be recognised. After all, the man who used to call himself editorial director could appoint me assistant editor as easily as he had just appointed himself editor; in this new role he had requisitioned Antony Armstrong-Jones to design an office for him, a place where he could lay out the proofs of the paper and stare at them silently until someone guessed what he wanted done with them.

He rarely ventured out of his office, moving swiftly through the perilous corridors where the possibility of someone asking him what he thought was always lurking. He would pass me in silence with the sideways look and faint smile which telegraphed enormous preoccupations. But recently I'd felt the smile was wintrier, and he may even have speeded up as he went by. There was a chill in the air, which was puzzling. I thought everyone liked me. 'I like you,' said my wife, 'and your mother likes you. People who see your programmes like you. But why should the editor rejoice when you turn up on the telly and knock the advertising industry?'

In some ways it was perhaps a pity that I had so easily got the better of the man they'd put up against me on the occasion my wife referred to. He was a hockey Blue or some such who had gone into advertising and had never been disagreed with before. But this was a programme about the morality of persuasion, and as a top dog in the advertising world – the Ad Gang, as Priestley always called them – he wasn't used to meeting people who had opinions different from his own. Indeed, as far as journalists went, he only ever met editors who buttered him up, and after I'd floored him not once but several times on questions of principle that no one had ever told him existed, he called on the editor for an explanation. Why had one of his journos been allowed out on ticket of leave to make a fool of him on the television (I think he knew for certain he'd been the loser when his own trade mag rallied to his colours by implying he'd won a great victory, rather spoiling the effect when it spoke of 'His opening peroration –').

All persuasion is impertinence, whether it seeks your vote, your conscience or your money, and that had been roughly my position. But the arrangements made by propagandists for the engineering of consent (the phrase is Frank Whitehead's) have a dimension that is more sinister than anything that can be brushed aside as mere cheek; in a variety of forms, advertising presents a world in which all decisions have been taken. This is the lie which underpins an apparatus inimical to the interests of people as individuals; the individual is the enemy, since the individual might not buy.

At the time it might have tickled me to know a day would come when I would be invited to collude in this deception – enterprises of great pith and moment like tinned dog food, the Milk Marketing Board, British Airways, were to offer me money if I would endorse their services in public. But a man who gets his living hiring out his capacity to form opinions is taking a very short view if he starts hiring out the opinions themselves: once he's seen to do that, why should anyone believe anything he says? Sometimes when I said this the chaps at the other end of the phone would think I was making a joke, which confirmed them in their feeling that I was just the right man, and they would say so. Then I'd put it to them, Isn't just the right man just *not* the right man, once he takes your shilling? They would laugh appreciatively. I laughed very appreciatively when a lady telephoned to ask me if I would do a voice-over for Andrex lavatory paper. Look, I said, there is one thing I must know: did you ask anyone else before you asked me? Oh no, she replied fervently, yours was the first name we thought of. After a time, my uncooperative attitude became known, though enthusiasts would still give it a go. 'All right,' said one, 'if you don't want to do it yourself, would you mind if we got a voice-alike to do it as though they were you?' I said, 'But wouldn't that be like losing your virginity and letting someone else have the fuck?' There was a silence. 'I don't think that is overstated,' I added.

But these bizarre moments lay in the future. I received a memo from the editor written as though under duress from a deputation of broken-hearted hacks who had begged him to tell me that unless I bridled my tongue we should all find ourselves selling matches on the streets. Assuming as usual that all bosses were really favourite uncles, I wrote back and said I was certain if he'd seen the programme he wouldn't have been ashamed of me – I sounded like a nephew in a school story expecting to be tipped a sovereign. I was about to enclose the telegram I'd received from Randolph Churchill which said 'Congratulations', but even my naïvety had its limits: already cast as a trouble maker, I probably wouldn't be doing myself a lot of good brandishing a reference from the leading anarchist of the day.

But the exchange made me broody. Quite apart from the particular incident, could it be that the boss had begun to find it displeasing that a member of his staff should have a base outside it? Had this begun to irk? Especially since the base was now enlarged. I'd started to present *Points of View*. Like most innovations, this was an accident. When they added up the time allotted for the new season's programmes, they found they'd got a spare five minutes, and instead of doing the decent thing and letting the viewers off early they thought they'd use it as a slot for the customers to say what they thought of the programmes. Not a blindingly original notion, but I suspect nervous administrators had to be reassured that in offering itself for criticism the Corporation would gain marks, and anyway it was only five minutes.

Actually, it was the five minuteness that gave the thing its bite. It's not impossible to bore people in five minutes, but it's quite hard. And anything sharp that is said in five minutes is sharper than when it is said in twenty-five minutes. I don't think they realised this. Of course, there was never any chance of criticism changing the nature or quality of the programmes, since in any given period television is a complex response to the temper of the time and the prejudices of the people who produce and consume it. But if you had an intelligent citizen sitting in the middle – and I mean me – who saw no reason to feel he needed to observe any sort of 'balance' save that prompted by his own sense of fitness, then a degree of reality would be conferred on the proceedings. I was neither tribune nor deputy, and *Points of View* was only incidentally about television: as far as I was concerned, it was a way of highlighting human idiosyncrasy, on the basis of the sort of letters people liked to write and the sort of programmes the BBC liked to make; here the five minuteness was invaluable, since if the thing had gone on any longer the level of my own self-satisfaction – already at the flood, according to some viewers – would have overflowed into the truly intolerable. Having the last word, and always having it, is a stern test of character.

I sat on a stool in the tiny Presentation studio and made my remarks in between the letters, which were read out by resting actors sitting round a microphone behind a screen. I had a little home-made bobbin with my comments on it, and it unspooled like an early Egyptian tally-roll underneath the camera when I pressed a button with my foot. If there were lines in the letters that particularly appealed to me I'd invite the actors to read them again – David Coleman's pronunciation of 'altitude' was given a well deserved reprise. We made a corner in small fantasies – I said I always imagined Wheldon humming the signature tune to *Monitor* while he was checking that his flies were done up before walking on, and after he sportingly came along and did just that, we got the Swiss ambassador to drop in and hum the Swiss national anthem: a viewer had claimed it didn't exist. We had the services of Jim Franklin, an inspired film editor who came to glory with *Monty Python*. Jim would spend hours putting together clips of films so that Sir Malcolm Sargent could be seen conducting the Beatles, and Maigret, in the long-running detective series, would seem to be talking confidentially on the telephone to Barlow in *Z Cars*. A question that much exercised our viewers was whether the panellists on *What's My Line* were cheating when the mystery guest came on – could they actually see through the masks which were supposed to blindfold them? Slipping one on I assured the enquirer that it was opaque. 'But Mr Riley is doubtful,' I continued, and still wearing the mask, picked up his letter and looking down at it said, 'He writes –'. We were not proud, we hoped to entertain.

Even the noted curmudgeon, Ingrams, my next door neighbour in

Chelsea, said he had been prompted by the idiom of *Points of View* when starting *Private Eye*. And the producers whose programmes were pilloried began by complaining they were being stabbed in the back but ended up insisting it would be an honour to be assassinated. That little programme and I were as one, and when I took a night off, the *Observer* critic said that *Points of View* without Robinson was like St Paul's without the dome. It was short and sharp, and when a viewer asked why we didn't have a long roll of credits at the end like other programmes we obliged with a list that included 'Hairstyles by Raymonde (Baxter)', 'Mr Robinson as a boy, played by Freddie Bartholomew', and 'Warmest thanks to the Spanish Airforce for their co-operation'. It left me with the suspicion that if more television programmes lasted only five minutes we wouldn't be missing much. The title has survived, but the thing itself is now indistinguishable from the decor, a sort of reception area where Can I help you means what it always means – that you are about to be processed. I seem to hear muzak playing throughout.

Back in the corridor at *The Sunday Times*, I listened to the horrorstruck Lambert. 'He's seen it!' he cried. He pointed at the magazine I was carrying in my hand. It was published in Scotland, and it featured the first of a series based on *Points of View*. I'd brought it along with the intention of reinforcing my claim to a small place among the *nomenclatura*. But as I went into the editor's office, waving my copy at him, he was waving his at me. 'What's one of my senior men doing appearing in a rag like this?' he hissed. I had to laugh. 'I can't be senior, I'm the only Other Rank in the whole building!' And talking of rags, hadn't he been responsible for the *Empire News*?' A theological discussion ensued: the man wanted me to pack in my extra-curricular activities and devote myself to the paper. I went home for lunch. My wife said, 'He sees himself as your patron. But now you outgun him. Did he sound solemn?' She said, 'Your naïvety will be the death of you, old sport.' Then she said, 'Mother never bred a jibber.'

I flinched at the idea of taking my toe off the bottom. I wrote earlier of my father having bettered himself, and my implication was that I would do rather more, in foregoing nine to five and risking a solo performance. Not quite solo, though. I'd had it both ways; being a member of staff meant anything I did outside could be laughed off as though it were no more than a hobby, like a man who sings tenor in a choir. But tenors get up people's noses ('You look like a *tenor*,' said Daphne Levens, when I played Cassio at Oxford. She was the wife of Robert Levens of Wadham, who was the statutory don on the board of the OUDS, and Daphne sometimes played mature women in undergraduate productions. When she said tenor it was a definite accusation).

Now I'd be singing my own tune entirely. And up on the high wire, no safety net. Neither my wife nor I really gave money a thought. Money only occurred to us in operatic or fictional terms; neither of us felt life was anything but happy endings; since nothing dreadful had ever happened to us, we didn't know what dreadful was – we didn't think dreadful existed. So after lunch I went back and told the boss I was leaving. I think he was quite glad – perhaps because he hadn't had to make a decision. Later, when Penguin brought out a collection of the columns I'd written for *The Sunday Times*, he dropped me a line in which he said he'd been the one who had argued fiercely that I should never leave the paper, as though a clamorous mob had shut him up in a cupboard until they'd seen me off the premises. 'But now you're a national figure,' he said, as though this status had been conferred on me by sitting next to a man who had said 'fuck' on television.

Captain Ferguson may have been annoyed when I declared myself a free man, for he tempted me out of a niche I had made my own: very unwisely, I abandoned *Points of View* and agreed to present *BBC3*. It was like selling the family silver. They'd fired Frost who had fronted the first two 'satire' series, possibly because of his criminal hairdo, and when someone asked me whether the prospect of taking over wasn't daunting I said If Frost can do it, anyone can. This was a serious error of judgement. Frost behaved on television like a man who couldn't believe his luck in being allowed into the studio at all – everything and everyone delighted him. What I didn't spot was that this was exactly what was required – the last thing the show needed was someone with reservations, and just as Frost's unalloyed pleasure could not be concealed, so my own grudgingness was involuntarily on view. What I couldn't suppress was a conviction that it wasn't satire. Satire is made out of material derived exclusively from what is to be satirised, reassembled in a form that makes the flaw in the original the source of the humour. But *BBC3* didn't bother about this, it just brought jokes and subjects together as people balance vases or ornaments on handy surfaces. And anything facetious was prized. The first show had a sketch about a nudist wedding, and poor Beryl Reid, naked, was handing out one-liners. 'Oh, what a lovely pair,' she said, of the couple. 'What a lovely pair.' Close-ups of bosoms. 'What a really lovely pair,' she went on, making sure you didn't miss it. I said to Ned Sherrin, We don't need that. He smiled courteously. It wasn't so much needed, as absolutely required.

I think I'd been wished on him. Alan Brien told me they'd asked Robert Kee to do it, but Alan had told him he had no sense of humour, so according to him Kee turned it down (but Alan liked adding spin to events: I was giving him a lift and stopped at a telephone box. Finding I hadn't got the right coins I got back in the car saying I'd do it when I got to the Television Centre. I suspect this turned up in a profile in *The Sunday Times* as 'He has been known to make a detour to the Television Centre to save threepence on a telephone call.'). They may have thought they'd get something of the asperity that had been the keynote of *Points of View*, but would it travel? Not a chance. Left on your own for five minutes, it works like a charm, but with a stage full of belly-dancers, fire-eaters, dogs in ruffs doing somersaults, and Dame Gore Vidal and the Widow St John Stevas flailing each other with pig's bladders, who needs it?

'Don't get shrill, Bob, don't get shrill,' said Harvey Orkin, a professional New Yorker hired for the talk section of the programme, who saw the veins standing out on my neck as I tried to get someone to take a bit of notice of me. The morning after the first show in which I had stared at every camera except the right one, banged into the scenery and insulted the actors, I walked into the production office and saw Ned Sherrin sitting bolt upright in his swivel chair with his eyes closed, apparently dead. My God, I've killed him, I thought. Not only did I perceive myself as having dissipated in a single evening the goodwill accumulated over my years in television, I had managed to do it clumsily. When Ned woke up – he had a knack of being able to sleep while sitting to attention – I believe he felt sorry for me. 'Some of the people in this show have never had a bad review in their lives. It hits them rather hard.' I think he really meant me. 'Just relax on it, Robert,' he said, which was a kindlier word than an anchor-man who had failed to anchor so much as a rowing boat had any right to expect.

Things could hardly get worse, and my spirits perked up when I was allowed to come on juggling with three oranges. After that, if two ladies in spangled tights had held a flaming hoop in front of me I should have leapt through it like a gazelle. 'The greatest gain has been in RR's chairmanship,' wrote Philip Purser in the *Sunday Telegraph*, 'he keeps the show bowling along at a sprightly canter, and his own dry humour is a great addition to the proceedings.' He had written more in sorrow than in anger about how dreadful I'd been on the first programme, but candour bids me admit that he may have been waiting to say something nice as soon as it was remotely feasible, because we were old friends. Not only that, we both occupied the same page in the *Sunday Telegraph*, he as the television man, me as the film critic. This was one of the jobs I did during the hours of daylight before slipping the oblong halo on as night fell. Since eighty per cent of the films I reviewed were drek it meant that eighty per cent of the time I had to write engagingly about rubbish – a little unfair. But I was rescued by Lady Pamela Berry.

ENTERTAINING LADY PAM

'YOU DON'T MEAN you invited her *back*!' Rosemary looked horrified. 'Well,' I said, 'she asked us to her election party at the Savoy,
so we thought it was our turn.' 'But,' said Rosemary, trying to get
me to see the enormity of the thing, 'you don't ask Lady Pam unless
– unless you're the *Prime Minister*.' 'Well,' I said, 'it's done now.'
'Goodness,' said Rosemary, 'I'd never have dared.' (Rosemary, no
mean hostess herself, had a keen sense of social nuance and told
me she was convinced she was lower middle class. 'How can you be
sure?' I asked. She replied. 'My mother never entertained.')

Lady Pamela Berry, daughter of F.E. Smith and wife of the Berry
who owned the *Telegraph*, was the Mrs Leo Hunter of her day. She
only ever invited lions, and their concerted roaring stirred envy as
far afield as Regent's Park Zoo. The party she held on election night
would have been regarded by her as a bun-fight, which is why as
a mere telly man, who was her husband's film critic, I scraped in
with my wife. But Pam filled in time between parties by going to
the pictures a lot, and since she was an enthusiast she thought I was
too stringent: 'I didn't agree with you on Sunday *at all*,' she told me,
and it dawned on me I was being accused of impertinence. Another
time she said, 'You don't really *like* films, do you?' and I realised
the more often my taste diverged from that of the mistress, the more
likely was it that my days at the *Telegraph* would be numbered. I
suppose inviting the lady to my humble dwelling with its earth
floor was another way of getting above myself. But ten to one she
wouldn't come.

I was fully occupied. I reviewed the newspapers weekly in *Punch*,
wrote a column in the *Sun* (hard to believe that in its first incarnation, the *Sun* was a broadsheet – it had once been the *Daily Herald*),
functioned comprehensively as book, theatre and film critic for the
new monthly *Nova*, and was Mr Manners in a weekly column
I did for the *Observer* colour supplement, laying down the law

157

somewhat airily on matters of social moment – the difficulty of deciding whether you were the sort of person who could convincingly pronounce Coventry as Cuventry, and how you should never ask to see the manager in case the waiter replied, 'He wouldn't come.'

Now that *BBC3* had ended, I presented an arts programme called (meaninglessly) *The Look of the Week* – why not *The Look of the Irish*? – and in addition fronted a series called *Divided We Stand*. This was a compilation of moments from local TV news magazines, illustrative of aspects of popular anthropology, and featuring such oddities as a chap who wanted to be buried in a sitting position, and a man in Bristol who sat on a seat in a public park, every now and again reaching down to pick up a pigeon and put it in a cake box. He was often beaten by old ladies wielding umbrellas, and when asked how he had learned his skills, which he deployed for the local council on a freelance basis, per pigeon, he said this could be attributed to 'Years of experience': he evacuated the vowels from this phrase, and it came out 'Yrs vxprnce'.

I also presented a book game on BBC2 called *Take It or Leave It*, in which extracts from famous authors were read out without attribution and the panellists had to say who the writer was. Betjeman was a regular participant and always referred to the programme as *Money for Jam*: he didn't feel it necessary to say much more than 'I say, it's awfully *good*', or if the passage in question featured names like Sergei or Alexandrovna he might opine that it was 'certainly *Russian*'. Anthony Burgess was often present, though in his autobiography he says he thought the programme put books to the wrong use. This surprised me, since the guessing of the author was only a preliminary to a discussion of the work – you can't really do books on television (as I was to decide some years later when I conducted *The Book Programme*) but at least on *Take It or Leave It* books were being entered into, their substance was being tested – which gets you closer to their nature than ever a profile of the author does.

And in the course of this enterprise, Burgess and I were the catalysts for bringing a forgotten rarity to light: quoting from a book my father had brought home from the Faringdon barrows when I was a boy, a book that had been part of our family *lingua franca* for as long as I could remember, I told Burgess he seemed to be 'in the full flower of his southern metropolitan Xtian manhood', and at these arcane words he jumped as though a pin had been stuck in him. 'Good God,' he said, 'I thought I was the only person in the world who knew that book!' It was *Augustus Carp: The Autobiography of a Really Good Man*, a sort of *Diary of a Nobody*, but with a much sharper edge: where Pooter is an old silly, Carp – a low-church humbug – is a swine. When it came out in the early Twenties it was published anonymously, but after our conversation Burgess dug about and found the author had been a certain Dr Bashford, a Hampstead physician.

His family were curiously stand-offish about the book, perhaps because it seemed to tilt at things religious. But it is written with unusual artifice, the prose hitting off the orotundity of the first-person narrator while displaying its inherent absurdity (if my earlier definition of satire is accepted, then this is a perfect illustration of it). Burgess wrote an introduction to a new edition which Heinemann brought out, and I contributed one to the Penguin version. So in addition to the incidental pleasures the programme provided – Cyril Connolly assigning a passage to Saul Bellow when it came from Baden-Powell's *Scouting for Boys* – it could plead, in mitigation of Burgess's charge that it wasn't true to books, that if it hadn't existed a comic masterpiece would not have been rediscovered.

So I was doing quite enough to prompt a favourite remark from my mother, who would say When you've finished those few little chores will you wash these blankets through for me. The *Telegraph* took up a disproportionate amount of time – you had to watch the films before reviewing them. I don't wish to sound victimised, but when the lights went up after two hours of sludge, and you had to go away and say something about it that would be readable, I sometimes felt I might have spent the time more profitably in a slot-machine arcade. There was a measure of consolation in observing the way in which one's fellow scribes set about the task: one elderly party arrived carrying a string bag with packets of Daz and knobbly lumps that might have been potatoes or onions distending the mesh, and the conviction you had that as far as he was concerned criticism came a poor second to a domestic life of unrelieved tedium was reinforced by a suspicion he still had his pyjamas on under his clothes. And which of them would fall asleep first? On this occasion, no contest. Freda Bruce Lockhart who was pushed respectfully in her wheelchair to a side aisle fell into the arms of Porpus just as the lights went down. Once one of the films was so restful, my old friend Milton Shulman slumbered, but far from peacefully, for his own snores made his sleep fitful and unrefreshing. Meanwhile, Jack Waterman (*Evening Standard*), Anthony Carthew

(*Sun*) and I would be filling the auditorium with the sweet savour of monosodium glutamate, as we munched our Wimpy cheeseburgers. Either before or after the show, canapés would be served, and while there was no telling which of us tucked into them with the greatest vigour, there was no doubting who got most, since a critic who was understood to be terribly poor always brought a brown paper bag in which he stowed the tiny triangular sandwiches when he thought nobody was looking, to provide himself with an evening meal. So the press shows were never without their interest, even though this might have nothing to do with the film. Sometimes the promoters would drag little old ladies in off the street to make an audience, in the hope that their enjoyment would infect the more sullen of the critics: but it only made them more sullen still, since they knew the old ladies didn't have to do any work afterwards.

But how wrong Lady Pamela had been to tell me I didn't warm to the genre. Would a man with no sympathy for the silver screen have agreed to play himself in Ken Russell's first feature film? This vehicle was entitled *French Dressing*, though when boasting of the assignment to my mother I had to pause before telling her the name of it, because sometimes a slip of the tongue turned the title into *Field Dressing* or *French Letters*. It was a comedy, though you wouldn't have thought so, looking at Russell's face as he sat cross-legged and glum in front of the camera. The scenario involved a French film star (Marisa Mell) opening a film festival at a fly-blown English resort called Gormleigh-on-Sea (oh dear) and I was to be the *Picture Parade* commentator covering it for television. Along with Schlesinger, Russell was an alumnus of *Monitor*. I think this showed to advantage in the camera-work – the mournful beach (Herne Bay) and the scrotum-tightening sea. But the fun and games hung a bit loose.

Listen, I said to Ken, I'll have to write my own lines. That's OK he said, you can write everyone else's, as far as I'm concerned. I thought he seemed depressed. But it didn't much matter what the words were since an actor called James Booth, playing a deck-chair attendant who was somehow in charge of the festivities, grabbed me round the neck as we pushed through the throng of fans on the pier, and as I tried to interview the visiting film star, ensured that I uttered every line into his left arm-pit. The film gets an occasional re-run on the telly, and watching it I'm not sure Booth wasn't trying to do me a favour, since in the sequences when I can actually be heard, I seem to be speaking in a funny accent ('eccent') that harks back to the days when actors spoke 'West End' – I sound like someone in an archive recording of *In Town Tonight*.

Chauffeured back from the last day's filming with a sexy little girl who'd been helping out on the production while waiting to be discovered, I asked her to the party – if Lady Pam turned up she'd see I was at home in the world of films, for John Schlesinger would be there as well. The girl said she'd come if she could, and she did; but in the event, perhaps it might have been better if she hadn't.

Everyone seemed to be enjoying themselves. 'Who is that man with the big face?' enquired the elderly Lady Armstrong from over the road, and on being told it was Robin Day she said, '*Such* a good listener!' (Zaida Armstrong was not quite au fait with current rankings, and when Esther Anderson who lived in the flat above her own at No. 9 had introduced her on the doorstep to Bob Marley, Lady Armstrong had tugged his dreadlocks and cried 'You funny little thing!') Rima, Marquesa da Guadalmina, arrived and my son let her in: 'Hello, Nick,' she said, 'guess what I've got in my bag? Fart powder. I'm going to put it in your Dad's champagne.' In earlier days, Rima had been a starlet at Pinewood when that's what they were called, and if Lady Pam showed up she might remember her: Rima had once been Victor Mature's girlfriend and had lived with him at the Savoy. Her mother was rather concerned – 'Do you think I should forward her mail?' she had asked neighbours in Sussex, anxious to do the right thing. We rented Rima's house in Spain and she used the money to buy an ice-maker which she christened The Robinson.

My housemaster Peter Smith was there, looking like the Russian ambassador with his dark pointed beard, and shaggier whiskers were brought by Michael Meyer, the Ibsen scholar. My daughter Lucy waylaid him while she sang him one of the household songs –

> 'There was a man called Michael Meyer
> He had whiskers like a bear:
> He cut them off to stuff a chair,
> And went on translating Ibsen.'

'Mamma sings it to us in the bath,' Lucy confided.

Peter Quennell arrived from No. 26, but Marilyn, his beautiful wife, was still at home. 'She is acting as midwife to our Siamese,' said PQ, 'and I am to return home to assist as soon as parturition begins.' The lady from the Ken Russell film said 'Oh, is your au pair having a baby?' and Peter replied a little testily, 'No, our cat.' Peter Quennell was the literary eminence of Cheyne Row – more cheerful than Carlyle, he wore a hat that outdid the gloomy Caledonian's, and he looked like an ironic monsignor. His style, his air, his very tread, took our little street back to its origins in a more cultivated age, and as he sauntered over the flagstones you felt he might just have come from Leigh Hunt's round the corner, having slipped him a guinea under the pretence that it was a subscription he had overlooked, pausing at the steps of what would then have been No. 5 to discuss the beneficent effects of laudanum with Mrs Carlyle. He brought bones for our great big dog and spoke of him affectionately as Foolish Fred.

Our younger daughter Suzy had climbed out of bed and was sitting on the stairs, naked, when John Betjeman arrived. She accosted him on his way up in the character of a waif and said 'None of my family loves me.' 'Oh dear,' said the Bard. Then added thoughtfully, 'Are you *sure*?' He and Quennell were old friends and Betjeman laughed about the letter he remembered Peter had received from his father when he'd been sent down from Oxford in the Twenties for being discovered in bed with Cora Pilkington at the Randolph Hotel; after being cast out from the dreaming spires he'd been taken on by the Sitwells as a sort of secretary and he was living the life of a great swell at Montegufoni. But his father's letter – quoted from memory by Betjeman so meticulously you could hear the punctuation – ran, 'But for this foolish escapade you would now be enjoying, in the company of your mother and father, a tour of the border castles of Wales.'

Prophecy and Walter Coles, next door at No. 18, had come, and very soon after they arrived so did their small son Alf; he was a close friend of Suzy and had climbed over the fence to join her on the stairs. He too was naked, save for a top hat. Lord and Lady Jessel came in from No. 11, and I was glad we had no music for when Teddy and Jessica visited restaurants where they had Muzak he simply said to the greeter 'Turn it orff'. A friend called Beryl from the suburb of my youth was being very vivacious, and as Amy – Amy Brown, who looks after the house for us – passed with the tray I saw her remove two glasses of champagne, one for each hand, from which she sipped alternately.

Sonia and Tony Berry dropped by from No. 22. 'The Queen's coming to dinner,' Sonia had told Josée earlier in the week. 'Would

Lucy and Suzy like to see her?' She meant, stand at the area gate
and watch her arrive. Sonia knew the Queen because they'd had
lessons together as children. I felt a little wistful – we hadn't been
invited; but there I was, peering out of the dining-room window
as the Queen jumped out of what looked like an old Rover and
skipped up Sonia's steps. Not many people have seen the Queen
ring a doorbell – you can't believe how quickly it was opened – and
the thought occurred to me that there were some occasions when
even Lady Pam would have been second-eleven. The girl from the
Ken Russell film was bending Schlesinger's ear, having discovered
who he was. 'He doesn't know a thing about films. Not a bloody
thing. Not the slightest bloody *thing*.' I shuddered. Did she mean
me? How fortunate Lady Pam was a no-show.

It was getting lateish for a drinks party, and having called for a cab
for Peter Smith I watched him from the drawing-room window as he
climbed unsteadily in and sat down, very carefully, on the floor. As
the cab drove away the doorbell sounded. Amy was seeing to the
canapes, and my wife greeted the newcomer. Unfortunately, there
was for that all-too-revealing three seconds and a half a look in her
eyes which made it plain she didn't know who the lady was. Then
of course it dawned on her. '*So* glad you could come!' Lady Pam
stepped inside. 'Such a pretty little house,' she said, rather crisply.

As soon as Lady Pam entered the drawing-room I turned into Mr
Turveydrop, hunching my shoulders after the style of the famous
master of deportment, sliding about among the guests like extra-
virgin olive oil and introducing her to all and sundry, avoiding Beryl
who was swaying like a cobra in front of Peter Quennell.

I made sure she met Schlesinger, and even edged the conversation
round to the time we had collaborated, but Lady Pam had got
him mixed up with another Schlesinger who was a South African
financier, and I didn't feel my cause had been advanced. At this
point the girl from the film who Schlesinger had managed to edge
away from (he often protected himself from actors who wanted jobs
by pretending on the telephone to be his own Japanese manservant:
Oh, solly. Mr Schlesingell in Horrywood) re-joined our group, and
taking up some earlier argument said, 'Now she,' pointing at Lady
Pam, 'will bear me out – she's quite old enough to remember the
young Lillian Gish. Now *weren't* her silent films,' she went on,
addressing Lady Pam with fierce sincerity, 'a revelation to everyone
when they first came out?'

Beryl joined us. 'Is it true you opened a dog's lavatory in the gardens at the end of the road?' Lady Pam jumped as though stung, thinking she was being addressed, for Beryl's eye now had a wandering quality. 'Ha,ha,ha,' I tittered, while grinding my teeth with annoyance, 'she means me.' No doubt Peter Quennell had relieved the tedium of Beryl's company by telling her the dogs' loo story, which had always amused him since his own dog Snaffy had no need of such an amenity, always using our doorstep; I'd opened the thing at the urgent request of the Borough Engineer, and had a terrible argument during the ceremony with a bearded heckler who said I'd be better employed supporting a prostitutes' collective – they filmed the acrimonious exchange for Thames News and Bill Grundy the presenter said at the end 'News at Six. The Bogside.' 'Pardon me,' said Beryl, and knelt down to rest her head against the marble column of the fireplace. 'The cat's having kittens,' bellowed Alfy Coles, bursting in naked in his top hat, followed by Suzy. 'Peter Quennell's wife says he's got to go home at once,' shouted Suzy, 'she's having trouble with the afterbirth.' Quennell pushed his sausage roll into the hired butler's waistcoat pocket and dashed for the door. 'Such fun,' Lady Pam said, looking at her watch. My wife escorted her down the stairs, while I hovered, smiling – this time like Mr Pecksniff. When I was fired from the *Sunday Telegraph* the following week, it may well have been (as someone told me) because the editor had heard that when the proprietor had asked some of us what we should spend extra money on for the good of the paper I had said 'New teeth for the editor', when in fact this remark had been made by the theatre critic, Alan Brien. 'How did things go?' Rosemary asked, 'Well,' I said, 'it was a roundabout way of relieving myself of watching a lot of dud films. But it certainly worked.'

ENCOUNTERS

Y OU MEET STRANGERS when you do interviewing, and that's what they remain when you've finished – material has been exchanged, a satisfactory transaction has taken place. Then once in a long while there's an exception. Sitting in his apartment in West End Avenue in New York, I said to Bernard Malamud, author of *The Fixer* and *The Assistant* and many magical short stories, that when I read his fiction I had the feeling I was looking through the eyes of his characters, and I had the feeling they were looking through my eyes as well. Malamud said, I have never heard it described quite that way. I'm delighted that what you say happens. I am happy to know it. And he looked happy. He smiled. He smiled as though he knew me.

Malamud wouldn't answer questions about how he made his fictions, he didn't want to consider the manner of their contriving in case he lost the power. But one way or another he tampers with the literal and transforms it; so when a bad-tempered crow comes flying through the window of Harry Cohen's apartment in New York and starts superintending his son's homework, you feel you were waiting for this to happen. So I smiled back at Malamud. I knew him too.

After the interview I went back to the Waldorf, where my wife had joined me, and that night Malamud telephoned and asked us to a party the next evening. It was a supper party, so not being sure whether we should get there late or on time we arrived on time, and were too early. Pretty soon a crowd showed up, and there was a lot of noise and a lot of argument. Some of Malamud's friends were incensed by William Styron's novel *Sophie's Choice* because his story was about a Polish girl in Auschwitz and they thought the narrative implied the Poles had had as bad a time of it in the war as the Jews, and they saw something anti-Semitic in this. I'd just come from Nassau where I'd visited Styron on the little private island he rented for the summer, and this was the book I'd gone there to get him to talk about (the itinerary, Nassau/New York, was known in telly man cant as a two-suitcase job:

165

summer togs for the blue skies of the Caribbean, overcoats for snowy New York. And you were paid as well).

Now Styron himself hadn't been too sure about the legitimacy of what he was doing. The story was about Auschwitz, and his uncertainty seems to surface when he lets the narrator quote George Steiner: 'It's not clear that those who were not themselves fully involved should touch upon these agonies unscathed', and Steiner also says, 'In the presence of certain realities, art is trivial or impertinent.' But when I asked Styron why he made Sophie Polish rather than Jewish he said, 'I wanted to show that the Nazis were out to get the whole human race.' He'd been in trouble before when he'd written a novel about the black slave Nat Turner, and some members of the black establishment felt it was presumptuous of a white man to do this. But in relation to the predicament of both Sophie and Turner, Styron's conclusion was that a novelist is allowed to imagine anyone or anything.

When I said some of this, I got shouted at by Malamud's guests, but not by Malamud, who was listening. I said how can you blame the man for what happens in a story, for what's made up? The condition of fictions is they are different from their makers – even the not very good ones; the fiction doesn't belong to anyone when it's finished, the fiction lives in its own universe, it's somewhere else, it's not anything but its own; people who do fiction are generating something that will be not themselves. And as I said this, Malamud smiled again, and reached out and squeezed my cheek gently between his finger and thumb.

Some months later I was in the kitchen at home and the phone rang. It was Malamud. I was filled with delight. He was stopping over in London a few nights later en route to Rome. Could he come to dinner? When he arrived, we sat down. The plane had been delayed, it was late, and I do believe the dinner my wife had cooked was the second one he ate that night, an exhibition of supreme politeness. 'It's so good to see you,' said Josée, and Malamud said, 'That's the kindest word anyone has said to me all day.' There were some other guests, and Malamud sat at one end of the table and I sat at the other. Looking up at one point I caught Malamud's eye. And he smiled, without saying anything. And I smiled back at him. Then I drove him to his hotel and he left the next day, and not a long time after I heard he had died. His daughter sent me a snapshot of him holding his grandchild. The business of knowing someone is quite mysterious. It can be sudden, like a blush or a stammer. But it's quite clear when it happens.

★

So, an encounter – what does this mean? It means that when both parties meet, they are actually present. I'll give you an example. When I was an undergraduate I went with the OUDS to France and we took a production of *Richard II*. They gave us *vins d'honneur* everywhere and at the university in Marseilles dancing had started. I was standing aside, waiting to claim as my partner the daughter of the house in which I'd been billeted; when we'd driven to Cassis for a day out the car had been rather crowded and to my great satisfaction Beatrice had volunteered to sit on my knee (how shocked I'd been when I heard her cousin who was driving shout '*con*' to another driver who had cut him up at a roundabout).

So I tapped my foot and looked round the room, but couldn't spot her. I was aware of a man standing next to me. I vaguely registered white hair and sharp chin, but I was watching the couples swirling about and as I looked out for Beatrice I saw a large porcelain bowl with a miniature Chinese tree inside it sway and rock every time the dancers swept past it – the floorboards must have been loose.

Then I heard a thin reedy voice say, 'Do you see that bowl over there?' I looked round and saw the man standing next to me was Bertrand Russell. 'The one in the corner?' I said. 'The one that wobbles every time the dancers go past. Well now – ' Russell raised his hand and pointed, and I knew that in the tradition of great philosophers he'd had a revelation arising out of his observation of something quite ordinary – I just hoped it wouldn't be beyond me. And Russell said, 'I can't think why someone doesn't just stick an old cigarette packet underneath it.' After a bit I said, 'It wouldn't be a bad idea.' And Russell nodded.

In an encounter there is no presentation, it is uncalculated. Nothing has to happen. And when, sometimes, something does happen you may wish it hadn't. Schlesinger rang and asked us to dinner. 'I need support. Bette Davis is coming.' Schlesinger was very nervous, because Bette Davis had made it known she wanted him to direct her in a film, and Schlesinger had told his friends he would sooner be fired from a cannon. Well, he just about was.

The mild-mannered Richard Rodney Bennett who'd done some music for Schlesinger was one of the guests, and there were a couple of young men who I couldn't help suspecting collected ancient actresses as others press ferns in albums. We arrived before the great lady, and I egged Schlesinger on to do his Field Marshal

Montgomery imitation, and we were all very mirthful, as though we knew our faces would have to be specially straight when Miss Davis made her entry. This she did, accompanied by a lady-in-waiting called Violet Rubber. Miss Rubber was a middle-aged frequenter of the world of show-business who partnered-out (as the old phrase used to go) when visiting celebs needed a companion, or even a keeper. It was understood that Miss Davis was fond of the bottle, but her poise was such as to make everyone else conscious of the need to sit up that much straighter as she took her place on the divan.

The conversation was perhaps a little stilted at first, for it was a bit like being in the presence of, well, Bette Davis, and we were all minding our manners. But the great lady smiled and condescended, and all went as merrily as a grig. There was a small silence, and our glasses were replenished, and then we were admiring Schlesinger's elegant new curtains, even unto the linings, which were of sumptuous brown wild silk. Suddenly there was a little cry – perhaps even a squawk – from Miss Davis. 'My ear-rings! They've gone. I've lost them,' she cried.

As one man we nose-dived to the floor, peering at the carpet, and I believe I banged my head against that of Richard Rodney Bennett as on all fours we both looked behind the same chair. Some mined the seams of the various sofas, others took up cushions and shook them reprovingly, while Miss Rubber knelt down and removed Miss Davis's stilettos in case the little fellows had gone to ground in her footwear. As we crawled round the room, watched narrowly by Bette Davis as though she had by no means discounted the possibility that if we found them we might pocket them, a single thought was becoming clear to me. On no account was a certain question to be asked. No sooner had I come to this conclusion than I heard the words being uttered. 'Are you sure,' said my wife in a kindly way, 'that you put them on?' There was a deathly silence. Bette Davis made a noise like a gas-fire before it is lit. Her eyes took on the full bulge. She said, 'You think I'm too drunk to remember?'

The evening began to disintegrate. The Gorgon complained bitterly of journalists in general and the British variety in particular. She was married to a second-rank actor called Gary Merrill and over the soufflé she claimed it was blasphemy the way the hacks referred to him as 'Mr Davis'. What with being a British journalist myself I thought I'd better enter a plea in mitigation. 'Maybe you don't understand British humour,' I said indulgently. 'Not understand!' shrieked the harpy. Tut tut, Bob. Oh, really, come on, said the others, as the woman stamped her feet under the table and Miss Rubber gasped as she caught the full force on her toe. 'Well, I mean, British irony is something of an acquired taste.' Bette Davis went off like a police siren. 'If someone doesn't stop this man I'm leaving!' I saw the two young men pretending to be as solemn as undertaker's mutes, while loving every minute. 'You see,' I said, 'we like to make fun of our sacred cows.' 'Cows?' she screamed, rising abruptly and knocking her chair over backwards. 'Get me a cab!' 'Time for bed anyway,' murmured Miss Rubber, steering her to the door. As the great lady banged into the portico, Violet spun her round and pointed her in the right direction, then turned and said philosophically, 'She won't remember anything about it in the morning.'

But she did. Schlesinger said that ever afterwards she shunned him and though as the *grande dame* of Hollywood she was invited, she always refused invitations to retrospectives of his films or indeed anything with which his name was associated. Was there a hint of reproach in his voice as he told me? I held up my hand. 'Don't try and thank me,' I said. 'When I do a friend a favour, it's for life.'

There's another sort of encounter where those involved stand shoulder to shoulder, as at Rorke's Drift, each of them sharing the same degree of desperation or dread. My partner in one such episode was a famous playwright. Let me picture him to you. I see him looking characteristically sheepish, but at the same time truculent. He is smoking a little cigar as though expecting someone to tell him to put it out. He stands with his back to as many people as he can, edging round whenever there is a danger of anyone catching his eye. He has the air of having entered the room where the party is going on under some misapprehension – that it is a Green Shield stamp redemption centre, or the annual general meeting of a public company – and resents what he takes to be a deliberate attempt to make him feel uncomfortable. He has a thin mouth, small close-set eyes that look as though they have been brought to the surface of his red pear-shaped cheeks with the aid of a buttonhook, and there is a faint air of provocation about his wispy grey beard, as though he is daring anyone to say he'd no right to come on like Chekhov.

I brought him over a drink and he said, 'Did you ever marry that actress, Josée Richard?' 'Yes,' I said, 'more than twenty years ago.' He'd been in California, and I asked him if he'd seen Tony Richardson, our mutual friend. 'That shit!' he said, 'I borrowed his house and a guy in jeans walks in through the french windows and sits down. I give him a drink and it turns out he's the gardener. I mean, what sort of a place is it where people dress so you can't tell the gardener from a family friend?' He spoke very quietly, in a faintly sibilant West-Endy voice that actors were still using just after the war. I said, 'This should cheer you up. When that play of yours was about to go on at the Royal Court I sat on the end of Josée Richard's bed when she was having 'flu. As you remember, she was understudying the bitch part. No play takes more than ten minutes to read so I picked up the script and skipped through it. I shied it back at her and said "This will never run." Doesn't make me much of a Prince Monolulu, does it?' Osborne had a puff at his little cheroot. 'But you were right. It didn't run. It was over two years before *Look Back in Anger* took off.' A man from Hollywood came in and whinnied with pleasure at running into Osborne. Osborne purred back at him, as though the encounter had been balm to his wounded spirit. The man went elsewhere and Osborne said, 'What a shit!'

Neither on this occasion, nor on any other, did we speak of the episode in which our joint fear generated a true encounter. It began with a telephone call from a man called Rudolph Cartier. This was a BBC producer who specialised in spectacular television productions of operas, though the little screen seemed to me to be essentially at odds with the booming effects he favoured. He was to produce a half-hour play by Henry Livings, a three-hander, in which one man's calvary was to be laid open to the view in the form of a television panel game. He had two people in mind for the husband and wife. Would I be the Quiz Master? When he said I was a natural choice, I knew what he meant: a day or two before, at the Ashmolean in Oxford, a woman had fled from one of the echoing picture galleries, crying, 'It is the Quiz Master!' as though I were a hobgoblin in a fairy-story. I explained that I couldn't act, and he was candid enough to say he believed me. 'But,' he said, 'everyone knows you as a quiz master, so even if you forget the lines you can just make them up.' I asked him who the two real actors would be, and he said Jill Bennett and John Osborne. OK, I said, if they don't mind, I suppose it's all right by me. 'Oh and by the way,' he added, 'it's BBC 2 – the Wednesday Play – so we do it live.'

I spent the early part of the week reviewing films for the *Sunday Telegraph*, so we rehearsed from Wednesday on, in a bleak drill hall out by Islington. We made an odd trio. No doubt about it, Jill Bennett was a funny-looking woman, and prickly with it. Her head was frozen into a backward tilt, as though an icy response to

170

some appalling affront was permanently on the point of utterance. I think Osborne's silences annoyed her, and she gave him a lot of actressy chaff well stirred up with a noisy laugh. She said she did the driving when it was the chauffeur's day off – 'I drive like a *man*,' she said, tilting her head even further back, with one of those looks actresses do when they are letting the audience know they are fiercely independent. She pronounced the word man 'mahn', then upbraided Osborne for apparently having reservations about being rich enough to employ a chauffeur. 'It's your *right*! Your talent gives you the privilege. He is *grateful* to you.' Then with a spine-chilling cackle, 'You Chester Square poof!' Osborne just stayed quiet. I had a feeling he had something on his mind, and a suspicion that it was the same thing I had on mine.

Doing it live. We hadn't thought much about it at first. Or perhaps it was just we didn't talk about it. But as the fortnight or so in which we rehearsed wore on, the thing about it being live started to surface. 'Don't you think it would be much better if it were recorded?' Osborne said, as he fluffed his lines again. He had the burden of the play on his shoulders, there were an awful lot of words he had to remember. Oh my *God*, I said, much more efficient if they taped it – why does everyone get moralistic about *live*? Live news, yes, but a television play is something you *concoct*. Jill Bennett was the only real actor present and didn't care. 'You're just a slimy old lounge lizard,' she said to Osborne, when he forgot the words once more. Meanwhile, Cartier held firm to his Kirby's Flying Ballet bias, and when the hero played by Osborne was dredging up fears from the depths of his psyche, he remorselessly illustrated them – the character had only to mention how much he was frightened of being ill for Cartier to interpolate a whole Soldiers' Chorus in which the halt and the lame were seen limping about in some nightmare hospital. 'If they record that section,' Osborne said, 'why not all of it?'

But Captain Ferguson had forbidden this. There were moments when we thought Cartier, a kindly man, might relent – after all, Osborne just couldn't remember the words. But it was a tradition: the half-hour Wednesday Play on BBC2 must always be live. And it was. To the last minute, we had hoped for a reprieve – if the thing was recorded we could do it, stopping and starting as necessary, and the paralysing tension of the live transmission, together with Osborne's inability to remember the lines, would pass from us like a poisoned cup. But we knew in our hearts we were for it. I believe I spoke Mr

Livings' lines accurately for I was rigid with claustrophobic fright
and clung to what I had to do like a man hanging on to a cliff. My
bit was over when I gave my arm to Jill Bennett and led her off.
Then Osborne was on his own. They'd rigged up a blab-off line
beforehand which cut off the sound, and a prompter was kneeling
down behind the camera, pushing the button while he gave Osborne
the words. A huge relief to be out the other side and just watching.
But I felt like a man who had slipped away from the firing-squad
and left a comrade to face the bullets. Not a mention of our ordeal
was heard during the splendid dinner, funded by the licence-payers,
that we enjoyed afterwards. And it was only then that the concealed
ingredient, stunning in its perversity, was revealed.

'A great addition to the archives,' said the Head of Drama, 'an
essential record.' I said, 'You mean, you *taped* it?' 'Well naturally
you don't want a piece of acting by the author of *Look Back in Anger*
to vanish in a single live performance.' I looked at Osborne. He was
pouring himself a glass of wine. Maybe he hadn't heard.

★

Some people seem to be more evidently themselves than others,
and J.B. Priestley was one of them. I thought his essays were
as good as Orwell's, and probably better – there was the same
casual accuracy when it came to hitting a nail on the head, and
an additional something, a note peculiarly his own, that was to do
with loss: if your ear was not in tune with what was actually going on
inside the words you might think here was an old-fashioned literary
gent mourning the passing of kindlier times which he may only have
been imagining. But this wouldn't account for the reverberation that
stayed with you after you read the piece; if it was simply a whimsical
descant on the decay of kindness, humour, generosity, in a style that
had something in it of the belles lettres of an earlier day, why did
the reader feel something altogether more absolute was in question?
Why did he feel the subject in hand hardly accounted for the force of
the regret it seemed to release? Priestley himself often said 1910 was
his golden age, which vanished with his friends who were slaughtered
in the First World War; but the feeling of separation that invades
him transcends even as dark an event as this; it permeates his plays,
where the unrevised, flavourless dialogue, and the often stereotyped
characters are hurriedly scrambled together to act out a drama of
alienation in which the divided self reaches for the completeness

that for ever eludes it. It wasn't any particular loss, it was loss itself that Priestley was besieged by: loss as a condition of existence. The unknowable garden from which by being born we are exiled was the place he continuously invoked, and he rushed out each play as though he couldn't wait to find out if this time he'd managed to identify what he'd been deprived of.

I met him at a party at the *New Statesman* – I know the exact date because that night when I got home I made a note of the conversation. It was 18 April 1963, and the note went as follows:

Across the room, I watched my wife talking to Nancy Thomas, one of the producers on the TV arts programme *Monitor*. Priestley came up to them and stared at Josée. Nancy said This is Mrs Bob Robinson and he said Oh he's a clever young man. In fact I did what I do once in a very long time, I sent him a letter telling him I liked something he wrote. Josée came over to me and told me this. I cottoned on he'd taken a fancy to her. I walked across with her and thanked him for his letter (of course, I had already written to him in reply).

Harold Wilson, then Prime Minister, came up, and Priestley talked to him. Then the PM went away, and Priestley said to the handsome woman who was his wife Come on, Jacquetta, I'm tired of this party. We shook hands, and he said he wasn't tired of us. Then I went across the room to find Nicholas and Claire Tomalin, fellow journalists we'd agreed to dine with, and while I was seeking them out Mrs Priestley came back and asked Josée if we'd go to dinner with them. I found Tomalin and said could we excuse ourselves, and he jeered, thinking we'd thrown them over for something better.

We walked to the Savoy. Jacquetta seemed to be scratching herself. Then she said I think I'm losing my knickers. I said Haul 'em up. JB and Josée were walking in front, and Priestley was wearing one of those low-crowned broad-brimmed hats you thought went out with the Thirties. His hair stuck out at the back. In the restaurant, the first waiter didn't recognise him. 'Have you a reservation?' Priestley said No, and I thought, He's got something better. The *maitre d'* knew him, and made this plain. We went into the gents and Priestley said he liked my film programme – said it was like a cold douche. He was very polite for a man who had no reason to bother to be polite.

He had gout so he ordered wine for the rest of us and whisky for himself. He ate onion soup followed by roast beef, salad and baked potato. He said the soup came out of a tin, but he knew the tin, and it was a good one. I had oysters. He spoke about William Haley, once editor of *The Times*: he'd said he thought Haley had two glass eyes because the first time he met him he started by thinking he certainly had one, then got round the other side of him and thought Poor fellow, he's got two. He made the mistake of telling someone this and had never had a fair deal out of *The Times* since then. He said he would like to wear Nancy Thomas on his watch chain, if he had such a thing as a watch chain.

Jacquetta said C.P. Snow and his wife Pamela Hansford Johnson had stayed with them for the weekend, together with Iris Murdoch and her husband John Bayley. Snow had accused Iris of lacking 'magnanimity'. The next morning Bayley and Murdoch had started talking at breakfast about how the Government had built special atom-bomb shelters for the most eminent people in their respective categories, and immediately Hansford Johnson and Snow had darted famished glances at each other – were they on the list? Priestley said to Josée, Tell me, or perhaps you think it's impertinent, about your background. She said her father was a merchant. Priestley liked the word. He said of me Was he at Oxford too? She said The same time. He said Oh he looks much older than you. Josée spoke of the blandishments of television notoriety and said I hadn't a great appetite for it. He said No, I didn't think he would. Where were you born, he asked me. I said Liverpool. Ah, he said, the Midlands.

Priestley said Let me give you some advice, if you don't think it tedious. Give up *The Sunday Times* and write another book. He said *The Sunday Times* stuff was good enough, but it drained off the fuel for a larger engine. I agreed, but I was only being polite. Jacquetta said the lady who was Kingsley Martin's mistress would not marry him on the grounds that she wished to keep her feminine independence. But when Jacquetta needed a single man for the weekend, she had invited Kingsley Martin on his own, and she had never forgiven her. Priestley recalled that I'd interviewed him on *Panorama*: he didn't mention that I'd had the best of the argument – he'd been urging unilateral disarmament, but I'd pointed out that when two sides had the bomb it wasn't dropped, but when one side had it, it was. I didn't mention this, either.

Priestley said Max Reinhardt had not always been in the publishing business, he had once exported bicycles to the Levant until Ralph Richardson had said he should turn to books. Priestley said he was three years behind with his income tax and had no idea what his financial position was, and didn't mind. He would have replaced direct taxation with a luxury tax, and I thought OK for anyone who's already got the luxuries or doesn't want them. He said he didn't care where he lived, he could live in a hotel room and still write, but when an author bought a house he would think Why here, since he could live anywhere. He kept regular hours, he said, only an amateur relied on inspiration. When the bill came I said Mr Priestley, may I share this with you? And he said Not allowed. We went into the gents again and he said he was to be seventy the next day. You don't look it, I said. Look it, he said, I look twice as old. Always have done.

I came under his command, he recruited me, as though he wanted me to know something by knowing him. When I was a boy he was doing the talks on the wireless that made Churchill so envious. My father didn't like him, something to do with his Yorkshire voice and his socialist views. I don't remember listening to what he said, I think I assumed it was all part of the 'war effort' and the propaganda that went with it; I wasn't interested in the war which was simply the prevailing condition, indistinguishable from our suburban life and equally without flavour. I had never read *The Good Companions* because I was too busy with James Joyce and T.S. Eliot. Priestley told me he didn't feel he was a natural novelist, real novelists kept the story moving and he didn't think he was much good at this. But when I read *Bright Day* I found I had been carried into the magical dimension he was always reaching for on the stage, and I wasn't surprised to hear that Jung had written to him to say the family in the story, the charmed circle the narrator is so desperate to break into, was both a real family and a magic one.

Priestley looked like a man in a hardware shop profoundly dubious about selling you a pound of nails, but for a man who might have seemed so down-to-earth he was curiously elusive. It went further than his versatility as a writer, he could transform situations by transforming himself; he would borrow the prevailing circumstances and reissue them. He led us one morning after breakfast to the garden gate of his house in Warwickshire – a little gothic door let into the red-brick wall. He was smoking his pipe, and was wearing a dun-coloured dressing-gown with a long tassel. As he unlocked the door he intoned 'Thus far may I bring you, but the rules of my order forbid me venturing further.' When playing tennis he wore a yellow pullover which had no sleeves and might have been knitted by an aunt: it didn't render him invulnerable, but it took the game somewhere else, beyond the en tout cas, which is more than you expect of a pullover.

He could beguile. When someone was talking about cruises to the Greek islands that came with lectures and were very educational he nodded gravely, saying he supposed it kept them out of the public houses. A man introduced him to his enormous dog. Was it a wolfhound? No, before he got fat he used to be a racing greyhound. He had the speed, but he was clumsy. 'Just about sums me up,' Priestley said thoughtfully. He was strolling one afternoon across his lawn, and his wife and my wife walked either side of him, and he saw me at work with the little home movie camera and as they all three moved past the lens he spread his arms to embrace both of them and announced, 'Captain Priestley and his two trained sea-lions.' He had a great *tendresse* for my wife, and when she had our second child she said she felt really grown-up, now that she could start talking about 'the children'. Priestley wrote to me and said, 'Tell Jo by the time she's settled down to talking about "the children" some of us will still be drinking champagne out of her slipper in the last private rooms in Soho.'

His spirit was truly humorous, his ability to amuse involved all of him. For a man with such a good conceit of himself ('I'm not very fond of public speaking, but if anyone's going to do it, it might as well be me.') what struck me was his willingness to share the conversation – he liked to amuse, but I think almost he liked to *be* amused even better. Once I was telling him about something that had happened, half acting it out as one does, and part way through I realised the narrative had hypnotised him – his lips were moving to the words I spoke, and he was looking not at but through me and into the story, and then I saw that for him tale-telling was a sort of magic, and I recognised what I had glimpsed in the small *tableaux* I've described above: that he was himself a magus.

When we first stayed with them Priestley told us at breakfast what we should call them. 'She's Jacquetta and I'm JB. JB – it's a very good name for an author.' Kissing Tree was a fine white stucco house, the sort of place that would have been built in 1830 for a Birmingham merchant, standing in its thirty acres, and there from a bathroom window Jacquetta had shot a hare and Miss Puddock, housekeeper and chef, had it up to the dining-room for dinner, jugged and delicious. Gertrude waited at table, smiling a sideways Welsh smile, and Jacquetta looked to the wine. There were dry martinis before dinner and beer and whisky afterwards, for in that house – wide and spacious, where the guests had handsome suites to themselves – food and drink were not despised. There were picnics. Jacquetta drove us out – I think it was an MG saloon, but the next time we stayed it had been replaced by a Mercedes. 'What on earth are you doing with a Mercedes?' I asked Priestley. 'Pure swank,' he replied.

'Do you ever get angry?' he asked me. I told him that I shouted at the least thing, that I would excuse this to myself as the spontaneous response, but now I recognised it to be merely childish and violent; though could not control it. He said he didn't have rows, couldn't bear them, because of the remembrance of the shattering rages that seized his father. 'We'd just be setting off for our holidays and some little thing would go wrong and he'd sweep all the things off the mantelpiece.' I thought of the shouts of my own father, frantic with anger. Priestley spoke of one of his favourite places, Askrigg in Wensleydale, and I told him my dad took me there to fish when I was in my teens, and how we stayed at the Temperance Hotel run by Mr Lomax. Priestley looked at me over his pipe and said, 'I thought someone must have done the right thing by you.' His voice was unlike any other voice, and you felt it was your voice as well as his.

He was defensive about his work because at this time it was not in fashion. 'Men have grabbed hold of me to tell me that once, years ago, they read a novel of mine, giving me the impression they had pulled me out of a burning building.' A guest at dinner in my house said to Priestley, 'I did so enjoy *The Good Companions*,' and Priestley murmured, 'I have written other books, you know,' and the guest – awash with Beaujolais – cried, 'Just reel off a few titles, I'm sure I'll recognise one.' Priestley spoke of a play he was in negotiation with H.M. Tennant about, and another of my guests said 'Oh, if they turn you down, could *we* do it? Our amateur group is run by the vicar, but he's very go-ahead.' I never heard the reply because I was up and away on the pretext of finding more wine.

He could put his own foot in it. One evening he telephoned to ask if he and Jacquetta and a friend could drop in for a nightcap – they'd been dining in a restaurant locally. When they arrived, JB and I lingered while the ladies went upstairs. Good dinner, I asked? He launched into a spirited critique of the service, wine, food and general amenity. When we joined the ladies in the drawing-room I said cheerfully Well, it seems to have been a disaster, from what JB's just told me. At which Jacquetta said 'Oh, Jack,' in a mildly reproachful way. He hadn't been the host, the friend had.

He might have made an actor if he could have been bothered, for he had the capacity to characterise, to identify aspects of personality

in others and give them for the moment a new imagined reality –
he wasn't 'on' as actors are, it would be a fleeting phrase, a look;
a possibility hinted at, a momentary revelation that made you feel
– as a good actor makes you feel – here was something you'd
always known. But I think he felt acting was not much more than
a knack, and his own needs called for something beyond that. He
told me about the time he'd taken over the comic turn in *When
We Are Married* ('a drunken Yorkshire photographer. Just about
my mark.'). He thought Right, now I'll find out about the thrill
of acting. He thought the special satisfaction he assumed actors
enjoyed when they acted might come his way when he heard the
audience laugh, and they did laugh, uproariously, but he didn't feel
anything much. So he wondered if he was destined to experience the
genuine frisson when he heard them clap at the end and he took a
bow. And they did clap, because they'd enjoyed his performance,
but still he wasn't tickled in the right way. Could it be that the full
deep down sense of accomplishment only came to you at the supper
afterwards, or maybe when the reviews came out in the morning?
But nothing happened at all and Priestley concluded acting was like
having sexual intercourse, with no orgasm.

But for him, nothing was ever quite enough. What he lacked we
all lack, but he felt it as few people feel it. He lived (as he put it)
'by admiration, hope and love' and his watchword was ever 'Be
cheerful, sir.' But study his face. He broods. He was one of those
who come close to the mystery, and the closer he came, the deeper,
surely, his disappointment that he was unable to enter it. I recalled a
little concert some of us once arranged for his birthday, at the house
of John and Diana Collins, where the trio had played the Schubert
piece which echoes from the house that the narrator so longs to enter,
in *Bright Day*. Watching Priestley listen to the music was like seeing
one enchanter enter the dream of another. But now music, which
had been the love of his life, no longer gave him pleasure. And he
had stopped writing. In his last days, in his ninetieth year, he was
silent. There was no getting any closer, Time which was part of the
mystery had defeated him. He had magnetised attention, he had
charged the particles, he was a source of power. But the power that
is stronger than any, the power that is without shape or meaning,
simply fell across his strings. If it had been a play, it would have
seemed wanton.

MR GOVIER'S LAND

A SMALL LIGHT brown bull with a white nose, I called him Rupert, looked round, more or less at me, though he seemed vague. I was sitting on the wall at the end of our garden which divides us from the valley – since we don't own it, my wife calls it a borrowed view. Like a child's painting of hills it rolls away in greens and browns until it turns up to the horizon across which a road runs: from the little guest-room window my mother loved to watch the lights of motor cars moving across it at night. It was September and the sun shone sideways, picking out tiny flaws in the surfaces of paths and stone walls.

The cows who surrounded Rupert sometimes raised their heads from cropping the grass and looked at him. He was a small elegant bull, and as I gazed across the tussocks thinking I wished Bernard would sell me the field so I could own at least the foreground of the view, Rupert cocked a leg across the backside of one of the black cows, while at the same time staring into the blue haze of the distance, perhaps thinking how everything was present in a way that couldn't be distinguished from the way everything had always been present, while the cow whose attention he had not exactly seized gave a mournful low. Rupert's leg slid off, he had forgotten the leg was his, he had lost sight of anything the leg might have been the preliminary to, and he dropped his head once more into the dandelions.

Mr Govier came towards me across the grass. 'Do you like parsnips?' he asked. He had a plastic bag in his hands, which also contained carrots and potatoes. Mr Govier grew the vegetables in his intensively cultivated patch of garden behind his council bungalow across the lane, opposite our cottage. 'We'll need your ladder – Billy Butt's locked himself out.' Frank, who was Mr Govier's brother-in-law, fetched the ladders out of the shed and I followed Mr Govier through the garden gate into the lane.

179

Mrs Butt and her son Bill who run the village shop had been jaunting off to Lyme Regis, and the key had been left behind. Mr Govier and Frank were shouting at each other like Laurel and Hardy, trying to get the two ends of the ladders slotted together, and Mrs Butt was saying Shhh. They got the ladders up to the top window which was slightly open and I played the wise old bird who always spots what everyone else has missed, and sauntered off to get a walking-stick so Mr Butt could hook the latch up, returning with an easy air as though the walking-stick inspiration put me on a par with the family that discovered radium.

Bell who had driven by while all this was going on, drove back a few minutes later and stopped the car. 'I didn't get what I came for,' he confided. 'It's a box. It's in the church, and the church is locked.' I nodded and slightly wondered whether the box contained hymn books, but I was concentrating on Mr Butt who was deathly silent at the top of the ladder; he was working away with the walking-stick, but I knew Mr Govier despised hesitation and might very well be including Mr Butt in one of his favourite categories, which was that of old apple-woman. Mr Butt got the catch up and the window open and climbed in. Mrs Butt said how easy it would have been for a burglar, but I urged her to look on the bright side since the burglar would not have had the help of my ladders or of Frank or of Mr Govier. Bell, who had been looking abstractedly at the window said, or I suppose added: 'The box has got flapjacks in it. We just fancied one.'

Mr Govier did the garden. 'It occupies my mind,' he said. Sometimes Mr Govier and I would walk round the garden talking about things and having a drop of whisky. He'd tell me about this and that; Mr Govier wasn't much in the listening mode, he was more or less permanently tuned to transmit. I found this restful. 'Moozing thing was,' he said, speaking of a recent marriage in the village, 'they didn't want us to hang out no washing.' The father of the bride came round to tell the inhabitants of the bungalows what he expected of them. The ladies kept their thoughts to themselves, but Mr Govier tended to laugh. 'It did tickle I,' he said, shaking his head, for he liked to shake his head against the daftnesses of the world, and while he shook it he would walk left and right, back and forth, in quarter circles and half circles. 'Then they had a party. But they didn't invite I.' He laughed again.

Mr Govier didn't believe in medicine, he drank the green water left at the bottom of the pan when he'd been boiling vegetables. 'Doctor told mother, that'll do you more good than anything I can give you.' He didn't believe in chemical fertiliser – what he called 'the artificial'. But even when it came to horse manure he was choosy, and checked it out closely, even when it was given away free, since stable manure often had wood shavings in it. 'If anybody could get a bag of peat and spread it round,' he would say. He liked to get what he called the tumours in early, and the height of his praise for the garden was 'Tain't looking too bad.' He went to bed about nine o'clock in the evening, saying the doctor had told him 'An hour before twelve be better than two hours after.' And he rose early, about five. What he liked was to keep an eye on everything, but most of all on Laurel Cottage which is the name of our house. He was full of stories of tourists peeping over the gate at the garden, and some of them opening the gate and going in. I used to say 'It's a tribute to the way you keep it, Mr Govier.' He reported the conversations he had with these strangers, rebuking them for being nosy. 'Who be you?' he'd begin, to which the response was 'What do you mean?' for the exchange was cast in ritual form. 'You can't just walk into other people's gardens.' 'What do you mean?' 'This be private property.' 'Who be you?' 'Never you mind who I do be, who be you?'

Mr Govier was in demand by the ladies who lived either side of him, but if he had been to help one of them tie up a rose bush or change a plug he had to be off the premises before the other lady arrived for her morning cup of tea in case she got jealous of her friend having another friend. They too liked to keep an eye on everything and would say 'The Robinsons' phone be ringing, I expect he'll have to go back to London,' and Mr Govier would say 'Why don't you go over and ask him?' Mrs Govier had died a couple of years before and in his time of mourning Mr Govier told us he found our garden a retreat. He'd cut the grass and fork the beds, then sit on the bench in the sunshine and maybe drop off for five minutes. He wrote a poem and gave it to me:

> As I sit in my old armchair
> On the lawn of Laurel Cottage
> The sun shining, the flowers nodding
> In the wind and as I look out towards
> The hills and meadows and see the
> Sheep and cattle grazing
> I think to myself of an English
> Country garden. Thank God for Laurel
> Cottage. My dream.

The past was a place of grace to Mr Govier and he often spoke of it. 'My father gave me three things, a knife, a piece of string, and a shilling. See, you could cut, tie and buy. I went to work when I were twelve year old. Father thought I'd go to the tanneries, CWS, up Street, but I didn't appeal to that, so I got a job on a farm.

''Twere all horses. 'Twere better than a tractor, because all's you had with a tractor were the fumes, and with the horses you had someone to talk to. In the summer you'd go and harness up about half past two in the morning for to go on out about three to mow. We used to go with the weather. We'd look across at Tor Hill and if Tor Hill had his nightcap on well then we'd know that in three or four days 'twere going to rain.'

When our children were small they'd go to the flower show. Mr Every always won. The Rev Mr Colledge would dance waltzes with the village ladies. There was a fancy-dress display and Lucy went as a gypsy and Suzy went as the Knave of Hearts. Josée made the tabard and I stuck the hearts on. Suzy was three, and won ten pence but wouldn't leave the stage and kept bowing and blowing kisses to the audience. Nick went ferreting – 'frrtn' – with the Every boys. He was thwarted in his constant attempts to ride Farmer Gready's fat pig, for though the pig only seemed to amble he always ambled faster than Nick could jump on his back. This pig was called Sir, and his sty was called Sir's House. Nick watched them geld the other pigs. 'Loads of blood,' he said. I yelped, for I was a cockney.

At this time I borrowed a Merry Tiller from Farmer Mitchell and was ploughing up a derelict part of the garden where I meant to sow a second bit of lawn. It made me awfully bad-tempered and I was cursing as my mother-in-law brought out cups of tea; she thought I was uttering old rural saws, since she wouldn't admit to herself she knew what the words meant. I tilled the earth, then raked it, then got the seed, and scattered it, and when fourteen days later I came back there was a green haze shimmering above the chocolate earth and I rushed into the pub which was next door to the cottage and there was Farmer Mitchell, and I cried, 'It works, it works,' and Farmer Mitchell said, 'They do say the devil looks after his own.'

The pub was a quiet alehouse with about eight or nine regulars, village worthies who sat round the sides of the bar on settles and might easily have been smoking churchwarden pipes and wearing smocks. The first husband of the lady who ran it had skipped, leaving behind a large fish in the deep freeze, perhaps in lieu of explanation. After this it turned into a hell on earth conducted by a ruffian, and

the car park ran with blood and the night reverberated to the thump
of moog synthesisers played by yeti. 'Too loud, too loud,' I cried
one night as the electronic cyclone boomed through the village, and
I stormed out into the car park. 'Even if it was Beethoven it would be
too loud. Though I don't suppose you've ever heard of him!' 'Oh yes
I have,' said the ruffian, stung all the way through to his cross-garters,
'I'm not *that* dim.' The children hung out of the window, choking
with laughter at an exchange whose primitive quality matched that
of the forest sauvage, when men swung at each other with the bones
of mammoths.

We sat out the ruffian, and the pub then passed from one hapless
noodle to another, each time falling into the hands of someone who
had as much chance of making a pub succeed as of being appointed
Astronomer Royal. When the place finally went under all the people
who'd never crossed its threshold got up a petition to preserve it. 'A
village isn't a village without a pub,' said the lady from the big house
in Mrs Butt's shop one morning. 'Then you should have used it,' I
said. 'Goodness,' said the lady, 'I don't go into pubs.' 'Then you've
only yourself to blame,' I said sententiously, as though if she'd done
her share when it came to shifting pints of Foster's none of this would
ever have happened.

Mr Govier didn't support the pub because he reckoned the beer
too expensive. Also unwholesome.

'When father's brother gave him beer at the pub he had three pints
and he were drunk, but he'd drink a gallon of cider and be as right
as ninepence next day. Father used to have his cider from Green's
out at West Pinner, because they reckoned all around West Pinner
were the best country for cider fruit. Father used to have a six-gallon
barrel every fortnight, and then he did buy a truckle of cheese off
them as well.

'We used to carry our dinner on the farm, we'd have top and
bottom, pull the loaf apart, a lump of butter and a lump of cheese
and put it together and tie it up in a red handkerchief and you
were well away. You had cider, and an onion in winter. Sunday
mornings we'd go up the farm rabbiting, well then you could come
back and sell thik rabbit for a shilling. See, they what bought it
made threepence on the skin, and that meant they got a cheap meal.
Sundays mother she used to cook two saucepans of potatoes and
she had to cook it over a fire, there weren't no electric, we never
had electric. Monday were a fry-up, cause Monday were washing
day. "First home from school can turn the mangle and get a piece

of cake," mother'd say, so Monday it were always a rush to see who were home first.

'You mightn't believe this, we had to hand over all our money till we were twenty-one. I used to get half a crown a week pocket money, that were all right, I'd go up Somerton, up the White Hart and have a drink, from there up the fish and chip shop, and from there up the Assembly Rooms to the dance, and there were still sixpence to go to the pictures with Monday night, which were threepence to go in.'

Mr Govier seemed just to appear out of the immediate whereabouts and be there one morning at his front door. He wanted to mend the mower I was loading into the boot for Crewkerne Horticultural to look at. Mr Govier was a stranger, but I never felt he was, or ever had been. I felt we were grafted on to him, as though he were the rootstock of the place we had so carefully yet so spontaneously chosen.

We'd found it after shambling around the west and staying at pubs and looking at places; sometimes I went maundering off on my own when there was nothing better to do, for as my wife put it, 'If things go off the boil for five minutes you like to go out and buy something.' After I'd been blundering about the landscape for some time she said, 'Do you really want a house in the country or do you just like looking?' At that moment we were walking down the hill past the pub and saw the house. The grass in the garden was knee-high, you could have let the keep. We made tracks through it and sat under an apple tree. We got the key from the pub and went inside. It was a house that let the light in, it had flagstone floors, and any window you looked out of you could see lots of country.

I was almost sick with excitement and wanted to stuff the cash into the owner's pocket that same day. I couldn't bear the thought he might sell it before we got to him. Only twice before had such a childish passion for getting something taken me over so completely, and then I actually was a child: once when I wasn't certain the Daisy air-rifle with the chromium-plated barrel was going to be at the end of my bed on Christmas morning, and once when I was trying to get money out of my father (17/6) for a pair of chukka-boots with inch-thick crepe-rubber soles. It's a feeling you'll disappear if you don't get what you want, and it's uncontrollable, like a child screaming in a supermarket.

I'd seen the two houses in which I live long before I did live in them, seen them in a quite literal sense, I mean. But I didn't remember seeing them, I didn't remember the houses at all since at that time, of course, they meant nothing to me; what I remembered in each case was windows that had been lit when I'd gone past at night. These memories of lit windows were single images, quite discrete, devoid of any context, devoid of any significance, just pictures that would come up in my head, extempore; I assumed I must have seen them but didn't know where. But when I went into the rooms that lay behind them I recognised the windows, the shapes were unmistakeable, then I went outside and saw how the house fitted round them, just as in the picture in my head. It isn't much of a mystery, if I were making it up I could surely do a better job. But it's a fact, and slightly curious. The window in the country has mullions and a dripstone. I've seen lots of windows like it, but it was that particular one I saw, when I drove past on a night I don't remember. Both houses have been there a long time and that's a relief; old houses share out the responsibility, you aren't the only ones to have chosen them.

*

When I saw the window in Chelsea I must have been about nineteen. David Atfield and I would go to the Cross Keys in Lawrence Street, or to the King's Head and Eight Bells at the end of Cheyne Row, wondering if we'd see Augustus John, and if he wasn't there we were always hopeful the girls would give us a try instead. The pubs were crowded in those days and you got close to everyone and people made noisy conversation as though it were a form of improvised opera. While I was coming on as Harlequin to a Polish lady, David was crouching down on his hunkers in the crowded bar as though somewhat fatigued, keeping up a steady though not competitive recitative – decent man, I thought, to give me a clear field, not always something I could rely on him for. His uncharacteristic forbearance was in part due to the fact that while playing chorus to my tenor he had his hand round the nylon-clad ankle of a complete stranger behind him, a girl whose face he couldn't even see, and though he hadn't exchanged so much as a word with her when the pub closed it was the Polish lady who bade me a polite farewell, whereas David squired the ankle home to Putney. I lost sight of him for fully a fortnight. It may have been that night while I was sprinting up Cheyne Row towards the King's Road to catch a bus that I passed the window and it got mixed up with the feelings of laughter, romance and possibility which was the micro-climate I carried about with me in those days.

When we were going to get married Josée looked at me and said, 'We'll have nice times.' Then we thought about somewhere to live. Ken Pearson brought the property section of *The Sunday Times* into my office from the printer one Saturday morning while we were going through the proofs, and I thought I'd got a day's start on everyone. We went to Cheyne Row and stood on the doorstep of the house we'd picked out and a lady with a rather vague look opened the door. 'Oh dear, there's a queue for it already, actually.' When we went away, Josée said, 'She's got a collecting box for the Crusade of Rescue. She's a Catholic.' So we dropped her a line. Said we were getting married at the Church of the Holy Redeemer at the end of the road. She was still looking vague when we went back. 'It worked,' she said. 'Do you think it's immoral, letting you queue-jump?' 'Certainly not,' I said, and we've lived there ever since.

Charles Vyse the potter had a studio next door and when he fired his kiln Nick, our first baby, got Mr Vyse's smuts all over him as he slept in his pram in the garden. Mrs Ingrams who had let us have the house lived in the one next door, the other side. She was Richard Ingrams's mother and called him 'Ditch'. Josée asked her why. 'Oh,' said Victoria, 'he's *so* dirty.' Alphonso de Zuluetta was the parish priest. One day over the garden fence we heard him talking to Mrs Ingrams: 'I invited Dame Edith Sitwell to open the bazaar,' we heard him say, and then there was a pause. 'I asked her because of course they lived in Carlyle Square.' Another pause. 'She hasn't replied.' Pause. 'I didn't like to say travelling and expenses paid. I thought she'd be offended.' Pause. 'I'm *rather* afraid I may have addressed it to Dame Edith Evans.' Alphonso was somewhat bleak. He told me of a parishioner who collected pictures of the Archbishop of Canterbury. 'Only he sticks pins in them.' Pause. 'I shouldn't like anyone to think I was encouraging him.' When the tree on the other side of the road fell over and smashed all our front windows, the journalists from the evening papers showed up and Zu was there to fill them in on background. 'It was a Tree of Heaven,' he told them, then thinking this needed a little colour, and looking up the road to Carlyle's house, said, 'Planted by Carlyle.' Then, a bit shiftily, 'In person.' He told them Maurice Baring had lived in our house, and how Belloc would come over from Cheyne Walk with Chesterton. Though I may be suffering from false-memory syndrome when I hear him add, 'And they'd end the evening with a sing-song.' After the scribes had gone, Zu said, 'I hope they got all they wanted.' I said, 'You're not the man to send them away empty handed.'

The tree fell at six o'clock in the morning and we were all outside in our dressing-gowns when Tom Iremonger from No. 34 came round with a petition to stop them cutting down the rest of the trees. He handed it to me to sign, but I looked up at my shattered windows and said 'Maybe tomorrow, Tom.' The roof was undamaged, which was a mercy since the Cheyne Row children liked to prowl at roof level from one end of the street to the other, sometimes to peep at the young lady in the room over the mews getting dressed, or to throw the replica of a body down, when Matty Coles from No. 18 was making one of his films; a police-car screeched to a halt, thinking it was real, and Lucy aged twelve, actress and co-director, coaxed the coppers into doing it again so she could include them in the story.

The deeds of the house date back to 1709. The Row was built by two men, a bricklayer called Oliver Maddox and a carpenter called John Clarkson. They'd bought the land from William, Lord Cheyne, and it was a strip called The Pindle – it had been the bowling green and orchard attaching to a pub called The Three Tuns, on the corner of what is now Cheyne Walk and Cheyne Row. The planks of our floors at ground level came from the timbers of decommissioned ships lying at the end of the road in the Thames: they are broad, not all of the same width, and of a deep honey colour. When we had the surveyor look round the place he said the walls were twice as thick as they need be, and I told him why: Maddox and Clarkson were churchwardens at Chelsea Old Church, and living among the people who bought their houses, couldn't afford to skimp the work. Many a time I walk up the wide staircase that takes its slow easy rise through the house and remember it was old fashioned even on the day it was put in – balusters and bannisters and newel posts were held in store for years until there was a call for them, and our staircase was made up from stock that had come off the lathes in William and Mary's day. It's the southernmost house in the terrace and it bears a plaque: 'This is Cheyne Row, 1708'. But here's the conundrum: did Maddox cement the stone plaque into the first house he built, or the last?

Our house was originally numbered 1. But just because the first house up from The Three Tuns was numbered 1 it doesn't follow it was the first to be built. They might have started at the other end. The date on the first deed is 1709, but the Row is dated 1708. Why is the deed a year later than the house? Did Lord Cheyne provide the capital for Oliver Maddox as an investment, only signing over the land when the job was done and the bricklayer, having sold a few leases off-plan, could pay him back, plus interest? But can you put up a terrace of ten soundly built houses inside a year? Or perhaps two years if they began at the start of one year and were finished at the end of the next (but would they start building in the winter? Not ideal, cold and wet, but there was plenty of cheap labour in Queen Anne's day). And one more thing: builders in the eighteenth century sometimes kept the end house for themselves. But which end?

Oliver Maddox was the driving force. I'm guessing this because his name comes first in the deeds, and because bricklayers are the top craftsmen; John Clarkson as carpenter came second, his name in the deeds appears after the bricklayer even though alphabetically it should come first (no law stationer, engrossing the deed, would have overlooked this, unless there were reason). And there's evidence that the bricklayer brought the capital into the business because thirty years after the houses were built there is a lease granted to a fishmonger – 'ffishmonger', to be precise – called Broughton, and the owner of the lease is called Westerband, but his first name is Maddox – Maddox Westerband. Why does he carry Oliver's patronym as his given name? Theory: because Oliver's sister had married a chap called Westerband, and this sister prudently christened her first son Maddox after his uncle, since Oliver was childless – Maddox had expectations.

Some nights when I stand on the pavement and look up at the end of the house in the lamplight I find it easy to see the open land that lay either side of the Row and people strolling down the half-built street to take a wherry across to Battersea to buy lettuce from the market gardens. And when I climb up to bed I know Maddox Westerband looked out of the same back window I do, across the tops of the mulberry trees that still grow in the gardens that his uncle Oliver carved out of the orchard of The Three Tuns. To the south-east, beyond the Tudor wall of the Cheyne Row gardens, he'd see the house that once belonged to Thomas More's bailiff; I see the gable end of it, though Maddox's view of the river is gone. And if he turned his gaze thirty degrees to the right he would see, a quarter of a mile away, the tree tops and the long wall of the Physic Garden, with the river beyond it; he might think how convenient to have been willed a house that was so close to his work. For Maddox Westerband was an apothecary, as the deeds record.

But the little conundrum I start with is unsolved. Do you put a plaque on the first house, or on the last? In private life, bricklayers are as excitable as anyone else, but not while they're laying the bricks. Would Oliver have hastened to proclaim a Row that he had yet to build? Surely not. So our house was last? On the other hand, he might have wanted to make it clear the work had begun, that this was no longer a bit of green that customers from the pub were free to stroll about on and pick a few mulberries: 'This is Cheyne Row, 1708' – a building-site, trespassers will be prosecuted. So our house was first? One of the old mulberry trees grows in the garden next door-but-one, and the pigeons sit on the branches and feast on the fruit and then come across and drop great purple splats in our garden. But did this start at the beginning of 1708, or the end of 1709? Is pigeon shit good for the garden? And have we been blessed with one year more of it than anyone else, or one year less?

*

Mr Govier arrived in the village after our garden fence got into the *Sunday Mirror*. When they put up the four bungalows opposite they ran exactly the length of our garden, and afforded anyone living in them the best possible view of it. I thought a fence was in order so I could go on picking my nose in private. While it was going up someone told the Council. There followed a protracted exchange about whether our fence was to be allowed. A cunning reporter canvassed opinion among the elderly newcomers who had been marooned in the four bungalows, far from a bus service on a hill in the middle of nowhere. 'It's like the Berlin Wall,' one old lady was encouraged to say. 'It's ruined our view,' said another. Since three of the inhabitants of the bungalows were blind and the fourth was registered partially sighted, I thought I'd give the News Editor of the *Mirror* a laugh by telling him. He did laugh, but said, 'You're paying the price of fame, Mr Robinson.' I thanked him kindly for promoting our cottage to 'West Country manor house' and told him I'd send the chauffeur to meet him at the station when he arrived for the weekend with his matched Purdies. The rest of the village laughed too, and sent the Council scornful letters. It was but a common or garden fence, and was allowed to stay.

It smelt of creosote in the due season, and this scent of all others seemed to mark the passing of time. The grandmas and the aunts spent summers and Christmases with us, and the children climbed trees and went riding and messed about round the farm, then bought sweets at Mrs Butt's. 'Money burns holes in the Robinsons' pockets,' Mrs Butt said. Grandma Mary who was ninety fell ill, and we sent for Father O'Brien. When he turned up, I tried to tell him just to pretend he'd been passing and was looking in, but the good man simply laughed at my atheist sentimentality and read grandma the prayers for the dying, and heard her confession – what *could* she have found to tell him? – after which she was out of bed in no time and said she wouldn't be ready to go until she'd had her telegram from the Queen.

We walked among the wild daffs by the little stream, and the buttercups stained my wellies when I dropped over the wall at the end of the garden with my gun, and the pigeons flew up out of Mr Gready's copse as they saw me coming three fields away. Sometimes a faun would break cover in the dappled shade of the wood and leap away to vanish once again in the unchecked growth of trees and bramble. A brown fox with a black tail sat in the middle of the lane, then went through the hedge like a coloured handkerchief disappearing up a conjuror's sleeve. I turned a bend, and Nick and the Every boys were hanging in the branches of a tree chattering like starlings. These scenes were like pictures. Perhaps I turned them into pictures. But when Mr Govier came to the village he so much looked beyond and through such artifice that I felt he took me with him into what he knew and what was his by ancient entitlement. The past he spoke of seemed to be a past that was longer away than his own years would literally account for; he had access to something further off. There was something of Hobden in Kipling's fairy-stories about him, and as the owner of it all by ancient right, he gave the place to me, he made me free of it.

'One of my brothers went to work for Lotty Wall, he were in the quarry business, and they used to say When Lotty Wall's out of money the King's out of soldiers. And father used to haul for Lotty too, Tommy Wall's father, he used to haul stone in those days from Seymour's quarry, they used to dig out the lias stones in Street, and he'd haul it from Street to Bridgwater.

'My father, he were a horse man, and you ain't going to believe this, my brother went to Bridgwater fair and bought a pony, twenty-five shillings, brought un halfway back, got to Woolavington and got fed up with un playing tricks and tied un to a gate and came on back home. Father said Where's the pony, and he said if you want thik damned pony you go down and fetch him. So father had my sister's bike and rode down and fetched un back. And he were a good pony.

'Well then father went down Norman Bartlett's, that were in Street, he were a wheelwright, and saw this carriage and said I'll have ee for the pony. So Bartlett said all right Freddy, you can have him for fifteen pound, and father had un. You had to pay 17/6 a year for a licence for a carriage, see, and 7/6 for a trap, rubber tyred trap. We went down the moor one day and coming back we called in up the pub. We had to go in because father were deaf and couldn't hear.

'Then I were outside holding the pony and a chap came up in a big car, 'tweren't often you see cars like that round our way, and this chap said Who does that turn-out belong to? I said My father. Oh, he said, where is he? Just then father came out of the pub and this chap said Is this yours? And father held his hand behind his ear and said What d'ye say? And he said Is this yours, and father said Yes. I'll tell you what I'll do, young man, said the chap, I'll swap this car for your turn-out. Oh no you won't, sir, said father. Why ever not? Well, said father, 'tis like this. If I get drunk, the pony'll take me home. But that car – he 'on't.'

Mr Govier died suddenly one morning, and was found by Frank who'd been doing his paper round. He was on the floor, with Max the abandoned Labrador he'd taken in crouched against him. Max whimpers when Frank takes him into the churchyard to tend Mr Govier's grave, and backs away and sits in the grass. He knows Mr Govier is not there and feels he should be, and when I walk round our garden I feel the same. He was the genius of the place. 'I can't believe Mr Govier won't walk in through the gate any minute,' said Mr Carter who was mending one of the outside lights. I expect to see him beyond the little ruin at the end of the garden, his back turned towards me as he stoops over the primulas he always put in round the pear trees, and which lasted ever so long.

AUTHOR, AUTHOR

W<small>HEN I LAY</small> in bed with measles Dr Roberts would come round to prescribe the bitter medicine and my mother would tell him I got headaches from reading too much. As I lay there I thought it wasn't for her to make the diagnosis, since he probably already suspected a tumour on the brain. But all he said was, 'It's a good fault.' As a child I ate books, taking the bones back to the library the same day to get another helping, and it disturbed the librarian: I was her best customer, and customers are what you want, but she felt that the stamp, the one she shoved down to register the date in red ink on the lined slip, shouldn't be used twice on the same day for the same person, shouldn't be the instrument of a small boy's greed. She said, 'You're not supposed to read them so quickly.' I shovelled them down as I shovel down spaghetti.

So when Will Wyatt asked me to run *The Book Programme* on BBC2 I felt I'd come into my natural inheritance. For seven years thereafter I tried every way I knew to throw the books open and wave the viewers inside, but in the end I had to face it. Whatever you did with books on television – whether you got biographers to tell you about biography, novelists to tell you about novels, whether you took the books individually and set the critics on them, whether you visited literary sources in the form of geography or birthplace or shrine, you never really met the books, you only met the authors. This was not to be despised, since people who write books are interesting even when as individuals – and it often happens – they are dull: for as you listen to what they say you're wondering out of what odd crevice the fantasy escapes. But it's a consolation prize. There's only one thing you can do with a book, and that's read it. In America there's a TV channel where they put a camera on a book, and turn the page; the electronics make the act of reading seem acceptable.

But there's a nice touch of the black art in entering an author's work and trying to reconstitute him from within. Doing it that way round, you're making him up, just as he made himself up in writing what he wrote: you're doing fiction, in reverse. You arrive at a character rather than a person, but then the author *is* a character – the character of all the characters in everything he writes. This was my premise in a film I called *The Auden Landscapes*. My proposition was that the landscapes were a secondary incarnation of the man: you began with a limestone upland, from which you get a clear view of the rest of the topography. Lead mines and slagheaps lying derelict, gasholders standing like border castles beside by-pass roads that run out to Hindhead and beyond, past preparatory schools and ruined summerhouses. It is often August, tramlines glitter, brambles choke the orchards. There are signs of life – a Bristol bomber flying overhead, a pederastic Colonel eyeing the gardener's boy from the gun room window, a corpse in the reservoir – but the landscape itself is stirring. The landscape is like a giant in a fairy-tale who is about to stand up, the landscape has one inhabitant, itself. Auden is this territory, whose location is the poetry, whose geology is the words.

It's a dodgy business bringing other people to see what you see, especially when it's film making and all concerned are ever apt to confuse what's best with getting their own way. And I've never been a believer in the theory that conflict is creative: personally, I think a row is just a row. We cut and re-cut the film, and I think in the end the reservations of Anthony Rouse the executive producer, and Adam Low who directed the film, faded as at last we managed to kick over the bottle and the genie appeared. We had the depositions of bystanders such as Isherwood and Spender and Robert Medley, as well as the reminiscences of the man who was the schoolboy who had been in Iceland with Auden and MacNeice. And when they spoke I suspected they felt what I certainly felt, that though Auden *was* the landscapes, at the same time they were also an unvisited outpost of yourself, where –

> Altogether elsewhere, vast
> Herds of reindeer move across
> Miles and miles of golden moss,
> Silently, and very fast.

But in *Book Programme* terms, *The Auden Landscapes* was a special endeavour, and I usually came across authors more conventionally by turning up on their doorsteps and asking them questions. Some liked this more than others. Saul Bellow turned off the air conditioning, or let me say, did not turn it on; afterwards he said he didn't like the noise. But it was a hot day in Chicago, and though I wore an elegant light-weight suit, my face turned red and swelled, as I got closer to Bellow than I think he wished. For it was not 'Saul, you old bastard, I believe you're a bugger for a party,' an approach which might have paid dividends, but a knowledge of the work he produced which – I'm guessing – made him feel I had my fingers in his tripes: I knew too much. I think he found it close to intolerable to discuss the springs of his own work, and he put on a display of bewilderment when we'd finished, saying he'd thought we'd been visiting him for a general address on the state of literature. But there was a sheet of paper in his typewriter which showed how daily and continuously he produced material which was uniquely his own, and who would want him to talk about anything else? He asked me how old I was, and I felt he wasn't as pleased with the answer as he was hoping to be. We only used ten minutes of the interview, because he wouldn't let me in. But when we got home I was given a transcript – I'd asked him if he'd ever been back to his origins in Russia and he said he'd got as far as Warsaw and the tea-ceremonies and the wall-hangings were so like those he had heard about from his parents as typical of Russia that Warsaw was the end of his journey, he hadn't felt impelled to get further than Warsaw. This sounded strange, but nowhere near as strange as the transcript made it, for everywhere Bellow had used the word Warsaw the typist had it down as Walsall.

And on the subject of wall-hangings, nothing that Hammond Innes told me about his adventure stories was quite as gripping as his account of his appearance in an advertisement for wallpaper. I asked him where in his fine house in Suffolk they had done it, since the ad featured Mr Innes at his ease in an oak-beamed interior, complete with log fire, surrounded by his chosen decor: 'Very Hammond Innes, Very Sanderson', read the caption. 'Oh it wasn't here,' said the best-seller, who had a rather literal, slightly frozen delivery in ordinary conversation. No, he said, it had been a studio in Putney, fitted up to the advertiser's requirements. The log-burning stove they installed looked convincing but they couldn't get it to stay alight, and had been obliged to pump air into it from behind, through yellow plastic tubes. The effect of the draught caused a flurry of soot to descend on the storyteller as he sat bootfaced in front of the camera. This wouldn't do, so they hosed him down and tried again. The resulting picture was passed off as his own house.

This fiction seemed neither to amuse nor discomfit him, and the stony visage with which he told the story bore comparison with Buster Keaton. Later he said he had been born in one county but had moved to another. 'There must be a touch of the gypsy in me,' he said solemnly, though perhaps he intended to entertain.

Gypsies intervened as I travelled to Cologne to interview Heinrich Böll. Having scooped up a profile of Alberto Moravia en route (there was sometimes a touch of the hoover in the way *The Book Programme* swept its territory clean), Phil Speight the producer and I were lolling outside a cafe in Rome when we were approached by two gypsies carrying babies. They begged for alms, but we indicated No, and once you've said No you feel committed to it: maybe we thought we could reverse the literary vacuum cleaner we carried so that people who were unsuitable for interview could be blown away. But the gypsies stuck at it. So we did the same. The thing was – I think, the basic thing of it all – was that we knew we only had to do this once, the necessity of standing our ground wouldn't come our way again: next time we could say Yes. But to the two women it was a life, a *métier*, even a vocation. They were a damned nuisance, but what they were doing, they meant. And we were just spoilers, and in some important way I can't put my finger on, you aren't allowed to do this.

They went at last, but not before cursing us. So then we paid the bill and got into our hired car, and I think it's worth saying it was from Avis because, as you know, they try harder. But you can't blame them for not seeing the gypsy dimension, and the car went dead in the Piazza Navona. I laughed and Phil said Do you reckon this pays off the curse? We got to the airport and waited for our flight to Stuttgart, until we realised it was now fifteen minutes after the flight should have been called.

The lady at the desk said It left fifteen minutes ago. But, we said, there was no announcement. Then she laughed. No, there was no announcement, they must have forgotten. When we arrived at Stuttgart we couldn't land because of fog – a little unusual, the pilot told us, since it's the wrong time of year and it seems to be confined just to the airport. We got to Böll's flat in Cologne and shot three rolls of film. The cameraman set the focus and locked it on. When we got home one of the rolls of film was blurred. It was the *middle* roll – the lens had slipped out and slipped in again, all on its own. The neatest touch in this comprehensive display of gypsy magic was the way they managed to disable the gum on the labels you use to identify the cans of film. The gum lost its virtue, and the labels wouldn't stick.

Böll had the kindest most parental face of any writer I ever met, and it was no surprise to me that it was with the owner of this face that Solzhenitsyn sought sanctuary when he was turned out of Russia. What writers say about their work when the camera is turning is serious and to the point, but of course it is calculated, and you might feel you were closer to that obscure little vent which I mentioned earlier, the chink from which the fantasies emerge, when you are talking to them in between – the human being is closer to the surface. Böll said how relieved he was the builders had finished the inside lavatory at his cottage at long last, just before Solzhenitsyn arrived. You get round to these things, Böll said, and I think it was a mercy, Mr Solzhenitsyn wouldn't have minded the outside privy, he's not that sort of man, and it's a nice little spot with a heart-shaped motif in the door. But it wouldn't have been right – it's like the blotch on the carpet, you see it, no one else does, but Mr Solzhenitsyn, a world figure, a great artist – I was glad.

Böll said You have a guest in your house, but you don't know what time he likes to get up, you are going on tiptoe past the door of his room not sure what you should do. And he is lying awake in bed wondering what time he should rise to please his hosts, and so it was with us and Mr Solzhenitsyn, because this is what he told us afterwards, and what we told him. He is a very humorous man. He had been confined, in prison, and he told us what he had hankered for in all that time. A notebook and pencil, and a clean shirt, soft and nicely pressed.

So of course Heinrich Böll was pleased that he had provided his guest with just such a shirt on his arrival, and something to write on. I wondered if the face of Böll might not have seemed to Solzhenitsyn to be the face he'd been hoping to find, somewhere in the world, at long last. When I met Solzhenitsyn in London to talk to him about his novel *Lenin in Zürich* I was daunted by the thought of being with a man who was a writer and a hero as well – a hero who had not attained that status in a moment of valour, but over the years, resisting a systematic assault on his humanity that began afresh every morning when he woke up. I saw his thick black suit and his unprepossessing beard, and the way he kissed the hand of Miss Cyrilova who translated for us and I couldn't think how to get on terms with my own feelings about the man who I was in danger of treating like a public statue. When he came back from the lavatory he had a bead of moisture on his trouser leg, but it only seemed to emphasise how little I shared with him. When I said it they put it in Pseuds' Corner in *Private Eye*, and I suppose I was trying too hard.

All the authors I encountered were responsive to the questions I asked, but were not quite so much themselves as they were in between. R.D. Laing the psychiatrist was a gloomy fellow whose book *The Divided Self* was much admired. We took him to Zürich to meet Erich Fromm, the jolly Freudian who wrote so clearly about similar matters, and was so affable and fluent; we hoped he might get Laing to loosen up, because when I met him at the railway station in Zürich he seemed to be like a tap that had been turned off too tight. Good journey? I asked him, and it seemed a long time before he managed to get out the one word, 'Uneventful'. But though Fromm worked delicately and with great understanding, trying like a midwife to deliver Laing, the encounter was not fruitful. But Laing said something the night before that made the hair stand up on the back of my neck. Morose at dinner, he had muttered something about the unconscious. I said, 'You mean, we may have lost touch with it?' And Laing looked at me dubiously. 'Supposing,' he said, 'it's lost touch with us.'

Catching a glimpse of the private man is disconcerting, it isn't what you're there for, but it may be what you remember. When John Cheever, in his smart suburban house in the shadow of Sing Sing, holding a glass of cold tea instead of whisky, spoke of his brother and he having gone through a time when they'd been too close, Will Wyatt, who was producing, and I both went hot and cold: was Cheever talking of his brother in sexual terms? We could never decide, and the thought still hangs around, in all its uncomfortableness, undefused. But this was while they were loading the camera, for the interview itself is a branch of the Greek theatre, where both the interviewer and the interviewee are showing faces that are also masks; no one is on full view, anything that is said must be understood in terms of the ritual.

In Nabokov's case, more than ordinarily. I had to send him the questions a fortnight before, and he sent back his answers. Then when we met we each shoved the words into the situation, and it was like a practical demonstration of taxidermy: how to kill, skin and stuff an interview, then stick it on a wall like a moose's head. But his carefully crafted, Nabokovian responses were defter than his conversation. This had a sort of thud to it, and the heavy-footedness may have been accentuated by the way he continuously dragged the chat round to Lolita. He seemed to be importuning me for a response, wheedling me into an enquiry. 'There are journalists who think my feeling towards this character was rather more than that of a father towards a daughter,' he said roguishly. Bit crass of them, I thought – he wasn't going to tell anyone anyway. 'I wouldn't feel like asking you,' I said. 'Oh, I think *I* would,' he replied, 'I think *I* would.' Then he said, 'Do you think Lewis Carroll did anything with those little girls he photographed?' Then he added musingly, 'There was a lay in it somewhere, there was a lay in it somewhere.' Perhaps it was a game he was playing, some sort of tiger trap he was trying to entice me into so that my own coarseness might be irretrievably exposed in response to what seemed to be his own. But maybe I'm inventing the idea of such a stratagem to protect myself from a Nabokov I did not foresee; one wouldn't be easy with him, whoever he turned out to be, but some versions would be a little easier than others.

Some got away. With enormous delicacy we baited the hook for Patrick White, whose novels, written in their ugly irrefutable prose, stand in the Australian landscape like deformed monuments. White had never at that time been interviewed, he kept house with a Greek, his long time partner, and shaped a life in bad-tempered solitude. But our letter must have caught him in a good mood, because he wrote back as though actually entertaining the idea, and then he wrote again telling us June would be the best time to come out to Sydney, when it was nice and cool. We were cock-a-hoop, it looked as though we'd be the first to get to this strange man and produce him to the world. Not a chance. Shortly before the off we received a long rambling telegram. 'Must have been crazy to think of it. Daresay Robinson would have done as good a job as any, but don't want any job done. Don't want to be stuck up there to be perved on by everybody.' To be 'perved on' is Australian for being looked at, as part of someone's fantasy, usually sexual. White thought of himself as a freak, so didn't want to put himself on show, but I've sometimes wondered whether it isn't willingness to be on show that makes you the freak.

When Helen Gardner and John Betjeman met at our house their instant sympathy for each other generated the idea of a book which might have appealed to many. Both were fans of the 'Georgian' poets – the versifiers of the inter-war years whose soft lamplight was extinguished in Eliot's high beam ('Eliot spoke the still unspoken word; For gasworks and dried tubers I forsook The clock at

Grantchester, the English rook'). They talked about an anthology, and Helen wrote to Josée afterwards to say, 'I'm very tempted by John B's idea of us doing the Georgians. I think I am like him in being "singularly moved to love the lovely that are not beloved". But it's a difficult form to define.' Both were gone before they got so far.

It took me long enough to make up my mind to visit Betjeman after he had the stroke. 'Just go on up and read to him,' said Elizabeth Cavendish when I arrived at Radnor Walk. She was doing the dishes, someone had made his bed, and he was sitting in a chair in the corner of the bedroom. 'Must be dreadful to lose your speech when it's the thing that makes you who you are,' said Elizabeth in a matter of fact way which she must have used to other visitors, to let them off having to say something themselves. I'd brought *The Everyman Book Of Light Verse* of which I was editor, and told him it had just come out.

He sat, the expression on his face pleasant but fixed, quite unchanging. I read a few poems out of the book, some of his own, wondering whether he would like the familiar echoes or resent some chump barging in and making free with the stuff. I offered a sort of commentary, making it sound like a conversation, as one does, but wondering whether things he'd said to Josée and me over the years was anything he could put up with hearing again. I told him his own jokes in the Do you remember mode: as when he'd overheard a lady buttonholing T.S. Eliot and asking him, 'Do you pronounce your name Leon M. Lyon or Layon M. Lyon?', and someone else who always pronounced the word 'poetry' as 'poytry'. And when I read him a verse or two of 'How to Get On in Society', a smile appeared, but oh, from a long way away.

*

This was the company I kept in these times, both in my private life and as an interviewer of authors on television, and it was good company. 'Have you ever thought of writing a novel?' I asked Jorge Luis Borges, master of the brief, surreal short story. The Argentinian fabulist was eating the soup which his landlady had brought him for lunch. 'No,' he said, 'and I've never even thought of reading one, either.' But the authors didn't often say strange or amusing things, they gave little hint that they were any different from managers of DIY stores, yet my assumption always was that anyone would have liked to have seen Shelley plain. On television, I showed the authors to the readers, and I believe I was of service – no butler would be ashamed to put it on his CV. The authors appeared in a light that was in part generated by my own idiosyncrasy, but that aside, what I did had no claim to originality.

Then I thought of something that entitles me to a D.Phil. 'Why don't we be the chaps who finally solve the mystery of B. Traven?' I said to Will Wyatt. 'Be the first ones to find out who he really was.' It was a bit like saying let's track down the real Robin Hood. A lot of people had had a go at it and got nowhere, because the author of *The Treasure of the Sierra Madre* devoted himself to being invisible. He was so successful in this that people began to wonder if he was a real person at all, and his anonymity generated myths: that he was the last President of Mexico but three; that he was Jack London or Ambrose Bierce, that he wasn't one man but two, that he was a negro slave, an American millionaire, a German prince. They couldn't quite say he was Francis Bacon because a certain awkwardness of expression (a Traven trademark) and a moral intensity that's always close to the surface, probably restricts his imaginative range. He wrote a dozen novels and many short stories, tales that are fiercely provoked by the plight of the anonymous, the eternal victims of the political injustices of the world. There are classical resonances, for Traven draws on material that has haunted the work of European writers for centuries: *The Treasure of the Sierra Madre* is a reworking of *The Pardoner's Tale*, for which Chaucer looked to earlier Italian analogues, which themselves had surfaced in Europe from the Orient by the slow, endless osmosis by which stories travel the world; and in *The Death Ship* a man is doomed to stoke the boilers of a ship that is falling apart, unable to land because he has no papers, placeless and unidentified, going nowhere, like another Flying Dutchman. The theme of pursuit is so frowningly present in the work that it connects with the paranoia of an author who refused to be known. No publisher ever met Traven. In correspondence the author typed his signature. He prohibited any biographical detail: he would have liked his name left off the title page. Book jackets were to be blank. Was there a touch of PR to all this? Facelessness made him more real rather than less, and the legend helped to sell the books. Only the work was tangible, nothing else was known about it except that the envelopes containing the manuscripts bore Mexican postmarks.

So we went to Mexico. We called on John Huston who had made *The Treasure of the Sierra Madre* into a successful film with Humphrey Bogart. He was at his Mexican retreat in Puerta Viarta and had once been in no doubt that he had met Traven. 'He called himself Croves – Hal Croves – and he turned up in my bedroom one morning at my hotel in Mexico City with a note that purported to be from Traven saying Croves was his intimate friend and would tell me all I needed to know.' Croves hung around during the shooting of the film, a small skinny man in long baggy shorts. Huston decided at last that he couldn't be Traven – there was no trace in this little scarecrow figure of the obsessive assurance that marks Traven's work.

Then we called on Louis Spota, a Mexican journalist. Spota had decided as a young reporter that Traven was someone he was going to winkle out, and was tipped off that there was a deed-box in the local bank in the name of B. Traven Torsvan. What he found in the box led him to Acapulco, and a little tea-garden run by a lady called Martinez. She lived with a man called Berick Torsvan who Spota supposed was American. Spota, posing as a tourist became a regular customer, and Torsvan would sit and chat with him, even on one occasion telling about two men who killed each other with machetes in the south of Mexico. It was a story from a Traven book.

Returning to Mexico City, Spota searched government offices for the immigration card he was sure would be there. And he found it, in the name of Traven Torsvan, listing the man's birthplace as Chicago. Then bribing one of the clerks at the post office, he steamed open a letter that was going to Torsvan from a friend. He photocopied it and turned up at Torsvan's place and said to him 'You are B. Traven.' Torsvan said to him, 'You are the son of a bitch.' Spota printed the story in his magazine *Mañana* and won a prize for investigative reporting. The man Torsvan disappeared from the tea-garden in Acapulco and the man Croves turned up again in Mexico City, and anyone who looks at photographs of both of them sees they're the same person. But this doesn't make either of them Traven.

Croves married a lady called Rosa Elena Lujan, so we thought we'd go and see her. Yes indeed, said Mrs Croves, at her house in Calle Rio Mississippi in Mexico City, my husband Hal Croves was B. Traven. Well, that was interesting, but – was Traven his real name, where did he come from, what was his nationality, and why was he Croves? *Who was he*? Mrs Croves showed us a home movie, and there was her hubby, old and meek, and he didn't look like a fellow who might have been the hectoring Traven who wrote bullying letters to publishers telling them how he wanted his books to appear, and who told them that if a writer 'wasn't recognizable in his works, then either he is worth nothing or his works are worth nothing.'

But just because someone's wife says her husband was a famous writer, doesn't mean he wasn't. Mrs Croves had a tape recording of her husband. Now this should have told us something about the way the man spoke English, and thus it might have shed light on what his native language had been. But the tape was indistinct – a 'foreign' accent, but so blurry you could imagine the speaker planning ahead to baffle nosy parkers who would try and strip him of his mask after his death. Mrs Croves believed him to be American, but one day she looked over his shoulder as he was typing and saw the words were German. 'But I thought you told me, dear, that you didn't know any German,' and Croves went on typing in German without looking up and said 'I don't.' One thing Traven and Croves had in common was secretiveness: Croves insisted they give false names when they checked into hotels, and on one occasion his wife couldn't remember what name she had registered under and had difficulty getting back into their room.

What about the language in which the Traven stories were composed? We went to Bernard Smith who had been an editor at the publishing firm of Alfred Knopf. He remembered the day the English typescript of *The Death Ship* turned up on his desk. He assumed it to be a literal word-for-word translation of the original edition which was in German, for the sentence structures were German not English. Smith put the text into acceptable English, but when the book had first come out in Germany, even the German had been odd: a student of both Traven and the German language reported that in a stretch of forty pages he had found over two hundred barbarisms of style – once every second page there was a glaring error in simple German grammar.

Croves had first shown up in Mexico in 1925. The Indians of the jungle region of southern Mexico were Croves's particular interest, and his diaries (as Torsvan) record his travels there. Some of the best of the B. Traven stories are set in the same jungles – the Chiapas – and tell of the Indians as though the author were reworking their own folk myths. But if Croves was Traven, why did the Traven books dry up round about 1939? After all, Croves himself lived on for another thirty years. One further novel appeared later entitled *Aslan Norval*, but it was turned down by a number of publishers on the grounds that it didn't read like Traven. If Croves was Traven, why couldn't he write like Traven?

This is where Croves himself adds spin to the mystery: he often said that Traven (whose note to Huston had introduced Croves as a great friend) was not one man but two – one man had the experiences, and the other man wrote them down. So if the writing half of this collaboration had disappeared in 1939, it would explain why the remaining partner didn't know how to do it. But then Croves's widow produced a piece of evidence that co-opted a third man. She showed us a first edition of a novella called *An Das Fräulein von S . . . (To the Honourable Miss S . . .)*, published in Munich in 1916, and the author's name was Ret Marut.

Now Marut was a real, even historical figure, who had been part of the anarchist movement in Germany in the early 1900s. He'd edited an anarchist newsletter called *Der Ziegelbrenner (The Brick Maker)* and Mrs Croves had copies of these too. Marut fled the country as he was about to be shot, and that's why Croves told his wife on his death bed that she could now reveal that he had been both Traven and Marut – he was no longer at risk. All this sounds like second-rate fiction, but there in Mrs Croves's possession were the indisputable souvenirs of a previous life – the novella and *Der Ziegelbrenner*. And there was another item: when Croves died, German newspapers ran articles speculating that he might have been the old anarchist, Marut. Whereupon Marut's secretary, who was still alive, sent Mrs Croves a painting; she took us to see it, hanging in her husband's study. It is a portrait of Marut, but it is also a portrait of Croves.

The United States Freedom of Information Act now came to our assistance. Yes, there were documents on Marut in the files of the CIA, the FBI and the State Department. They showed that Marut had been in London in 1923 and 1924. And at the Home Office, following up the references found in the American files, we brought to light two hitherto unpublished photographs of Marut taken by the British police; he'd spent two months in Brixton prison for failing to register as an alien, before being deported on a Norwegian ship called the *Hegre*, bound for Tenerife, via Brixham. The pictures clinched it. The man who was Marut was also Croves. And as a grace note, we know from a document in the American consul's office that Marut worked his passage on the *Hegre* and the job he was given was that of fireman. The hero of *The Death Ship* by B. Traven was also a fireman, and the assonance is attractive.

So was the man Marut the man Traven? He was certainly Croves, but the evidence that he might have been the author of the B. Traven books was still tangential. And there is an internal crux, at this point. How could a man who did not arrive in Mexico until the middle of 1924 have absorbed sufficient of a strange milieu to have been able to complete the manuscript of *The Cotton Pickers* – an account of Traven's adventures among the poorly paid Mexican Indians – so that it arrived at his German publishers early in 1925?

Some Traven scholars believe an incomer would have found it impossible to have won the confidence of the Indians, and to have written a book so much imbued with the authentic feel of their lives, in the space of nine months or so. They think Croves may have been telling the truth when he said Traven was not one man but two: their hypothesis is that the first man – and a Swiss Traven reader has called him the *Erlebnisträger*, the bringer of the experience – was the original author of the B. Traven books, an American writing in English, and that Marut met him and recognising that the material would be welcomed by his own left-wing publishers in Germany, translated it.

The possibility of the other man haunts the Traven mystery, and personally I hoped it might be so – the *doppelgänger*, the shadow walker, stepping out from behind the puppet he had possessed, to claim his own. Alas for the romantic twist, no scrap of evidence exists. And to answer the question how a writer might convert a place and a people he had never before seen into imaginative fiction of great force, one has only to remind oneself that fiction is not a process of finding out, of research, it is a process of divination. And at the merely documentary level, Mrs Croves showed us the diaries kept by her husband when he was in the jungle, and they closely parallel the incidents in the Traven book.

What is it, to find out who a person is? In a purely scientific sense, it is to find out who his parents were. The aliases swarmed around us like gnats: Croves had (we discovered) been Ret Marut, he had been Fred Maruth, Rex Marhut, Richard Maurhut, and of course Torsvan and B. Traven Torsvan and Berick Torsvan, as well as B. Traven – for now we felt that if we identified Croves we would have identified Traven. We ran down every name to its source, and each time there was no collateral – there was no such address, no such name, no such record. We had one last name, one final place, to try. It was a name and place Marut had given the London police in 1923. A telegram went off to the place he claimed was the town of his birth. Back came a copy of his birth certificate! From the little town of Swiebodzin on the Polish–German border came the typewritten evidence: Hermann Albert Otto Maximilian Feige had been a real live human being, born in that town on 23 February 1882.

Had we done it? Feige existed, but it didn't mean he was Marut. Marut could have borrowed the identity. We looked again at the birth certificate. Marut had told the police the occupations of his father and his mother – his mother was a mill-worker, his father was a potter, and this was confirmed on the certificate. If he'd been an impostor, would he have known the occupations of the father and mother of some other person, forty years before? We looked again at the certificate. The mother's maiden name had been Weinecke. On the list of aliases used by Marut, preserved in the police files of 1923, the same name appears – Weinecke. Would an impostor have borrowed the maiden name of the mother of someone else?

And the man had said his mother was a mill-worker. In the record of births in the town hall at Swiebodzin her occupation was listed more generally as 'factory worker'. At the time of Feige's birth there existed only one place where a factory worker could get employment: there were no factories in Swiebodzin, there were only cloth mills. It was Marut himself who had specified 'mill' in his deposition to the police. Could an impostor have been so precise?

But there was a deeper, more internal chime. At the time of Feige's birth Swiebodzin had been Schweibus and a part of Germany, and so the town hall records were all in German. His father's occupation was listed as '*Cupfe*' – he was a potter. I thought of a potter as a man who made cups and bowls. Yes, said an elderly citizen of the place, who was telling us where the pottery had stood, but the word *Cupfe* indicated he made other things – tiles as well. And the pottery in Swiebodzin was attached to a brick works. I asked the man whether a tiler might also be thought of as a brick-maker. He nodded. Marut's father had been *Der Ziegelbrenner*.

Then we got very lucky. Feige had brothers and sisters, all named in the town hall records. Two of them – Ernst and Margarethe – had moved to Germany. They would now be eighty-three and eighty-six. It was a long shot that they would still be alive, but they would be the only two people in the world able directly to confirm what we had discovered. We found them in a tiny village in Lower Saxony and the portrait of Marut/Torsvan/Croves/Traven was touched in for us at first hand.

They called him self-willed and intelligent, but a strange boy who lived in a world of his own. He had no friends, he was a loner. He wanted to be a priest but the family couldn't afford to let him. He was apprenticed to a locksmith and then joined the army, and they never saw him again. He'd been a political activist from his earliest days, his room stacked with placards and leaflets, all preaching the socialist cause. And in 1922 the police had called at the Feige house, where his mother, fearful of the consequences, denied that he was her son. He wrote once – from London, as he was about to be deported.

The old people produced two photographs, one when he was fifteen years old, one when he was about twenty. It was Marut/Torsvan/Croves/Traven. We showed them photographs of the man in later years. Their recognition was the final endorsement. 'Yes,' said Margarethe, 'That's him.' We had found B. Traven.

Can I claim my D.Phil? At the time, I had no doubt. Here was an investigation of the facts which scrupulously excluded the circumstantial, and was founded on unassailable identification at every stage. It was not a hypothesis, dependent on internal textual evidence with all its ambiguities, though there was suggestive support from within – no wonder the German in which the books were written was odd, since the town of his birth was neither German nor Polish but a mixture of both: and the anomie which assails his heroes comes as no surprise from a man whose parents didn't marry until a year after his birth, and who was later sent from his mother's house to be brought up by grandparents. Here was a mystery solved – no loose ends, no weak link, a chain of events in immaculate sequence, marvellously complete.

Except for just one tiny thought. Torsvan was Croves was Marut was Feige was – but did anyone ever see him actually *writing* the Traven books? Well, you might say, who saw Wordsworth in the act of composition, who saw C.P. Snow? But these writers do not conceal their authorship, there is no scope for doubt: their claim to be who they were is unchallenged. All his friends in Mexico City were convinced Croves was Traven, they knew they must never mention this to him, for he would fly into a rage and leave the room; as one of them said 'Why would he act in this elaborate manner unless what he objected to was true?' But Croves claimed *not* to be Traven. Spota's story establishes Torsvan was also B. Traven Torsvan – and Torsvan told him a story that turned out to be in a B. Traven collection. Then there were the diaries in the possession of Mrs Croves, detailing Croves's time in the Mexican jungle when he called himself Torsvan, and the details match the details in Traven's Indian stories, *The Land of Spring* and *The Cotton Pickers* and *The Bridge in the Jungle*.

But even so, but even then. We have shown that Croves was Torsvan and Marut and Feige. We have photographs of all of them and they are the same man. But we have no photograph of Traven. Have we *quite* shown – beyond dispute, on first-hand evidence – that Feige was Traven? I asked Will Wyatt. He thought awhile. Then he said, 'How can you have a photograph of someone who didn't exist?' I liked this reply. On the basis of it I began thinking the terms of the equation are the givens – and they equal the unknown, the x. But I had to stop there. There is no equation – the terms are all on one side. The value or identity of x is still unknown, in any mathematical or purely factual sense, because there is no opposite side of the equation to shake it out of.

The ghost of the *Erlebnisträger* still walks.

RITUALS

A MAN KEPT COMING round to my house like a policeman trying to get a confession. 'If you don't do it,' he said, 'you're a cissy.' A week or two would pass and he'd be on the doorstep again. 'If you turn this down you'll never be able to face yourself in the shaving mirror.' Sometimes he'd vary the approach and say, 'Mind you, the DG's not keen. He thinks you're a Maoist.' But mostly he went for the jugular and implied I lived the life of a wastrel and he was offering me a chance to reclaim myself.

It was perfectly true that nothing I'd ever done as a journalist or broadcaster had been of the slightest practical use to anyone. I simply told people what I thought. The essential services – current affairs – were supplied by others, and I suppose I classed them with men who turned the gas, water or electricity on and off in the street: indispensable, but anyone could do it.

I lived on my wits. This phrase, with its hint of unwholesomeness, appealed to me (though it brought me low at Dulles airport. The plane for London was delayed and people were belabouring the man behind the BA desk. One American complained stridently of a chickenshit airline, which was no more than the truth, but his bullying way with the man in the uniform was irksome. After a bit I said, 'He can do nothing. Why don't you leave him alone?' The American was a dead ringer for the ferrety lawyer whose alopecia and two-day stubble suggest a loser, until by the time they change the reel you realise he's an update on the stereotype and is really the hero. I hadn't spotted this, and maybe the rolled umbrella I was carrying, the camel-hair coat and the Borsalino hat made me think I had the George Sanders part. When I spoke, he gave me an appraising glance. Was I above or below the title? 'And what do you do?' he asked. What would George's line have been? Nonchalantly I replied. 'I live on my wits.' His pause was immaculately timed. 'And *is* that a living?', he asked).

Anyway, as a phrase it was a bit fancy: maybe Patrick Campbell came closer when he said being on the telly was showing-off for money. 'Listen,' I said to the man from the press-gang, 'I've got enough to do. Why should I bother?' But as I said it a line from a profile a man had done about me in the *New Statesman* came into my head – he'd listed me as presenter of *Ask the Family* and *The Book Programme* and *Call My Bluff* and *Points of View* and *The Fifties* and *Vital Statistics*, and he'd added, 'You don't have six programmes running at the same time unless, deep down, you're yearning for a seventh.' I was being threatened with community service, but if I did it, vanity would be playing its part as usual.

The arm twister wanted me to get up in the middle of the night and present the *Today* programme. I was to replace Jack de Manio, a figure left over from the BBC's waxwork era, when a plummy voice and a double-breasted blazer passed muster; he did the *Today* programme in a style that recalled the ice-and-slice end of a pub in Surrey – you felt that for Jack it was always the weekend. He had just been named Radio Personality of the Year by a group of shopkeepers who sold thirteen-amp plugs – the Radio Industries Club – and of course had been fired; their prize had a touch of the mummy's curse about it, for the previous year's winner Kenneth Horne had died of a seizure, while John Dunn, a mild and inoffensive disc-jockey, brought the trophy – a sort of brass frankfurter – back to the office to find the High Command had deprived him of the programme he'd won it for.

A nagging suspicion that I'd never done anything that I could offer as proof that I was grown-up, and a feeling that those who ran the media thought grown-up meant asking questions of politicians, decided me to give it a try; it would be a form of graduation. I'd never heard the *Today* programme because I'd always been in bed, though I was bashful about telling anyone this, and as I drove out into the dark roads that lay between Chelsea and Portland Place round about ten to five that first morning I felt a bit peculiar. People were still in bed, and they'd be deep in their own domestic otherness when I pulled the cosies off the microphones and started doing it to them. I'd be entering bedrooms and bathrooms and kitchens I didn't know, sneaking in between the lavatory paper and the shaving foam and pushing my mouth up against the ear of strangers. Driving in, and going pretty slowly so I shouldn't encounter the reality a moment before I had to, I stirred up such an image of an intruder on the order of the dark figure in M.R. James's 'The Mezzotint' that the first person I thought I saw flitting about the small chilly studio was Captain Ferguson. As the microphone came live and I told the world we were open for business my voice shook like an aspen leaf. But the shape I'd seen was only the studio manager who had been filling the water jug, and by the time my first interviewee was sitting on the other side of the green baize table, hands folded piously in his lap, it occurred to me that no one at home was going to notice me, and that though I'd dumped myself unasked into their early morning privacy I would be as unregarded as the egg cup and the half-fat milk.

This cheered me up enormously, as did the realisation that I was up and about and cutting mustard when the rest of the world had yet to start. One jump ahead of everyone, an energising thought, and sometimes in the early hours as Timpson and I sat across the room from each other, scowling at our typewriters, I'd look up and catch his eye, and I knew he thought the same. We jogged along as a duo, sour as lemons when we arrived in the office, grumbling that the stuff the overnight shift had prepared for us was threadbare, and the overnight shift nodded smugly for it knew its responsibilities were over and it would soon be tucked up in bed, a sanctuary from which we had been untimely ripped. No wonder they called us the Brothers Grim.

A paper knife for the mail, for there was always too much of it for just a thumb. As a presenter, I subdued myself to the business in hand: the news was part of the early morning, and not getting in the way when you were mediating it was the overriding obligation – the style you use has to fit the function. But it doesn't mean you have to use anyone else's style, and if you're suited to the job at all your best chance of getting it right is to do it in your own voice. These letters I opened came from people who wrote as if they'd caught a cadence that took their fancy, they wrote endorsing an idiom they hadn't been expecting: as though some familiar source sounded slightly different. So our listeners joined in and Timpson and I used their letters to fill the odd empty seconds; used them sparingly, I hope, for banter steams up the lens if it goes on even a fraction of a second too long.

The paper knife, and then my appliance. It sounds like a truss, and in a funny way it did hold me together, for along with the knife I invested it with a beneficent power beyond its function, cried aloud for it in the dark mornin ˜˟ I might for a talisman or amulet to take me unharmed through ˬ ˸ shabby corridors to the biscuit-box studio and out again. It was a little plug to stick into the socket in the table in the studio, attached to an ear-piece by means of a thin wire that looked like the sort of thread you use in embroidery. It was for interviews with people who were too far away to come in, or politicians who had learned the trick of getting the radio-car to come round to their houses so they could walk to the front gate and do the interview in their dressing-gowns, then go back to bed.

I thought interviewing politicians would be like interviewing anyone else, but it wasn't, since politicians are prevaricatory and evasive. Favourite openings by a Minister of the Crown when asked a plain question were 'What we've said –' or perhaps 'We've made it quite plain –' or possibly 'I've said very clearly –' followed by rambling evasions. They replaced answers which would be readily understood, such as 'We haven't made up our minds' or 'We're going to wait and see how things turn out' or 'I'm not going to tell you' or even 'I don't know'. I used to wonder why it didn't occur to any of them to try the truth, once in a way – how it would attract attention! Of course, politicians can't always tell the truth, because you sometimes need to be covert in the world of affairs – you don't hand over your plans to the enemy. But this habit steadily encroaches until everyone seems to be the enemy, and you find you are only telling the truth when it coincides with your interests; then of course it's only incidentally the truth.

As I sat in the *Today* studio listening to a fatheaded MP assuring me from unfathomable wells of sincerity that it was every citizen's duty to round up stray dogs – 'But how,' I cried wildly, 'how do we distinguish the stray from the unstray? Do we lasso them? Is it done with butterfly nets?' – or interviewed a logrolling woman who presented herself regularly, being chairman of a political society of which she was the sole member, I began to devise a new politics. Its basic principle would be simple: that a desire for the job would automatically disqualify you for it.

Thereafter citizens would be deputed for parliament just as they are for jury service, by lot. The six hundred thus randomly selected would assemble in the House of Commons and bingo cards would be handed out. Black Rod would be the caller, and there would be two winners. Each would then step forward. A coin would be flipped – by the Queen, of course, who might enjoy the little ceremony – and though there could be some seemly diffidence on the part of the two winners ('You call', 'No, no, I insist') one of them would do it, and thus Government and Opposition would be instituted. The captains would then choose their men as men are always chosen – because the chooser likes the look of them. The offices of state would be matched to names at random from the computer, and every man of the six hundred would vote as he pleased. A five-year term to be adhered to, and those pressed to serve would be consoled for being snatched away from their ordinary avocations, for the remuneration would be handsome and the experience a novelty.

I constantly mulled this over while listening to Ray Buckton telling me his lads were very, very angry and William Whitelaw sternly insisting that he didn't want anyone going round stirring up apathy. My ruminations were only interrupted on those rare occasions when a human being strayed into the studio – it might sometimes be my old friend Shirley Williams (Shirley Catlin from Oxford days) who when the Labour Party lost an election actually admitted that to be the case, or the engaging Lord Carrington who seemed to be the only politician to speak in public as I imagined him speaking in private. He had in those days been given the thankless task of getting the horse-trader Dom Mintoff to do something he didn't want to do, and each morning I'd be on the line to Malta: 'Still there, Lord Carrington?' and he'd say, 'No time off for good behaviour, I'm afraid.' 'Well,' I'd tell him, 'so long as you're there I know I'm here, and the world is the way I left it yesterday,' and he'd say, 'Got to keep trying,' and I'd say, 'No doubt about that.' He was the last politician to resign when he need not have done, about something he deemed to be a matter of honour. No wonder he is not forgotten.

Sometimes the overnight shift grew desperate towards dawn, and items of a spectacular irrelevance would appear on the menu: we had two and a half minutes from a nightwatchman who had fallen into the hole he'd been watching. 'You've stood guard over many holes,' said the reporter, who got A for effort. 'Oh yes,' said the nightwatchman. 'I have.' 'And this time you fell in.' 'Yes,' said the nightwatchman, 'I did.' And once – and I think it was the same poor fellow who'd copped the hole in the road – we got a full minute and a half from a lady whose knickers had fallen off in Selfridge's. At the end of this item I heard myself saying to the listeners, 'If that's news, on what principle is anything ever left out?' It may have been my tendency to say things out loud that Trethowan, the DG, identified as Maoist: he was a simple-minded man who looked like a Labrador, a political journalist by trade who had run a fifteen-minute filler about parliament in the late evening on the telly. How he ever got the top job seems more of a mystery than such things generally do.

He had a head of protocol, an elderly party called Arthur, and they would exchange memos about me as though they were two maiden aunts deprecating the behaviour of a wilful nephew. These they copied to the editor of *Today*, who showed them to me for my amusement. Not once did this excellent man ever tell me to keep the information confidential – a display of real grown-upness unique in my experience of *apparatchiks*: he was Marshall Stewart, the admonitory presence who had haunted my doorstep until, like Marley's ghost, he had caused me to change my ways.

Or if not change them, amend them so that while I continued the usual round, I did it as a soldier on jankers does it, with a full pack – after the *Today* programme closed down round about nine in the morning, I was free to go out to work.

I might slide over to the British Museum newspaper library at Colindale to dig out stuff for *The Fifties*, a weekly tot of nostalgia-and-bitters for BBC1, or if it was the end of the week, I'd be at the Television Centre for *Ask the Family*, 'a quiz show for clever accountants and their wives,' as Julian Critchley, assiduous as ever in his masquerade as a grandee, remarked snootily in *The Times*. Thursdays – for I did a four-day week with *Today* – I'd nip up to Manchester, arriving at the Piccadilly hotel with barely strength enough to toy with a dozen oysters and the tiniest tankard of champagne – 'You must look after yourself, sair,' said the waiter solicitously, as though administering beef tea to St Sebastian – prior to arriving at the converted Methodist chapel in Dickinson Road to record four instalments of *Call My Bluff*.

It kept me off the street corners. Some mornings I'd come back and have a snooze, but I never got the sleeping right. Getting up so early, I arranged to go to bed at nine in the evening and would leave dinner-parties after the drinks and before the actual food was served. This is the sort of behaviour hostesses pretend to be amused by, but aren't. So I started going to bed at any old time and kidding myself it was nine o'clock. No pattern developed. I was awake on and off all through the night wondering how much longer I'd got left. The alarm call was never allowed to go off, since I was wide awake by then and always took the phone off before it rang. Except once. I came awake with a start, saw the clock. Good God, it was six-thirty! I'd missed the show. I rang the duty editor. 'What can I say? How can I apologise?' 'What do you mean?' he asked. 'The time – I missed the alarm. It's six-thirty!' There was a small silence from his end of the phone, then he said 'Six-thirty. But in the evening.' I looked at the light slanting through the windows – I'd slept the afternoon away. 'I think it's getting to me, Mike,' I said, and put the phone down.

There were pleasures incidental to the *Today* routine: Branca the lovely Yugoslav lady who brought the tea had a figure on the order of Raquel Welch and was in fact a geologist. There wasn't much doing on the geology front so she filled in by pushing a trolley. She would plump herself down in my lap of a morning, and as we exchanged compliments Timpson would look up and say, rather bleakly, 'And I thought I had a strong stomach.' Branca had a friend, a girl who worked for *Who's Who*, and one morning as she held the tea cup to my lips Branca told me that while waiting in her chum's office she'd seen my name on a list due for inclusion in that year's volume. I wouldn't be a bit surprised if I'd been on the Reserves list, and the loyal Branca hadn't transferred me to the actual Players when her friend's back was turned.

Gloria cleaned. She used one of those day-glo dusters on the end of a stick, flicked it across the dandruffy typewriters and saucers of fag-ash. Her voice was gravelly, her laugh creaked like a swing in a playground. 'Gloria, you dusky enchantress,' Denis Frost would cry, and she would ask, 'Are you Agriculture correspondent, Religious Affairs correspondent or Court correspondent this morning, Mr Frost?' for his prodigious energies took many forms. The damn thing being done with for the day, a convalescent hilarity would grip us all and in the mild hysteria I'd sometimes deliver spontaneous monologues on anything at all or nothing in particular, for that's the way the post-coital surrender took me. And the others, in their cheerful lassitude, the fever having abated, were content to listen. During one such flight Gloria, her fluffy tickling stick tucked under her arm, her chin on her hands as she leaned on her elbows across a desk, waited until I had hit the last high C. Then she asked, 'Mr Robinson, you been drinking?'

We clubbed up for a racehorse and it raced under my name, bearing the programme's colours – toast and marmalade. It was no bigger than a good-sized alsatian, and didn't like corners, trying to gallop straight on as the jockey wrenched it into the bends, as though it wanted to reach the stands before someone ate its sandwiches. I was so overcome with excitement the one time it came second I couldn't get my breath as Timpson and I were up in the box doing the commentary. It never liked the fifth furlong, so we sold him to Hong Kong where they run races over four.

I was slagged off by Jean Rook, 'The First Lady of Fleet Street', only the article got such a negative response they had to print another, under the reluctant headline 'Smirking Killjoy Makes Good'. The *Sun* ran a competition to find out how much people disliked me: 'He sneers at everything, politics, religion, war, peace, even the grass growing in the fields if he gets the chance . . . Write to *Sneer*, the *Sun*.' So they did, and I joined them, dropping them a line and saying they didn't know the half of it, signing it with my mother-in-law's name. But so many people thought so well of me the *Sun* had to tuck the result away in a small box down-page. Even Arthur, the DG's dusty chief of staff, seemed to be coming round. Trethowan had sent him a testy note, clucking about my saying that MPs have longer holidays than anyone else and only turn up half-day when they're actually working. 'Such ignorance,' noted Trethowan, who had the lobby-correspondent's natural deference to politicians. Arthur snuffled back. 'I think it may have been deliberate contrariness. Part of his alleged "charm"!'

Things go wrong in funny ways. Timpson and I sat at the green baize and it was his turn to speak. The item concerned a man who was going back to Africa to solve a family mystery. Timpson hadn't quite decided what note to strike. He opted for the solemn. 'He is going back to Africa,' said Timpson, 'to find the lion that ate his grandfather.' I put my head on the table and my hands on my head and though it was silent laughter I couldn't control it.

And then things go wrong in uncomfortable ways. New Year's Eve, and it was Man of the Year time. One of the editors telephoned Lord Longford. Would he come along to hear me say his anti-pornography crusade was the lost cause of the year, and at the same time dub him sportsman of the year for turning up to talk about it? To these terms he amiably agreed. He arrived, sat down at the microphone and, after I'd made my point, it was as though a button had been pressed, and he began to foam at the mouth.

He said he was 'shocked' and 'revolted' by what I had said and that I had no right to editorialise. Shocked? He'd been told days before what I was going to say. I looked at him in amazement, which was all I could do since he was raging incoherently like a man having a row in his own kitchen – had there been any plates I daresay he'd have thrown them. I couldn't contain him, the man was coming down round me like shrapnel, and I caught the horrified gaze of the people behind the glass – guests had been invited, for it was supposed to be something of a party; but even as the storm raged I thought I caught a hint of some secondary emotion hovering like an aura over the assembled company – something was going badly wrong, but wasn't there a measure of satisfaction in watching a smartarse sitting in the middle of it, unable to do a thing?

Longford apologised. Publicly, of course. 'I am writing a note to Mr Robinson to apologise. I was too rude and I am very sorry,' he told the journos who doorstepped him next morning. I liked the 'too rude'. The touch of a master.

And then things go wrong, and it matters. There were special rules at the height of the violence in Northern Ireland – never written down, of course, they never are, for if you leave people to guess what they mustn't say you have the most effective censorship of all. The news had just broken: a committee had found that the authorities in Ulster had not used torture when they made IRA prisoners lean on their hands against walls for hours together, their heads encased in dustbin bags, and with white sound playing continuously – it was just something called sensory deprivation. 'Truly the barbarians are among us,' I wrote in my introduction to the item. '1984 is at hand and Newspeak is upon us. Torture is a word that from this morning is no longer acceptable usage, it has been replaced by the officially approved phrase "sensory deprivation". We remember that Orwell warned us – those who wish to distort reality first distort the language.'

I gave the sheet to the typist to be incorporated into the script. The editor of the day picked it up and read it. 'You can't broadcast this,' he said. I looked at him. 'Then I'll quit.' 'Do what you like after the show,' he said, 'but you can't broadcast this.' There was no chance of me being able to say the words, he would have pulled the plug and gone to the next item. So as soon as the programme was over I banged into the office of the Controller of Radio 4 where the first thing I didn't do was resign.

Tony Whitby who was the Controller was a clever sensible man and what he said was that had *he* been the duty editor we could have devised an introduction that would have suited both of us. This was such a seductive formula – and he was an honest caring man – that I began to reflect: supposing my words *were* in some way subversive of endeavours to bring order to the situation in Northern Ireland, supposing their effect were in some way to promote the violence we were trying to contain? I didn't want to hand out propaganda to be used by a bunch of murdering thugs who killed at random; I had good personal reason not to, since an anonymous caller had rung the office to say the IRA had a contract out on me because of something uncomplimentary I'd said about Edward Kennedy, and a copper kept the house under surveillance as I left every morning (though the way my mother took instant cover by moving her chair smartly between the windows when I told her about the threat seemed a mite self-absorbed).

But isn't this the way censorship always works – getting you to think twice? If I'd been allowed to say the words, I would have been saying no more than the truth. I was censored. And I didn't resign. Does this mean I connived? I think it does.

But now I braced myself for the Bloody Flux of Lombardy or a dose of St Anthony's Fire, for it was my turn to receive the trophy made out of melted-down stair-rods. The Radio Industries Club had voted me Radio Personality of the Year, and *Today* was getting a prize too, as top programme. We were bidden to a party at the Connaught Rooms, a temple dedicated to Functions. We hacked our way through a legion of retailers to a table where drinks were being very carefully dispensed indeed, and the price you paid rung up on a cash-register. There was no sign of host or even greeter. I spotted Timpson, who said Get drinks from that table at the end – *if you're convincing* they don't ask you for money! I think Timpson was *au fait* with the conventions that prevail on such occasions, having absorbed them over the years at many a Rotarian dinner where he made speeches. ('If anyone plays God Save the Queen, I automatically get up and speak for forty minutes,' he told me once.)

The toastmaster was concerned to put the guests at their ease – 'I should like you to meet my sister, old chap,' I heard him say to Timpson, prior to announcing lunch was served with the words, 'This way, girls and boys.' When all were seated he enjoined silence for someone I thought he called Mrs Elrick Nuit-St-Georges, but this turned out to be a Mr George Elrick who was chairman of the occasion, an elderly musician who when the wireless was still in its infancy had always been introduced as 'Mrs Elrick's Wee Son George'. I was sitting next to Frankie Howerd who had once come up to me while Josée and I were looking at the ducks in Holland Park and breathed down the back of my neck, like a horse. He was suffering from actor's paranoia, blaming wars on the young, and I was getting it all wrong, making facetious remarks about hair, my own and others, having entirely forgotten he wore a toupee about which he was very sensitive; maladroitness seems built into these institutional festivities – how else at a Lord Mayor's banquet could I have got my foot into one of those copper troughs they use as

217

ashtrays, and thundered to the floor? I received the trophy from John Dunn and pushed it home on a sack-shifter. Next year I handed it on to Terry Wogan. For just a split second I saw myself letting it slip from my fingers, on to his toe. How awful.

I was into my third year. Wasn't that the year you graduated? The never-ending effrontery of elected persons, their sonorous drivel, was unchanged. Every word was spoken for advantage. The endless loop of threadbare justification was halted only by the next question, after which it resumed. I recognised that my own system of government by lot wouldn't do – it would be far too exciting, and those randomly selected, having nothing to lose, would opt delightedly for change; all change is for the worse (the obvious exceptions springing to mind) and I suppose that's why we pit self-interest against self-interest, allowing those who hanker after the job to form Government and Opposition in the way a thief is set to catch a thief; while there are two groups vying for re-election, nothing much is ever going to happen. We preserve the democratic process in spite of politicians, and avoid revolutions, for although there may have been revolutions after which power was returned to the people, offhand I can't think of one.

All I ever did while involved with the *Today* programme – if I did do it – was bring my status as individual to the public discussion of affairs. Affairs become ritualised, but the individual stands against this. I don't think it was brash or cocksure to believe – or rather, simply never to doubt – that this could be done. But after three years I got fed up with doing it: the ritual never had the slightest chance of getting the better of me, but the satisfaction of sitting there morning after morning, and making sure of it, wore thin. Rituals are indestructible, the individual bears witness against them but they can only be discarded by popular consent. No sign of this. Rituals are pleasing, they're less effort than the individual encounter, they dim the view with incense and incantation, they replace speech with ullulation, and within their echoey spaces what can you identify? The trick of ritual is that no one is there.

Poor old Jack hadn't known any better. He was a sort of Master of Ceremonies whose business was to dance his partner gently round the microphone and return him to a comfortable seat in the hospitality room. This ritual was succeeded by another, the one in which the interviewer appears to be wrestling rather than dancing with his partner, except no one ever gets hurt, there are no bruises; so it is really a ballet, with each of the performers versed in all the armlocks, throws and falls. In a three-year interregnum between these two forms of ritual – each, when you consider it, intimately related to the other – I asked questions I'd have liked to hear answers to. Perhaps that's what made it such hard work, for the politicians preferred the ritual, whether it was a minuet or a bout of catch-as-catch-can; actual questions disturbed them – they wanted a partner.

So I gave my employers six months notice, and quit. At least with *Call My Bluff*, you knew it was a game.

STOP THE ROT

I̲T̲ ̲W̲A̲S̲ ̲A̲ 'working breakfast'. This is a fairy-tale concept to assure the participants they are busy important people who can spare no other part of the day. All those invited know this to be a prevarication, since in the ordinary course of events they arrive at their place of work at ten in the morning, fetch a cup of coffee and spend the next forty minutes reading the newspapers.

Nobody present had the slightest idea what the meeting was intended to produce. Nonetheless, the boss of the department was there, there was I, and there was the man who had been detailed off to be the producer. We were piling into the orange juice and scrambled eggs with very serious faces because though we weren't convinced there was any such thing as a working breakfast, we didn't want to let on to the waiter.

I eyed the man who was going to be the producer. Some of the egg had stuck on his lip and he was trembling violently. Just my luck, I thought, they've landed me with an alcoholic. I learned afterwards that he was actually shaking with rage at the prospect of having to change his ways: Michael Ember had spent the last couple of years in the peaceful cloister of a morning show where all he'd had to do was stroll out into Portland Place, buttonhole any stray author who happened to be passing, sit him down in front of a microphone on the promise of paying his bus-fare home, and get him to publicise his latest book. Now he was being asked to take responsibility for something new, and what made him additionally fretful was that nobody seemed to know what this new thing was supposed to be.

We managed to define it by doing it: for the eighteen years that this programme was a part of Radio 4's Saturday evening, Ember and I very often told each other what it was we were doing, but when you really know what you're doing you don't have to keep on saying what it is, and I have a feeling we never once entirely convinced each other. We could recognise that we'd done it when we'd done it, we knew what we'd done the Saturday before, but the next time seemed always to be the first time: we spent many hours over the years trying to devise a formula which would spare us this effort, for when you've got a formula you only have to fill in the spaces, but we never managed it – the absence of any structure meant it had to be extemporised each time, for conversation was all there was.

It was conversation from five people to whom speculation was a genuine pleasure. Nobody ever said anything they didn't mean, though it pleased them to say it for effect as well; all spoke as though expecting or even demanding to be disagreed with, so that a view of the matter from a number of unpredicted locations might be prolonged. This is by no means the conventional media style; conversation in the media looks for finality, it seeks a rule, it wishes to discover and enforce an orthodoxy, and thus – paradoxically – it wants to put a stop to conversation; it insists on capitulation. But on *Stop the Week* we spoke as though conversation was endless, as though it were a way of reflecting the eternal flux that could never be explained but only acknowledged. We were full of questions, to which we knew there were no answers, but which invoked a variety of scenarios, tissues of speculation, skeins of possibility: we disagreed as people do who are trying each other out, we held our opinions, our opinions didn't hold us. We liked to find ourselves in unremarkable savannah where the territory required close study, and after a consideration of whether stiffeners were integral to the concept of the shirt collar or evidence that the concept was essentially flawed, something of the contributors had been laid bare, for it is surely true that we never open our mouths but we speak of ourselves.

You can't have endless conversations with people you don't like. Mind, you don't have to dote on them, but if you really don't like them the animus displaces far more than its own weight, and then everything becomes a matter of victory or defeat. So we were all friends, but we didn't know this until Ember had done his recruiting – he had an instinct for it. The conversations were artificial because they were designed to be overheard, and this may have given us all our fine competitive edge; but I think our main impulse was to entertain each other. We were aware of no constituency which we had to keep on the right side of, we had no agendas on behalf of any group, and our improvisations were our own.

But well prepared. Conversation is extempore at the point of delivery, but you can't simply turn up and hope to think of something. Ember and I spent our lives on the telephone, finding out if the topics we were drumming up were part of a conversational route which would reveal itself as we talked, or were cul de sacs leading nowhere. We both knew we couldn't afford to wing this, we had to keep at it until we had convinced ourselves we had a road, preferably minor and circuitous, that was going somewhere. Then Ember would feed it out to the others, acting as a sort of placenta. We were invariably doleful when we began, for we were beset by the conviction we would never be able to do it again; Ember and I resented the fact that having done it once it hadn't gone away – or at least left us with a stencil we could send round to Harrods to have filled in for us next week.

You had to stare hard until you recognised the subjects. The *Sun* said seventy-five per cent of Belgians preferred Mrs Thatcher to their own mother, but it was some time before the question suggested itself: how does anyone manage to see their own mother clearly enough to compare her with any other female, what sort of perspective on their own mother does anyone have, since from day one, mother filled the entire horizon, mother was the universe? Then we were in the pub once and Ann Leslie's voice rang round the saloon bar proudly announcing there wasn't an ironed sheet in the whole of Kentish Town, and a man drinking Foster's with a lump of ice-cream in it said wasn't Kentish Town where they spread the sheets out on the hedgerows? Milton Shulman said No, he must be thinking of Eaton Square where the peeresses pounding the laundry with stones were a colourful sight, and Laurie Taylor said sheets must always be ironed but the iron must never singe the silk. I began a short address on the subject of the ironing board as symbol of our fallen state, and only then recognised laundry as one of the great topics.

Are they the same seagulls all the way across the Channel from Dover; at what point are English seagulls joined by French seagulls? Is it possible to name six famous people called Stan? Why put a shelf up, since someone is sure to fill it with things they didn't know they had? In what sort of household would you expect to find *Old Moore's Almanac*? Why is it easy to imagine the pubs in Ilford to be the sort where a man with a sawn-off shotgun rushes in and shoots an old friend? The subjects were almost invisible to the naked eye, the very viruses of conversation, with which Ember and I had to infect ourselves before we knew they were there. It was personal currency we dealt in, the sort that actually changes hands, that people can touch and feel as something of their own, for the public topics are owned by no one in particular, and anyone who had something useful to contribute about Bosnia or Northern Ireland wouldn't be wasting time talking about it on the radio.

It was claimed I talked too much – 'How unkind of your guests to spoil your attempt to speak uninterrupted for thirty minutes,' someone wrote – but I only sounded as if that's what I was going to do, with the idea of making the others think they wouldn't get a chance – it stirred them up, they were always falling over themselves in their anxiety to be heard, and so there was a restless edge on the proceedings which I rather liked. The thing became a bit of a cult and we got letters saying We never get conversations like yours at our dinner parties, and I'd write back and tell them how lucky they were because if they had half a dozen people sitting round their dining table each of whom had very thoroughly mugged up his own thoughts on every subject, talking *without pause*, the effect would be intolerable.

And being something of a cult, it was passionately disliked by many who never missed it. 'Dear Sir,' wrote Tom Gazeley of Willesden, 'I have listened to your programme for the last five years. It's crap. All best wishes.' And Mrs Jean Mallinson of Harwich wrote saying, 'You compete in an ill-mannered way, and make a dreadful noise. I could switch you off but inexplicably your contentious programme has a soporific effect on my dogs, and I am loath to deny them this small pleasure.' While Mr Thomas Dyer said, 'In my last letter I said I should not be writing you another. This is it.'

Quite few people seemed able to do *Stop the Rot* (a description first applied to it by Phil Speight, my friend from *The Book Programme*). Do what? Well, as I've said, I'm not sure. Ember once asked me how you recognise a good conversationalist and I said by the way people cross the road to avoid him. But it's something to do with chucking a subject up in the air with a bit of spin, so that for a moment or two everyone sees a facet that wasn't visible before; but above all, you have to chuck it up so that when it comes down it's caught by someone else. The thing became, indubitably, a club. There were members who were there all the time, and there were country members who turned up once in a way. Michael O'Donnell and Nicholas Tucker and Sarah Harrison and Celia Haddon joined Ann and Laurie and Milton, along with

Edward Blishen, Brenda Maddox, Anthony Clare, Stephen Oliver, Matthew Parris, Tessa Blackstone, Roger Royle, Gillian Reynolds, Jasper Griffin, Christopher Page and Susan Jefferies. We had music in the middle. It was good stuff – Instant Sunshine, Dilly Keane, Jeremy Nicholas, Peter Skellern, Kit and the Widow – and we needed it because talk that's an end in itself is abstract stuff, even when it's only for fun, and the songs gave the talk a sort of face.

I held the ring for the occasional visitor, but it was hard on them – the regulars all spoke as though they belonged to the same Old Boys society. Dennis Barker, the journalist, who had been a regular contributor, spoke of 'cronyism' and he was right – people who keep each other's company develop a common style and a common style is excluding, it's an inevitable side effect; I believe this factor made some people impatient with the thing, though there were those who found the exclusivity alluring.

I was a fictional version of myself, my whims and prejudices seemed often to be the main course when they should have been the seasoning, and even then the conversational garlic would have been strong. Yes, everyone chooses a character for themselves when they encounter the rest of the world, but here I was doing it with the aid of collaborators. All of us found it difficult to fall out of the fiction and go home. Sometimes at dinner my wife, who knew the rough deposits from which the fiction was hewn, would smile and say 'After you've been doing that thing, nothing is good enough for you.'

*

I take life itself to be meaningless, with the individual chalking out a hopscotch pitch for himself amid the chaos of unnumbered universes. I use 'meaningless' in the literal sense: 'meaning' describes the relationship between something and something else, so the process of which we are a part would have to be able to be compared to something other than itself. But the process is all there is, so this can't be done. You can believe that the meaning exists in some 'revealed' way, but that remains a belief: so far, no one's turned up anything in the way of objective correlative. And as far as individual existence goes, no one ever chooses to be alive but arrives unconsulted, and equally unconsulted, departs; this robs the event of any significance beyond that of being the latest term in a random series – life has no meaning, but constructs meanings: hence the allusion to hopscotch.

If this is so, it's the given condition and cannot be otherwise. No need to rejoice, no need to repine. But as a view of the matter I don't think it's very popular: after all, we live each day as though we were immortal. I can hear myself arguing the point on *Stop the Week*, a weekly serial that in some ways was re-run of early times.

When I was a child my relationships with my friends were often proprietorial. I could hardly bear the thought that they had other friends, that they could ever not prefer me to all others: even when applied to a lover, a passion for faithfulness may be a desire to possess, proof of possession being a proof of identity – your own. When I was a boy I sometimes heard through my bedroom window an owl hooting in the fields beyond the brook: 'Who *are* yoo-oo, who *are* yoo-oo –?' – and over the years my eagerness to jump in with a convincing reply suggests a certain anxiety in this department: Captain Ferguson often materialised out of nowhere and took me by the throat. Nowadays he is a shadow of his former self, for though the forces he commanded were always considerable, they are as nothing when they meet the reality of a loving wife, and children with kind hearts.

INDEX

226

Index

Index

Index

231